THE COST OF THINKING:
Information Economies of Ten Pacific Countries

COMMUNICATION AND INFORMATION SCIENCE

Edited by
BRENDA DERVIN
The Ohio State University

Recent Titles

Susanna Barber • News Cameras in the Courtrooms
Jorg Becker, Goran Hedebro & Leena Paldan • Communication and Domination
Lee Becker, Jeffrey Fruit, & Susan Caudill • The Training and Hiring of Journalists
Herbert Dordick, Helen Bradley, & Burt Nanus • The Emerging Network Marketplace Revised Edition
Sara Douglas • Labor's New Voice: Unions and the Mass Media
William Dutton & Kenneth Kraemer • Modeling as Negotiating
Fred Fejes • Imperialism, Media, and the Good Neighbor
Glen Fisher • American Communication in a Global Society Revised Edition
Howard Frederick • Cuban-American Radio Wars
Gladys Ganley & Oswald Ganley • Global Political Fallout: The VCRs First Decade 1976–1985
Gerald Goldhaber & George Barnett • The Handbook of Organizational Communication
W. J. Howell, Jr. • World Broadcasting in the Age of the Satellite
Heather Hudson • When Telephones Reach the Village
Meheroo Jussawalla, Donald M. Lamberton & Neil D. Karunaratne • Information Economics in the Asian Pacific
James Larson • Television's Window on the World
John Lawrence • The Electronic Scholar
Thomas Lindlof • Natural Audiences
Kenneth Mackenzie • Organizational Design
Armand Mattelart and Hector Schmucler • Communication and Information Technologies
Kaarle Nordenstreng • The Mass Media Declaration of UNESCO
David Paletz • Political Communication Research
Everett Rogers & Francis Balle • The Media Revolution in America and in Western Europe
Jorge Reina Schement & Leah Lievrouw • Competing Visions, Social Realities: Social Aspects of the Information Society
Herbert Schiller • Information and the Crisis Economy
Jorge Schnitman • Film Industries in Latin America
Jennifer Daryl Slack • Communication Technologies and Society
Jennifer Daryl Slack & Fred Fejes • The Ideology of the Information Age
Keith Stamm • Newspaper Use and Community Ties
Charles H. Tardy • A Handbook for the Study of Human Communication
Robert Taylor • Value-Added Processes in Information Systems
Sari Thomas • Studies in Mass Media and Technology, Volumes 1–3
Lea Stewart & Stella Ting-Toomey • Communication, Gender, and Sex Roles in Diverse Interaction Contexts
Tran Van Dinh • Communication and Diplomacy
Tran Van Dinh • Independence, Liberation, Revolution
Barry Truax • Acoustic Communication
Georgette Wang and Wimal Dissanayake • Continuity and Change in Communication Systems
Frank Webster & Kevin Robins • Information Technology: A Luddite Analysis
Carol Weinhaus & Anthony G. Oettinger • Behind the Telephone Debates

THE COST OF THINKING:
Information Economies of Ten Pacific Countries

edited by

Meheroo Jussawalla
East-West Center
Honolulu, Hawaii

Donald M. Lamberton
University of Queensland
Queensland, Australia

and

Neil D. Karunaratne
University of Queensland
Queensland, Australia

Ablex Publishing Corporation
Norwood, N.J. 07648

Printed in the United States of America

LIBRARY OF CONGRESS
Library of Congress Cataloging-in-Publication Data

The Cost of thinking: information economies of ten Pacific countries/edited by Meheroo Jussawalla, Donald M. Lamberton, and Neil D. Karunaratne.
p. cm. — (Communication and information science)
Includes bibliographies and indexes.
ISBN 0-89391-419-3
1. Information technology—Economic aspects—Pacific Area.
I. Jussawalla, Meheroo, 1923- . II. Lamberton, D.M. (Donald McLean), 1927- . III. Karunaratne, Neil Dias, 1937- . IV. Series.
HC681.3.I55C67 1988
338.4'7004'099—dc 19 87-22937
CIP

Ablex Publishing Corporation
355 Chestnut Street
Norwood, New Jersey 07648

Contents

Foreword
Concepts and Issues on Information Sector Measurement

Bjorn Wellenius*

This book is about measurement of the information sector. It presents case studies from 10 countries in the Pacific region: two advanced industrial nations (Australia and New Zealand), two newly industrialized countries (Singapore and Taiwan), and six developing countries (Fiji, Indonesia, Malaysia, Papua New Guinea, the Philippines, and Thailand). This widens a field of analysis heretofore limited to advanced economies. Furthermore, the use of a common approach establishes a basis for comparability across this range of countries. Besides measurement, there are theoretical considerations, as well as some analysis and interpretation of results.

Before taking the plunge into this wealth of data and statistical elaboration, the reader may well ask: What is the information sector? Is it important? Why measure it? How is that done? In this foreword, each of these questions is addressed in two parts. First, a brief answer is given, reflecting basic concepts that run through the book. This may help the reader get started, especially if he or she is not familiar with the sector. Second, selected issues arising from these answers are discussed. This may help the reader gain a sense of balance. He or she may wish to return to this latter part of each answer after reading the book.

---

* Dr. Wellenius is a senior economist with the World Bank's Industry Department in Washington, DC. The views expressed in the foreword do not necessarily reflect those of the Bank and its affiliates, and do not imply endorsement of the material presented in the book.

What is the Information Sector?

Loosely speaking, "information" is interaction essentially realized through symbols, as opposed to the physical production and handling of goods. The "information sector" comprises all information activities in the economy, as well as the goods required to carry them out. This includes numerous activities and outputs of the conventional tertiary sector, such as education, banking, and services (e.g., those provided by libraries, engineering firms, and data processing bureaus). It also includes organizational activities, such as administration, management, and research in the traditional secondary (e.g., manufacturing) and primary (e.g., agriculture) sectors.

The emerging concept of an information sector leaves considerable room for uncertainty regarding which activities, goods, and services are part of the sector and which are not. Case studies in the main text partly overcome this operational difficulty by defining the information sector in terms of a list of activities taken from a standard industrial classification. Inconsistencies arise, however, when the list is adapted to each country's particular national accounts. Further differences are likely to build up quickly as activities are added or deleted over time.

Two examples illustrate practical difficulty resulting from conceptual ambiguity. First, the manufacture of information goods (e.g., television sets, typewriters, ink, and paper) is often included in the information sector, which overstates the sector's size and growth rate. The fact that certain goods are used in information activities bears no logical relationship to the information activity content of their production. The same applies in other sectors. For example, tractors and fertilizer are part of the agriculture sector, as capital goods and materials used to produce food; however, making them is counted under manufacturing and chemical industries, and their distribution and sale to farmers fall under trade, not agriculture. The distortion is largest when the notion of information goods is extended to include all electronics manufacturing, many products of which are not even used for information activity. This sometimes carries over to the discussion of information policy. For example, the growth of electronics assembly may be important to expand industry and exports, but cannot be construed to add to the information economy more than similar operations in any other industrial subsector.

Second, nontraded organizational information activities are mostly excluded from the case studies, which understates sector size. This "secondary information sector," which includes information activities of private and public entities as well as of households, is roughly comparable to the "primary information sector" (i.e., traded components) in several advanced countries (the U.S., United Kingdom, and Japan). It may be even larger in relative terms in less developed countries, where public and private bureaucracies commonly flourish ahead of information-intensive activities in industry (e.g., research and development) and services (e.g., engineering). A related question is whether the primary and secondary components of the information sector are additive. That partly depends on their definition and how they are measured. Contributors to this book argue it both ways.

Is the Information Sector Important?

Advocates of information economics view the information sector as dominant in advanced industrial societies, where it has taken over from manufacturing as the main contributor to gross domestic product (GDP) and employment. In newly industrialized and developing countries, the information sector is small but thought to be growing at a faster pace than the rest of the economy. Where not mature, the information sector is believed to offer exceptional opportunities for economic growth, both from its own output and by facilitating productivity improvements in other sectors. The focus of economic development efforts may be inevitably shifting from industrialization to "informatization," partly in response to increasing world economic interdependence and associated trade and communication needs. More broadly, some authors perceive the information economy as the desirable ultimate stage of economic development, beyond agrarian and industrial societies.

The case studies (and related references) support and qualify some of these expectations. In particular, it appears that the shift from agrarian and industrial societies to information economies is real and important, but slow and gradual rather than explosive and revolutionary as often assumed. To the extent that advanced industrial nations seem to have gone a long way in this process, while newly industrialized and developing countries have barely started, a large and potentially lasting information gap may have already built up.

The advanced industrial nations' transition to information economies started roughly 80–120 years ago, and by now may lie largely in the past. (Should economists, having arrived late at this scene, now press ahead and start thinking about the post-information society?) For example, the U.S. information sector appears to have tapered off, at somewhat less than one-half of GDP in the 1960s and at a similar proportion of the workforce in the 1970s (after 100 years' growth from about 6 percent of workers in the 1870s). Japan's primary information sector settled at about 35 percent of GDP in the 1960s, while "knowledge workers," as a proportion of the workforce, continued to outgrow the rest of the economy (suggesting, as in the U.S., lower than average information sector productivity gains at this stage).

Among the newly industrialized and developing countries, the evidence presented confirms the small size of the information sector. For example, in each of the four largest ASEAN countries reviewed (i.e., Indonesia, Malaysia, the Philippines, and Thailand), notwithstanding growth of telecommunications, computers, and other infrastructure, the information sector accounts for a lower share of GDP than either the tertiary, secondary, or even primary sectors. In both Singapore and Taiwan, where the information sector reportedly developed at an outstanding pace, it is still considerably smaller than either the tertiary or secondary sectors.

The limited data do not support the belief that a rapid transformation from agrarian and industrial structures to information economies is already well under way in less advanced economies. For example, the primary information sector's share of Singapore's GDP remained roughly constant (at about 25 percent) between 1973 and 1978, and labor productivity appears to be no higher than average for the economy.

This is only the beginning. Much of what is expected about the information sector is neither supported nor refuted by the data. In particular, key hypotheses have not yet been tested. The assumption that the information sector poses exceptional opportunities for economic development needs to be substantiated. The presumed desirability of major structural shifts from agriculture and industry to information in the developing world should be examined in terms of broader macroeconoic considerations.

Why Measure the Information Sector?

Some analysts argue that prevailing economic policies and strategies are not well suited to dealing effectively with information sector development opportunities. Moreover, they claim that world informatization exacerbates distributional and other problems within and among countries, adversely affects the least developed among them, and thus requires specific corrective actions. Quantification of the information sector and its interrelations with the rest of the economy should help examine these concerns, facilitate understanding of trends and strategic options in contemporary economic development, and eventually result in improved economic policy and planning. The 1960s and 1970s witnessed a boom in information sector measurement in the industrialized nations, especially in the U.S., United Kingdom, Australia, Japan, and few European countries. Little was known, however, about the situation in less advanced countries.

The studies presented in this book suggest various ways in which information sector measurement can be used to guide policy, expecially in newly industrialized and developing countries. Practical viability, however, is not yet demonstrated. The possible inadequacy of policies that promote economic development in general (and industrialization in particular) regarding the information economy has yet to be proven in practical planning situations. Formulation and assessment of economic policy and strategy, based on the case studies, has been largely deferred to later stages of the research program of which they are part.

How is the Information Sector Measured?

The studies reported in this book share a common basic approach of structural economic analysis utilizing input-output techniques. Broad definitions of the information sector and subsectors are applied to the country's standard industry classification. National interindustry accounts are recast to show the information sector separately from the traditional primary, secondary, and tertiary sectors. The information sector's value added, total output, and coefficients that measure relationships with other sectors, are calculated from the recast input-output tables. The information sector's share of employment is likewise determined by reorganizing labor data. The studies focus on the primary information sector. The secondary information sector is largely excluded for want of separable data.

Extensive use of input-output analysis in terms of the traditional primary, secondary, and tertiary sectors shows the approach to be useful but subject to important limitations as a tool for economic analysis and planning. These limitations are likely to apply as well in information economics. Three examples follow.

First, quantifying the information of an activity is very dependent on assumptions, unless it is based on major (and costly) reworking of the national accounts. Accounting categories are highly aggregate (e.g., "transport and communication" often includes telecommunications, posts, radio, television, the press, and publishing, besides all modalities of transportation). Disaggregation of a particular activity may require going back to the original data. Objective determination of coefficients to allocate a part of each activity to the information sector requires close examination of the activity. These coefficients are likely to vary considerably among countries and over time. Informed judgement and other shortcuts suffice to obtain rough initial estimates (as in the case studies presented in this book), but cannot be expected to meet the data requirements of more detailed quantitative analysis.

Second, simple cross country comparisons may be of limited value for purposes of analysis and policy guidance. For example, the data show that the information sector accounts for a larger share of the economy in industrial and newly industrialized countries (average 21 percent of GDP for nine countries quoted in this book) than in developing countries (12 percent average for seven countries). This is consistent with expectations. Individual country results, however, are baffling. Fiji's primary information sector's share of GDP is high as in Sweden (17 percent), New Zealand compares with Japan (19 percent), and Singapore matches the US (24 percent). A cursory review of these economies suggest they are quite different in the extent to which they are information-intensive. This is only partly attributable to the definition and measurement problems discussed above. Often, more elaborate analytic tools (with more stringent data requirements) will be needed to draw meaningful lessons.

Third, the numbers admit alternative interpretations leading to different conclusions and prescriptions. For example, were the information sector found to exhibit larger than average scale economies, a high proportion of GDP in this sector could signal a small economy rather than an advanced one (this could explain the apparent data inconsistencies above). Likewise, the growth of services (which are partly counted in the information sector) can either be a positive sign of economic modernization or indicate a bloated public sector, which is a serious disease in many developing countries and the target of economic policy reform efforts. The analysis, in its present form, does not provide an objective basis to make these important distinctions.

Concluding Remarks

The studies presented in this book add considerably to knowledge about the information sector, especially regarding the less developed countries. Much remains to be done, however. Unresolved conceptual ambiguities undermine comparability with other sectors, among countries and over time. Sector expectations are only partly tested by available data. The practical value of the approach, in terms of guiding economic policy, largely has not been demonstrated yet. Methodological diversification will eventually be needed to overcome limitations of the analytic techniques used. All this adds up to a formidable agenda for further research.

One final comment. The idea of an information sector can be elaborated in terms of concepts of information and communication that are well established in the physical, social, and behavioral sciences (with which it is broadly compatible). Besides strengthening measurement, a better defined sector concept will help reduce confusion in information economics between information as commodity, resource, and relationship, between information and telecommunication, and between telecommunication services and specific technologies used to realize them.

PART I

OVERVIEWS

CHAPTER 1

Preface: The Cost of Thinking

Donald M. Lamberton

The title of this book, *The Cost of Thinking,* derives from the writings of Jacob Marschak and was adopted in recognition of his pioneering role in the development of information economics. His 1966 essay, "Economic planning and the cost of thinking," first appeared in *Social Research.* For Marschak, economic planning was simply "the process of arriving at an optimal decision," optimality being achieved "if, in the decision-maker's well-considered view and allowing for the cost of making the decision, its results will be, on the average, not worse than those of any other available action" (Marschak, 1966, p. 193). He argued that planning in this sense involved questions about organizational costs and informational efficiency. The notion of optimality had to be extended to the obtaining and processing of information in order to determine and carry out those optimal strategies. This cost of thinking he thought "formidable" (p. 199).

The contributions brought together in this book, despite their focus on the primary information sector (which includes only traded information goods and services), lend support to Marschak's assessment. In this respect, the studies replicate earlier work on the information sectors of such industrialized countries as the United States, Canada, the United Kingdom, France, and Australia. However, in another important respect these studies break new ground, in that they relate to both newly industrialized countries (NICs) and less developed countries (LDCs) of the Pacific Basin. It is hoped that, in due course, this line of researach will throw light both on problems of development and of structural adjustment.

Success in this venture will require important changes in the way economists think about central features of the economy and in the way economic analysis is carried out. First, achieving informational economy or, in practical terms, keeping down the cost of thinking, requires specialization in information handling. Such economies are sought through modern forms of organization of the firm and the economy, but are partially offset by higher internal communication costs (Arrow, 1985). Second, the cost of producing information is independent of the scale on which it is used. Therefore, if information costs are substantial, as the studies in this book show, there are important implications for integration and industrial organization generally. Third, user cost of information is also substantial, and this exerts much influence upon the utilization of information. Fourth, the stock of information and the organizations created to handle information have the characteristics of capital. Information costs, even such knowledge production costs as R&D, are often not conceptualized in this way and mostly are not accounted for separately from other costs. Fifth, the demand for information equipment, e.g., computers and telecommunications switch-gear, is a derived demand. It must, therefore, be related to the demand for the information flows that it makes possible. Sixth, taken together, the main characteristics of stocks of information and of the organizations created to handle information—i.e., uncertainty, indivisibility, and capital intensity—lead to a lack of responsiveness to change. And seventh, there are usually significant information differentials, in terms of possession, access, and capacity to use, which affect economic performance and have major implications for equity.

All this takes us to the heart of information economics, which was described recently as "the general framework of the present generation for formulating any problems about the efficient allocation of resources" (Weizsäcker, 1984, p. 1085). Strong endorsement of the achievements of information economics has come from others. Green (1985) contends that "the recent literature on the economics of information stands as a remarkable achievement in economic theory. It has demonstrated that useful, empirically testable conclusions can be derived in complex situations previously beyond analytical tractability. It has raised new theoretical questions and has solved some of the more puzzling older ones. It has given us a framework within which welfare analysis can be carried out. Though its interaction with game theory proper is still in its infancy, there is already reason to be hopeful about the fruits of this union" (p. 178).

Further recognition comes from Stiglitz (1985): "Traditional economic theory has ignored the central problems associated with costly information. When due attention is paid to these information theoretic considerations, the basic propositions of neoclassical analysis no longer remain valid: market equilibrium may not exist, even when all the underlying preferences and production sets are 'well behaved'; when equilibrium exists, it is, in general not Pareto efficient; it may not be possible to decentralize efficient resource allocations; the separation between efficiency and equity considerations which characterizes traditional neoclassical theory no longer obtains; market equilibrium may be characterized by an excess demand for credit or an excess supply of labor (that is, the law of supply and demand no longer holds). The theory which has been developed explicitly incorporating information theoretic considerations provides an explanation of phenomena about which traditional theory simply had nothing to say" (pp. 25–26).

The expression of such views marks the coming of age of information economics, and offers strong encouragement to go further along the route mapped out in this book. The studies included have yielded some quantitative indications of the importance of the cost of thinking in the functioning of the economy. However, much remains to be done.

References

Arrow, K.J. (1985). Information structure of the firm. *American Economic Review, 75,* 303–307.

Green, J. (1985). Differential Information, the market, and incentive compatibility. *In* K.J. Arrow and Honkapohja (Eds.), *Frontiers of economics.* Honkapohja. Oxford, England: Basil Blackwell.

Marschak, J. (1966). Economic planning and the cost of thinking. *In* his *Economic information, decision, and prediction, selected essays: Volume II* (pp. 193–200). Boston, MA: D. Reidel.

Stiglitz, J.E. (1985). *Economics of information and the theory of economic development.* (National Bureau of Economic Research Working Paper No. 1566). Cambridge, Mass.: National Bureau of Economic Research.

Weizsäcker, C.C., von. (1984). The costs of substitution. *Econometrica, 52,* 1085–1116.

CHAPTER 2

The Growing Asia-Pacific Economic Interdependence

Seiji Naya

Introduction

Economists have traditionally assumed that information is a free good and that search and information costs can be ignored in our models. However, it is evident that, in the real world, acquisition of information is very costly and its availability plays a crucial role in development. Over the years, many great economists have devoted their efforts to this area. They have, however, been confronted with theoretical and empirical difficulties of establishing the value of information. Kenneth Arrow declared in 1979 (p. 316) that information economics involves "the most fundamental questions of economic organization." Also, D.M. Lamberton, who is a major contributor to the volume, edited the classic *Economics of Information and Knowledge* in 1971.

Information—The Development Process Trade and Welfare

The importance of information gathering is evident in the Japanese development process. The Japanese are well known for their inability to communicate with people from other cultures. In spite of this, they are very succesful exporters, due to the establishment of agencies specializing in information gathering and dispensing, that is, trading companies. Much of their export is carried out by these trading companies, which provide Japan's small firms with market information as well as brokerage services. Following the Japanese model, Korean firms have also relied on such information specialists to expand their exports. Some have said, perhaps with exaggeration, that Japan, being highly developed in this area of information gathering, can anticipate changes a few weeks or even months ahead of the event, and, therefore, can act ahead of the others.

In its application to international trade, the information sector has grown in importance. Today's multinational corporations and financial institutions have their own computerized networks to communicate information and policy decisions between the home office and the subsidiaries in host countries. Global markets are becoming so integrated that, in the future, it will be difficult to distinguish between national and global policies, because they interact with each other. It should be noted that the instantaneous speed at which information can be transmitted, and transactions made, has some negative consequences. For example, telegraphic transfers of funds by international banks may have contributed to the debt crisis, especially in the case of government-guaranteed loans.

The welfare effects of the growing information sector have to be closely watched, because rich and poor nations will be characterized by those which are information rich and those which are information poor. Information will give power to those who already have it, and, if access to information can be limited to a select group, the potential for misuse is great. For example, advance knowledge of an impending devaluation can be very profitable for those who know about it. The developing countries will have to invest in information skills to catch up in the race for superior information technology. Unless developing countries are aware of the changes and can act on a timely basis, they will be at a distinct disadvantage.

Information and communication have been especially important for the rapidly growing and developing Asian countries, as they are open to trade and have become increasingly integrated into international financial markets. This integration into the world economy, however, makes the Asian countries extremely sensitive to external conditions. A market-oriented economy must be information-oriented, responding quickly to changes in the international economy. The newly industrializing countries (NICs) of Asia, in particular, have shown this ability to adapt to changing conditions, and, thus, it is not unreasonable to say that their development success has been information-based.

Macroeconomic Performance of Asia-Pacific Developing Economies

The developing countries of the Asia-Pacific region have been quite successful in terms of macroeconomic performance. I refer here to the Asian NICs of South Korea, Taiwan, Hong Kong, and Singapore. These countries have been outperforming all others, not only in the region, but in the world. Neither the 19th century development in European countries, nor the more recent achievements of Japan, can compare with the rapid growth of these countries. They had growth rates of 8 to 10 percent annually during the turbulent period of the 1970s. Although growth rates have dropped in the 1980s because of extremely poor economic conditions, the sharp appreciation of the yen improved the competitiveness of their manufactured goods relative to those of Japan. This has improved the prospects for these Asian countries.

The development success of the NICs is largely the result of market-oriented, outward-looking policies. In particular, international trade and investment has been an important component of their rapid growth. Their export-to-income ratios range from 40 percent for Korea and more than 100 percent for Singapore. These ratios are much higher than those of the United States and Japan, which are 7 percent and 16 percent, respectively. In addition, the external financial flows into these countries increased more than four-fold between 1972 and 1982.

Other Asian countries, namely Indonesia, Malaysia, and Thailand, also grew rapidly in the 1970s by adopting more outward-looking policies. Depressed prices of primary commodities and high debt servicing obligations have forced these countries to cut imports and slow growth in the 1980s. The longer term prospects for growth, however, are still strong. Inflation rates remain low and saving rates are high. This is in great contrast to the poor economic performance of other developing countries, such as those of Latin America and Africa.

Implications of Asia-Pacific Region Developments for the United States

In contrast to these outward-looking Asian countries, historically the United States has looked inward to find resources or to seek solutions to her problems. Not long ago, the United States was virtually a self-sufficient economy, and trade accounted for only a small percentage of total economic activity (or GNP). Recently the U.S. has become more open. A large part of this increase in trade has been with Asia and the Pacific. U.S. trade with Europe has become surprisingly small. Trade with Western European countries—including England, France, Germany, Italy, Belgium, and Switzerland—now amounts to only a little more than 20 percent of the total. On the other hand, trade with the Asia-Pacific region is nearly 30 percent of the total. If we include Canada as part of the Asia-Pacific region, the figure becomes more than 50 percent. In other words, the U.S. trades more with the Asia-Pacific countries than with Europe. Moreover, this Pacific trade flow has been growing more rapidly than that with any other region.

U.S. exports to the NICs, in particular, have expanded dramatically. In 1970, little more than 4 percent of total U.S. exports went to the NICs. By

1985, the share of U.S. exports to the NICs almost doubled to 8 percent. The rapid growth of these countries led to the large need for imported capital goods and equipment.

In contrast, Japan's share of U.S. exports has not increased. The era of rapid growth ended for Japan in the 1970s, and Japan's growth rate now is only 3 or 4 percent annually. In the past, that growth was like a magnet, attracting exports and pulling up the growth rate of poor, neighboring countries. In the future, it will be the other way around. The growth of the developing Asian countries will pull the Japanese, and also the American, growth rate upward.

For these reasons, Pacific cooperation invariably involves the participation of the Asian developing countries. Their participation would not consist of the traditional North–South relationship, but would require active participation. Unlike other regional cooperation groups, the Asia-Pacific region would group together in strength rather than in weakness or fear. The long-run objective of this group would be the realization of Samuelson's factor equalization theorem; the large growth rates of the developing Asian countries involved makes this a possibility.

The Importance of Japan in the Region

The region is fortunate in that its economies were linked to the two largest free enterprise systems in the world, the U.S. and Japan, which served as locomotives over the postwar decades. Japan has been the largest trading and investment partner of most Asian developing countries, but it would be a mistake to delegate Pacific economic leadership solely to Japan. Instead of the domination of one country, one would prefer to see the evolution of a situation of mutual interdependence and multilateral cooperation. If trade and investment activities are to continue to expand in the Pacific—and doing so would make the Pacific countries better off—there are certain hurdles that must be overcome.

First, many people think of Japan as a protectionist economy. But, over the years, the Japanese have liberalized their trade and tariff structure. Hence, tariff and nontariff trade barriers are no longer very high. Japan is also moving in the direction of financial liberalization, although this is occurring in response to pressure from the United States. However, the Japanese agricultural sector is still heavily protected. Also, imports of manufactured goods comprise only 20 percent of total Japanese trade; in this sense, Japan can be considered a protectionist economy. The comparative figure for the United States is more than 50 percent.

As is well known, the United States has a large trade deficit, and this is due, in part, to its deficit with Japan. The Japanese claim that their persistent trade surplus stems from the structure of their economy and, thus, is very difficult to correct. They are very high savers. For example, in 1984, the Japanese saved 31 percent of the GNP, as compared with only 16 percent for the United States. In addition, they do not spend as much as they produce. The difference shows up as exports. But this does not explain why their imports of manufactured goods are so low. They conveniently forget that the excess export-saving identity is an ex-post, and not necessarily ex-ante condition. The Japanese social welfare system, particularly in housing and social security, is very poor. If they improved housing conditions, the Japanese would have to increase imports. The inner structure of the Japanese economy will have to change more quickly in order to allow trade and capital flows to play a bigger role for the mutual benefit, not only of Japan, but also of other Pacific countries.

The Impact of the United States' Economic and Protectionist Policies

It is important to emphasize the enormous impact of U.S. policy on the rest of the world. The recent strong U.S. recovery has had a favorable effect on other countries as well as on the U.S. But high interest rates, which were meant to solve domestic economic problems, have had profound and sometimes negative effects on the rest of the world. For one thing, they have raised the debt burden of developing countries. They also attract capital inflow into the United States. The capital inflow supports the high exchange rate of the United States, so that a high exchange rate is due more to capital inflows than to the competitiveness of the U.S. economy. In fact, high exchange rates make U.S. goods more expensive than those of other countries. Exports are penalized, and imports increase. It is no wonder that the U.S. has more imports than exports!

But the rising protectionism in the United States is also a cause for worry, since the United States economy provides a large open market to other countries, especially to developing countries. The United States is the world's largest market for the manufactured exports of developing countries. For both the NICs and ASEAN, (Association of South East Asian) the United States has been the largest market for manufactures. For example, in 1981 the United States' share comprised 32 percent of all manufactured exports from the NICs, and 28 percent from ASEAN. In contrast, Japan took only about 7 percent from each of these groupings. Thus, both the NICs and ASEAN countries were exporting four times more manufactured exports to the United States than to Japan. Historically, the United States has led the world in promoting trade liberalization. It has urged the poor but growing developing nations in Asia to be market oriented and outward looking. Thus, it is somewhat ironic that, today, many Asian countries are liberalizing their trade and economic policies, while the developed countries are becoming more protectionist. It is clearly inconsistent for developed countries to close the door to exports from developing countries at this time.

Conclusion

Fortunately, the tide is slowly changing. The United States is adopting a Pacific orientation. This shift could be seen in a comment made by Secretary of State Schultz in his address to the Honolulu Council on Foreign Relations in July of 1984. He said that "to understand the future, you must understand the Pacific." Official interest in Pacific cooperation has also been exhibited by the United States, as evidenced by the attendance of the Secreatry of State at the ASEAN meeting in July, and the appointment of Mr. Fairbanks as Ambassador in Charge of the Pacific. Moreover, the National Committee for Pacific Economic Cooperation was formed in response to the creation of similar committees in other Pacific Rim countries, comprised of business leaders, scholars, educators, and government officials in their private capacities. The East-West Center has been participating in these endeavors. For example, the Center hosted a meeting of a task force on Pacific economic cooperation in the areas of capital flows and technology transfer in October, 1984.

In this, as well as in other ways, the East-West Center is promoting better regional understanding and cooperation. Due to the interdependence among the nations involved, regional cooperation will become even more important for economic development and improvement in the levels of living for all Pacific Basin countries. Only in this manner will the full potential of the "Era of the Pacific" come to fruition.

References

Arrow, K.J. (1979). "The economics of information." In M.L. Dertouzas and J. Moses (Eds.), *The Computer Age: A Twenty-Year View.* (p. 316) Cambridge, Mass and London, England: MIT Press.

International Monetary Fund (1970–76, 1986). *Direction of Trade Statistics Yearbook.* Washington, D.C.

Internation Monetary Fund (1986). *International Financial Statistics Yearbook 1986.* Washington, D.C.

International Monetary Fund (1986). *Direction of Trade Statistics Yearbook.* Washington, D.C.

Lamberton, D.M. (1971). *Economics of Information and Knowledge: Selected Readings.* Harmondsworth, U.K.: Penguin Books.

Samuelson, P.A. (1948). ''International trade and the equalization of factor prices.'' *Economic Journal, 58,* 165–184.

Shultz, G. (July 18, 1984). ''Asia-Pacific and the Future''. Address by Secretary of State Shultz before the Honolulu Council on Foreign Relations, Honolulu, Hawaii, p. 1.

United Nations (1982). *Commodity Trade Statistics 1981.* New York.

United Nations (1983). *Yearbook of International Trade Statistics.* New York.

World Bank (1986). *World Development Report 1986.* New York.

CHAPTER 3

Information Economies and the Development of Pacific Countries

Meheroo Jussawalla

Introduction

Communication technology over the last two decades has revolutionized global interdependence in economic, political, and social relationships. Technological and scientific innovations are now transmitted so rapidly across continents that it is possible for developing countries to weigh the options offered by off-the-shelf technology, calculate their opportunity costs, and decide on investment policy. Equally rapid is the rate of obsolescence in telecommunications technology, which makes it feasible for less developed countries (LDCs) to invest in the latest and most sophisticated networks, provided the cost of scrapping existing equipment is not too high. At the same time, decision makers in LDCs must exercise caution so that they are not saddled with equipment that soon becomes dysfunctional and involves costly maintenance. The control of technology has become the control of development, and this makes developing nations recognize that a growing infrastructure in telecommunications foreshadows widespread benefits for peripheral areas which have hitherto remained isolated (see Jussawalla, 1983). The welfare effects of the new telecommunications technology upon LDC society will need to be assessed as carefully as when modernization of the manufacturing sector was considered the engine of growth. There has to be a recording of our intellectual framework, so as to better understand the changes which communication technology brings to society.

The improvement in the scientific management of micro and macro processes of development has become a major tool in dealing with scientific and technological progress. The whole gamut of knowledge about various processes taking place in society constitutes socioeconomic information.

Hence, an information base forms the foundation on which policy makers and researchers draw to evaluate the impact of new trends and events initiated either by technology or policy change. The value of such an information base, and findings from it, relate to the identification of key sectors in the economy and their interaction with the rest of society. This increasing reliance on information introduces significant changes in the structure of an economy as well as in its product mix. As information technology changes, it imparts a more powerful communication environment to economic development in the future. Therefore, Arrow (1974) emphasized the economy of information as essential for a market system. There are special functions in producing, acquiring, and disseminating information which are part of routine economic activities. These functions are adding greater value to the GNP of industrialized countries than are the more traditional sectors, like agriculture, mining, and manufacturing. The economic implications of changes in telecommunication technology lie in the creation of new markets, changes in existing markets, and changes in national productivity.

Developing countries are no longer passive spectators of the information explosion and the communication revolution. While the Industrial Revolution passed them by over a century ago, this will not happen with the current changes in communication technology. The developing world is so keyed up to participate in the ongoing changes that they are laying their claims to balanced new flows, a priori planning for allocation of spectrum and orbital resources, and their own information networks. They are prepared to invest heavily to leap frog technology, as witnessed by the commitments to Palapa, Insat, Arabsat, Satcol, Brazilsat, and the plans for domestic satellites in Papua New Guinea and Thailand. Clearly, the developing world is conscious of the social benefits of new telecommunication technology.

Policy makers and planners in developing and newly industrializing countries want to know how best to invest their scarce foreign exchange in alternate new media systems. What are the opportunity costs of communication systems as against other, more urgent, development projects? Communication economics, and the measurement of *primary information sectors,* enable them to analyze the costs and benefits of communication systems. *These have a theoretical and a pragmatic focus which is of relevance for* development, inasmuch as it seeks to apply economic tools to decisions that will generate development strategies and combat poverty. This is true insofar as development is a process of structural change,—something more than simple growth of GNP.

The heterogeneity of developing countries makes it difficult to devise uniform packages through which the technology and equipment for telecommunication infrastructure can be transferred to them. These countries are, in fact, in a situation in which their domestic development is conditioned, not only by the technology transferred, but equally by the logic and dynamism of technological advances in the industrialized countries. The microelectronics revolution promises to make the international division of labor even more skewed than it is at present, because of the concentration of information-intensive industries in the advanced countries, generating high levels of productivity in all forms of economic activity.

The importance of communication infrastructures led the United Nations to declare 1983 as the World Communications Year, so that an awareness of the linkage between communications and economic development might be generated. The ITU (International Telecommunication Union) made special efforts to prove this linkage by wide dissemination of the MacBride Commission's Report entitled, *Many Voices One World,* (International Commission for the Study of Communication Problems, 1980) and also by setting up an independent commission to examine the issues in 1984. Popularly known as the Maitland Commission, its report, entitled *The Missing Link,* (Independent Commission for Worldwide Telecommunications Development, 1984) further goes to prove that information can no longer be treated as a residual factor in the socioeconomic system. The costs and benefits of information flows have become part and parcel of economic activities. The ITU has held a Space WARC (World Administrative Radio Conference) (1985) to discuss the allocation of the orbital spectrum to which LDCs have staked their claims.

The Information Economy and Development

UNESCO constructed a Commindex to indicate the relationship betwen development and communication, using indicators like newspaper circulation, mail flow, radio, and telephones, and their relation to GNP. Colin Cherry (1978) correlated media and wealth indicators. Schramm and Lerner (1976) related communication and change in developing countries. Rogers (1976) reexamined the dominant paradigm or percolation theory, and related modernization among peasants to the impact of communication. Boulding (1966) considers economic development to be essentially a knowledge process. Because economists have neglected the role of information in development theory, and because communication is so fundamental to all types of economic systems (free market or centralized or mixed economies), the possibility of establishing a new and fruitful area of interdisciplinary research could have a significant impact on society.

While we can correlate communication variables with indicators of economic growth, we are unable to establish a cause/effect relationship. The analytical tools of economics can be used in the choice of communication systems, in the pricing of communication services, and in the measurement of the impact of these systems on economic growth. Most developing countries adopt an interventionist approach, assigning a bigger role to government in manipulating market outcomes. The information sector concept helps to identify the stocks of infrastructure in communication, and it also measures the flow of information through the networks relating economic activities. The interventionist doctrine helps developing country governments to create institutions and to protect contracts, which, according to Arrow (1979), is the role of government in development. Trading institutions, brokers, banks, stocks, and commodity exchanges are all part of the institutional network. Institutions will emerge with development because of potential benefits arising from scale economies and transaction cost, minimization, subject to efficiency differentials. The information society borrows from both the educational and commercial worlds, and, as the Nora and Minc Report (1980) affirms, "the transition to an information society is inevitable." Developing countries have found through experience that such a transition is necessary for their survival in an interdependent world.

So far, conventional measures of development have relied historically on the use of quantifiable variables, like changes in the composition and structure of the economy. Now we find that economic indicators of change do not tell the whole story, and that there is a growing interdependence among communication and development variables. But these variables vary from country to country, and we need to construct a few key indicators if we want to make international comparisons. Economic variables were defined over 50 years ago by Simon Kuznets, when he measured the GNP of the United States. But, with the information explosion, these very variables are changing within the system of national accounts.

In addition to the existence of an income gap between high-income and low-income countries, there is a very real technology gap, chiefely because of the barriers to communication between countries, or because of inappropriate technology transfer. It can be argued that, even if there were no communication gap, developing countries would still lag behind in technological change for development, because of capital scarcity and labor abundance. These countries face the constraints of inadequate growth in both scientific attitudes and institutions for fostering research and development. Streeten (1981) maintains that the effective transfer of communication technology has to be suitable to the recipient country's development strategy. The development effects of television in Indonesia, as a consequence of the Palapa domestic satellite system, have influenced neighboring countries like Malaysia and Thailand to lease transponders. India, having experimented with SITE, (Satellite Instructional Television Experiment) has a multipurpose satellite, INSAT I B, built by Ford Aerospace and launched by NASA in 1983. This trend indicates that LDCs are trying to telescope the stages of growth by expanding their services sectors and moving towards information societies. The major issue, however, is, can they afford to become part of the global information society? It appears as if many of them can. Even with a measure of selectivity in telecommunications technology, their investments are growing so rapidly in these directions that their markets are becoming increasingly attractive for exports from industrialized countries. This is particularly true of the Asia-Pacific region.

There is considerable divergence of opinion on whether communication is a dependent or an independent variable. In the process of economic growth, there is no conclusive evidence that communication can be treated as an independent variable, like capital and labor. Economists have been disillusioned from time to time by placing total reliance on a single development indicator; for this reason, they have not abandoned a range of indicators. Development planners realize the need for increasing the allocative share of investment resources for communication. They anticipate that informational efficiency will promote performance efficiency for the overall economy. Economic development concerns itself with resource mobilization. As long as telecommunication promotes resource mobilization through improved division of labor, it becomes an agent of development.

To those who claim great social benefits for communication satellites and computers in social transformation, Schiller (1981, pp. 153–176) poses the question, "who knows?" There are conflicting forces in the information economy which tend to overlook the hegemony of transnational corporations in the spheres of programming and software—the applications of technology that induce social transformation even in developing countries. Schiller provides empirical evidence to show global-distribution control of the mainframe computer, semiconductor, and data base industries. This control is mainly centered on American transnationals like Citibank, Exxon, IBM, AT&T, and RCA, and may involve privatization of scientific and technical knowledge in order to make information a profitable commodity. The question of "who knows?" is answered by "who can pay." Those who can pay are, again, large corporations like the U.S. library system, global financial and data networks, and remote sensing satellite systems. Does that involve greater inequalities in the distribution of information resources depending on private corporate growth? It appears that the information economy may experience problems of unequal distribution of income and wealth between core and peripheral societies, as well as within core societies, to some extent. Therefore, the question of the extent to which the information revolution impacts on the process of development requires further critical research within peripheral societies of the Third World. From data available from the World Bank (see Saunders, 1981), it appears that investment in telecommunications is 0.3 percent of GDP, whereas investment in research and development is less than 0.2 percent. The reasons stem from paucity in the supply of investment resources to the high opportunity costs of telecommunications. The economic rate of return on investment in telecommunications is increasing to 18 percent on average, and equipment costs are declining, but there is inadequate reserach into the overall social benefits of telecommunications to justify the high opportunity costs. Benefit–cost criteria need to be applied to assess the development effect of rural telecommunications and to ascertain its impact on reducing the rural–urban dichotomy. There are nonfinancial indicators that have not been fully researched. If output for basic needs satisfaction is one of the goals of development, then selective communication technology transfer may be a beneficial strategy for policy makers. Within the framework of opportunity costs, communications systems for development need to be analyzed in two categories, namely, development support systems and those which directly generate socioeconomic development.

Like the definition of information economics, the definition of development is open-ended. In general, development is conceived of as societal change for which conventional social sciences are unable to set parameters. Just as Keynesian economists sought a solution to development problems through the use of incremental investment levels leading to higher rates of GDP growth, so also communication scholars pinned their hopes on the mass media to provide multiple development. When the UN development decades failed to make any sizable dent on poverty, the very idea of aggregate growth, with its trickle-down effect, was called ito question as a social objective. The dominant paradigm was passing, even as the use of the investment multiplier failed to improve the physical quality of life index. Two major prardigms emerged in the 1970s; one was the dependence paradigm, the other was neo-Marxist. The dependency school drew its ideas from Latin American work in import substitution. The neo-Marxists merged with the dependency theory for measuring the external and internal dimensions of dependence. Since the Marxists had never accepted the concept of stages of growth and its reliance on urbanization and modernization, the emphasis shifted to challenging the existing international division of labor and the power of transnational corporations. In the emerging information economy of the developing world, the major focus is on basic human needs of the deprived majority of its population.

Communication has a special role to play in the new paradigm of self-reliance which LDCs agreed upon in the Cocoyoc Declaration (1974). Self-reliance is a strategy of improving the international division of labor without any form of dependency. Galtung (1980) warns that, if the positive effects of self-reliance are sought, then initiative should rest, not with the state, but with local communities. Communication theory has shifted its emphasis from hardware to software, as an integral part of technology transfer in terms of programming content and audience-oriented messages. This becomes necessary because developing countries have different content requirements, and software programs should be suited to deliver development-related messages instead of imitating program content from MDCs. The media, the message, and the manager should all be aligned to the same objective of self-reliant development.

The MacBride Commission, in its final report (International Commission for the Study of Communication Problems, 1980), emphasized the organization of local newspapers and community media as part of the developing information societies' provision of greater and more equitable access to information. How far such information societies should grow from indigenous models is another vital issue that warrants research. The populist model articulates the interests and values of peasant societies and rural cultures, but they are under scrutiny even in LDCs. There is speculation over the relationship between Western cosmology and populist models. However, institution building is vital to such indigenous models, and policy oriented research must be directed towards the intellectual emancipation that flows from the right type of institutions.

The connection between telecommunication infrastructure and development is vividly apparent from the data on telephones available to the inhabitants of LDCs. According to *The Economist* (January 26, 1985, p. 69) the 26 million people who live in the Tokyo metropolitan area have more telephones than the 500 million inhabitants of Africa. Of the 600 million telephones in the world, three quarters are owned by nine industrialized countries. Two thirds of the world's population have no access to telephones at all.

Policy Relevance of an Information Economy

There are very few countries in the modern world that have not been directly or indirectly affected by the industries and services that make up the information sector. The impact of this sector's growth, both in size and scope, is felt in virtually every facet of society, even as it has reverberated through the economies of the technologically advanced countries.

This same revolutionary change is now sweeping across the developing countries of the world, especially those of South-East Asia and the Pacific region. The effects of innovative communication technology are visible to a greater extent in the newly industrializing countries (NICs), i.e., Singapore, Hong Kong, Taiwan, and South Korea. They have become centers of production, assembly, and design in telematics activities, and are beginning to rival the region's two economic giants, Japan and the U.S. There is also evident an increasing desire on the part of the region's LDCs to become involved in the information revolution and, thereby, reduce their sense of remoteness from the world's political, financial, and technological arenas. This trend has significant ramifications for trade relations, employment patterns, and the growth of multinational corporations (MNCs), as well as for changes in factor productivities and demand for human capital.

As the over-all growth of the information sector at the primary and secondary levels increases in size and scope, *traditional economic relationships become altered.* This gives rise to the need for data which highlight these changes, and for establishing the trends and linkages which will be useful to policy makers in designing future investment policies. An information base forms the foundation on which policy makers and researchers draw to evaluate the impact of new trends initiated either by techonology or policy change. The value of such an information base relates to the identification of key sectors in the economy and their interaction with the rest of society (Jussawalla, 1982). The increasing reliance on information *introduces significant changes in the structure of an economy as well as the product mix.* Hayek (1949, p. 78) regarded information as fundamental for any theory explaining the economic process.

There are specialized functions in producing, acquiring, and disseminating information which are a part of routine economic activities. These functions are adding greater value to the GNP than the traditional sectors like agriculture, mining, and manufacturing. The economic implications of telecommunications innovations include *the creation of new markets, changes in existing one,* and *increases in national productivity.* Neoclassical economics assumed perfect knowledge. But even with perfect knowledge, uncertainty is difficult to eliminate, because prediction requires signals other than prices.

The next significant step in information economics came with the view that information itself is a marketable commodity, subject to neoclassical general equilibrium theory (Arrow, 1962; Boulding, 1966). Lamberton (1977) suggested that the quality of information is an important determinant of its price, so that, depending on its quality, information would be priced as separate commodities. The problem still remains, in that the decision maker needs to know the price of information in the information market as well as prices registered in all other markets (Newman, 1976, p. 486). Consequently, optimality in the information market becomes doubtful. Informational efficiency, then, is an important characteristic of decision making under uncertainty. However, if we strive for information efficiency, we often have to forgo neoclassical principles of rational choice such as profit-maximization. But, if the institutional structure of any economy is stable, then conventional judgment is used instead of rational choice. Perfect knowledge is not always a precondition of rational choice.

Measurement of the Information Economy in Advanced Countries

Information-intensive technologies have rendered economies of industrialized countries highly sensitive to information. Studies done for the U.S.,

Europe, Japan, and Australia provide considerable evidence indicating the emergence of information-based economies. As a result of specialization in economic function, information acquisition and dissemination have become activities in which "practitioners are rewarded by exchanges with other economic agents" (Hirshleifer & Riley, 1979). The information component of advanced economic systems is seen to have more than just a cursory role in economic growth and development. This aspect has been widely publicized through the writing of Machlup (1962), Gilbert Burck (1966), Peter Drucker (1968), and Daniel Bell (1973).,

The pioneering work of Machlup indicated that, in the U.S., the knowledge industry accounted for 29 percent of GNP and employed 31 percent of the total work force in 1958. By Machlup's estimates, this knowledge industry encompassed education, research, publishing, and broadcasting information machinery and services, and grew at 10.6 percent per annum between 1947 and 1958. He identified over 50 specific activities within these broad categories. That this growth rate is twice that of the GNP of the U.S. for the same period indicates the magnitude of national resources consumed by information activities.

Porat (1976) extended Machlup's work by assessing that 46.2 percent of U.S. GNP emerged from the activities of the primary and secondary information sectors. For the year 1967, the *primary information sector,* comprising the production, distribution, and processing of information goods and services, accounted for 25 percent of GNP. The secondary sector, as defined by Porat, covered the volume of information overhead required to organize firms and coordinate markets. This sector accounted for 21 percent of GNP. Machlup, in a more recent work (1980, pp. 23–24), refutes the charge that economists, in dealing with the information sector, put a dollar value on intangibles like education, research, art, and culture. According to Machlup, measurement of the knowledge sector does not involve "normative judgment." Rubin and Taylor (1981) estimated a lower value for the information sector in the U.S. for the year 1972—24.8 percent of GNP.

Trends similar to those in the U.S. were demonstrated in empirical OECD studies done in the U.K., Australia, and West Germany. These studies helped to launch an OECD conference on Computers and Telecommunications Policy which recommended that member countries explore the preparation of information sector accounts within existing national income frameworks (see Lamberton, 1981). The U.K. data for 1971 showed 36.6 percent of the economically active population engaged in information processing and information related employment (Wall, 1977). For West Germany, Lange and Rempp (1977) showed that 30.71 percent of the total work force was classified as information workers. Japan and Sweden had 29 and 35 percent, respectively, of their total work force in information handling occupations in 1976. Knowledge workers in Japan grew at an annual rate of

4.5 percent between 1960 and 1975 (Uno, 1982). Japan's value-added to GNP was 35 percent from the information sector (Komatsuzaki & Tanimitsu, 1983).

These estimates are based largely on the manner in which occupations are classified as information related or otherwise. A partial solution may be found by clarifying the rationale used for the concept of information. Once that is done, the differences in statistical measures can be explained. With the availability of current studies in both mature and developing economies in the Pacific Basin, we can begin to unravel the impact of innovative information technologies, and their implications for the pricing and investment of information goods and services.

It can be seen that the emergence of new technology in the information sector has led to the use of new conceptual and measurement tools for economists to identify and analyze this important new set of activities. So far, the national accounts data, or the input–output (I–O) tables available for many countries do not delineate the information sector. This impediment is overcome by identifying the information economy embedded in the macroeconomic social accounts. Extricating this sector enables holistic investment planning in telecommunications and information systems which are expanding rapidly with innovative technology.

However, there are conceptual difficulties in using the I–O methodology in measuring the contribution of information intensive production to the overall economy. Support for such analysis has been strongly stated by Marschak (1971) in his claim that the information sector has dominant activities, such as inquiring, communicating, and decision making through symbols, and creates value-added as well as jobs. Daniel Bell (1973) expressed the similar view that knowledge activities or encoded information play a crucial role similar to energy and muscle power in the production of a manufacturing economy. Despite this support, information activities create conceptual problems. This is because information exhibits characteristics of a public good, and free-rider problems arise because of associated externalities. Information can be treated both as a commodity and a resource because it is renewable and synergistic. These peculiar characteristics have far-reaching implications from the perspective of economic theory (Boulding, 1963).

Information Economies of Pacific Region Countries

For the purpose of this study, covering Pacific Basin countries, researchers from the East-West Center, the University of Queensland, and the University of the Philippines have used a common methodology of dividing each transaction into information and noninformation components. This leads to a four-way partitioning of a given transaction S matrix into I (information) and N (noninformation) inputs, which are assumed to be proportional to output regardless of its composition, based on the industry-technology assumption. Chapter 5 details the methodology used for empirical analysis of the information economy of the Pacific economies studied.

The Information Sector in Australia

Studies done for the information economy of Australia point to the rapid growth of the information sector even without any intervention on the part of the government. The Espie Committee, in 1983, recommended the establishment of venture capital companies with 100 percent tax deduction on equity capital, plus a $200 million deferred budgetary revenue to finance the adoption of new information technologies. The theoretical justification for special incentives for a rapid expansion of the information sector, or the "sunrise strategy," as it is described (Karunaratne, 1984), emerges from perceived externality-induced market failure in information sector activities. The public goods character of the sector leads to free-rider problems, so that investors are not always able to appropriate profits, and uncertainties render the investment risk high. Therefore, our study emphasizes under-investment by private enterprise in the information sector. The primary information sector in Australia contributed 19 percent to GNP, and accounted for 21 percent of the total employment in 1977–1978. Australia is not far behind the other OECD member countries with respect to the size of its information economy. With the launching of AUSSAT, Australia's national satellite system, the information sector will engage more workers and add greater value to GNP. However, this analysis refers only to the *primary information intensive activities,* which does not give a full picture of the changing structure of the economy. There may be underestimation of value-added, unless we are able to measure these activities at the secondary level and access the information overhead at the level of the firm. Bureaucracy is an important part of the information sector, and, as governments take on additional functions, information services in the sector of government bureaucracy grow commensurately and form part of the secondary sector. If we look at the transactions matrix for Australia, we find that the second largest output in the *primary information sector* emerges from education services, valued at A$4.1 billion in 1977–1978, while commerce is valued at A$6.1 billion. Information services yielded an output of A$2.8 billion and business services A$1.9 billion, all of which indicates the growing size of the bureaucracy. This data supports the hypothesis of Karunaratne and Cameron (1980) that markets for technological information, information support commodities, and market information are substantial in Australia. As such, they have implications for public policy formulation. In Australia, the shift towards an information economy is also revealed by the increasing proportion of the work force engaged in information activities. In our study, the Australian I–O matrix is collapsed to identify 20 sectors which cover the heterogeneous nature of information. Over all, the 20 sectors cover industries which produce goods and services that provide information intrinsic to the process, or provide information-support inputs. The *primary information sector matrix* constructed for Australia shows the interindustry intermediate information transactions, based on the Australian Standard Industrial Classification code. The multipliers and linkages derived from the inverse Leontief type matrix give evidence of structural interdependence within the information sector. From this analysis, we cannot estimate the self-sufficiency of the information sector, even though it is among the highest contributors to value-added. This is because we did not have access to data showing the dependence of the sector for imports, or whether import substitution policies would be profitable or not. Only if the I–O matrix were extended to cover the rest of the world sector could there by any conclusions regarding the balance-of-payment effects, and the interaction between the information sector and the economy as a whole.

The Information Sector in New Zealand

The information economy of New Zealand is in its early stages of development, since the country has relied mainly on its agricultural and farming sectors for value-added to GNP. In its external economy, agricultural exports are dominant, while most other capital equipment is imported. However, New Zealand has been quick in conceding the benefits of telecommunications and its related services. Its entry into the information age has been speeded with the use of teleconferencing services, computerized electronic funds transfer through SWIFT (Society for Worldwide Interbank Financial Telecommunications), and use of INTELSAT for overseas communications. The size of its information economy was examined, along with the linkages of the economy to other production sectors (see Chapter 15). The Planning Council of New Zealand has promoted traditional exports through the 1970s, but, simultaneously, has diversified its manufacturers to overcome the deficits in the balance of payments. However, the economy has faced severe problems of unemployment and inflation even through the 1980s. In the context of the benefits of the postindustrial society, New Zealand is actively pursuing a policy of initiating an information policy cycle, as evidenced by import duty concessions on computers launched in October 1983. Nonetheless, this is only a modest beginning which needs to be expanded if New Zealand is to maintain its economic relations with rapidly advancing technologies of its neighbors—the Newly Industrializing Countries (NICs), Australia, and Japan.

The study of New Zealand's *primary information sector* was done using the same methodology as for Australia, delineating 20 activities for the information matrix. Using the interindustry input–output table for 1971-1972, New Zealand's primary information economy accounted for 18.6 percent of national income in value-added terms, 15 percent of its national expenditure in terms of final demand, and 14.5 percent of total gross output. The linkage effects calculated by using the Leontief inverse shows that New Zealand is in the very initial stages of an information economy, where the information sector has an inputs demand (backward linkage) of 1.0236 and a supply creation (forward linkage) of 0.2112. These are significantly different from similar linkages of other sectors in the economy. This indicates that New Zealand's economy is determined predominantly by supply conditions in the noninformation sector. In any case, the three sectors which are highest in rank are education, infrastructure, and households. Thus, the information sector is still embryonic, its planning strategies need to be altered.

A further useful result of the study, which policy makers can take note of is the structural similarity between the economies of New Zealand, Australia, Fiji, and Papua New Guinea. This implies that these countries have not prepared for a global market for their communication goods and services by harnessing economies of scale and specialization according to product differentiation (Krugman, 1983). They have focused only on agriculture and manufacturing trade for regional cooperation. In so doing, New Zealand might not be able to meet the challenge of global competition as it gets drawn into an international information society. The comparative advantage of hypothesis of traditional trade models is giving way to the comparative advantage of information technology. Even so, we must give credit to the country for its information sector of NZ$1,247.1 million in terms of value-added to the GNP, contributing 18.6 percent of the total for 1972.

The Information Sector in the Philippines

The Philippines has 53 million people inhabiting an archipelago covering 7,000 islands. It has a predominant traditional sector and a small but growing modern sector. Surplus labor finds its major channel for employment in skill formation. The 1975 Census of Establishments in the Philippines provides a five digit classification of industries, from which it becomes clear that educational services have a high workers-per-establishment ratio of 36.89, whereas communications has 93 workers per establishment. The services sector as a whole has a ratio of 13.87 workers per establishment.

For measuring the information economy of the Philippines, the 1974 Inter-Industry Input-Output Accounts were used. They consisted of 120 industry groups, each of which was defined by an activity or aggregation of two or more activities described at the four digit level of the Philippines

Standard Industrial Classification code. As in the other country studies, information coefficients were used to extract the information component of an industry for which only a portion could be attributed to the information sector. The same information coefficient was used to apportion the number of workers employed in a given industry group. The data base for this procedure was the 1975 Integrated Census of Population and its Economic Activities. This study (see Jussawalla & Dworak, 1983) encompasses both measures of the information economy, viz, the size of the information work force and the value-added per worker, and the overall value-added per industry group for information goods and services. The *primary information sector* was measured by collapsing the 120-order IO table to a 26-order table.

Like New Zealand, the Philippines relies on a large agricultural and a diversified manufacturing base, and is beginning to grow into an ifnormation economy. It cannot yet be classified as such. In 1974, the largest sector in terms of total value-added was agriculture and fishing, adding up to approximately 28 percent of GNP. The government services sector from the available data did not lend itself to estimation, which led to an underestimation of the information sector's value added. This minor shortcoming in the Jussawalla and Dworak analysis was addressed by Patalinghug (1983), who estimated the wages and salaries paid to government workers by adjusting scalars used in the Porat analysis for the U.S. economy. He concluded that the total value-added of the *primary information sector,* adjusted in this manner, could be assessed as 18.6 percent as against 11.7 percent in the analysis by Jussawalla and Dworak (1983). While the conventional services sector made up 18.5 percent of the Philippine GNP, over 48 percent of these services were devoted to the production and distribution of information. The public sector of government services was not amenable to breakdown, owing to the fact that the original I–O tables included all current government purchases as a vector in the final demand sector, rather than as an intermediate product. Only the value-added component of labor could be extracted.

Even with a *primary information sector* (as measured by Jussawalla & Dworak, 1983) of 11.68 percent of the GNP in 1974, this sector was still ahead of the mining, utilities, and construction industries in terms of its total value-added contribution to GNP. Measuring the sector by the number of workers and compensation per worker in each sector, the results show that 5.7 percent of total work force could be classified as information workers, yet they were responsible for 11.68 percent of total value-added and 9.57 percent of compensation. Based on these data sources, the average information sector worker generated 16.14 pesos of value-added, while the non-information sector counterpart generated 7.49 pesos. Of the top 10 activities in terms of value-added per worker, eight were information sector activities.

If we omit the government services sector, ten, out of the top 10 activities ranked by compensation per worker, eight were information-related. As such, the information workers per capita contribute a greater share to GNP than the others. To ascertain whether investment in human capital will serve as an economic force over time in imparting strength to the information economy, we would need to analyze I–O tables of a more recent data base.

There are also measures of interdependence, of derived demand, and of output utilization that have been estimated by Jussawalla and Dworak (1983) with the aid of the technical coefficient matrix and its inverse, the Leontief matrix. The technical coefficient matrix shows the direct connections of an industry with others, e.g., what proportion of its output was sold to others for intermediate uses, and to final demand, and also reflected by the proportion of its inputs bought from other industries. For the Philippines, there is a 26-order I–O table defining such ratios. On the basis of output utilization for production purposes, education, electronic and telecommunication equipment, and nonelectronic office equipment show low values of intermediate demand, which implies that the products of these industries have a low use by other sectors in the production process, and go instead directly to final consumption. By contrast, financial services, manufacture of paper and pulp, manufacture of stationary, insurance services, and professional services all register high intermediate demand and low final demand. A study of the forward and backward linkage effects in the Philippines indicates that greater investment ought to be directed towards goods and information hardware sectors, whereas software industries do not offer as large a stimulus to further output.

In sum, the *primary information sector* of the Philippines was accounting for 12 percent of GNP in 1974 by the conservative techniques utilized in the study. Inclusion of the government bureaucracy raises this estimated contribution to 18.6 percent of GNP. It would be worthwhile to follow up this study, not only by estimating the secondary information sector, but also by repeating the macro level analysis with a more recent data base. As the information sector grows, its impact on traditional market structures will become more significant. It will also increase the productivity of existing structures.

The Information Sector in Singapore

Two studies of the *primary information sector* of Singapore have been done, covering the DGP of Singapore for 1973 and for 1978. Both studies show evidence that Singapore is moving rapidly towards an information-based economy in which specialization in information-support activities is growing. Not only is the services sector burgeoning, but the structure of industrial production is changing as a larger proportion of the country's work force is absorbed into service occupations.

As a compact city-state, Singapore has relied on entrepot trade. The character of its export trade is now altered from manufactures exports to exports of services. Even her manufacturing sector is geared to skill-intensive technology, yielding sophisticated outputs of electric typewriters, semiconductors, computers, television receivers, and other information goods. Its strategic location makes Singapore the center of global flows of finance and communications (see Jussawalla & Cheah, 1983). The results of two empirical studies done for Singapore bear evidence to the hypothesis that Singapore is fast becoming an information economy.

In 1973, the *primary information sector* contributed 24 percent of Singapore's GDP, and in 1978 this grew to 26 percent. This implies that, for every Singapore dollar received, about 24 to 26 cents are paid for the production of information goods and services. Public bureaucracies accounted for 49 percent of total value-added in 1973, and 58.8 percent in 1978. The bulk of these services emanates from public administration and education. Information services performed by stock and foreign exchange brokers and insurance agencies rose from 10 percent in 1973 to 11.1 percent of GDP in 1978. These studies also revealed that about 26 percent of Singapore's total work force was engaged by the *primary information sector.*

While the size of the information sector has grown in terms of value-added, the proportion of information sector output to total output has declined from 20.1 percent in 1973 to 19.3 percent in 1978 (see Cheah, 1983). This is due to the higher value of total output for the year 1978. However, in terms of value-added, the rate of growth of the information sector was higher than the rate of growth of the total economy. This is a significant aspect of Singapore's newly industrializing economy.

An analysis of the interindustry matrix shows that, of the top 10 sectors ranked by multipliers and backward linkages, five were information related, and that their productivity was built into the productivity of the overall economy. The four sectors related to the top 10 by way of forward linkages were information related, e.g., professional and business services, banking and finance, communication, and printing and publishing. In this context, the policy makers in Singapore are aware of the emergent information economy and of the relevant investment criteria for structural development. Therefore, we find Singapore planning investments in appropriate technology like videotext, cellular radio, and an integrated services digital network (ISDN). By identifying the stage of development of the information sector, policy makers can link this stage with the strategy for accelerated growth of national income and penetration of information activities in the economy's product mix.

The Information Sector in Fiji

Most Pacific island countries have depended so far on agriculture and fisheries for their affluence. During the colonial period, basic infrastructure for transportation was made available, and plantations and mines became sources of income. In the post colonial era, the isolation of these economies was accentuated, leading to unequal income distribution within the nations (see Karunaratne, 1982).

Fiji's eighth development plan, 1981–1985, is a blueprint to coordinate national resource allocation for diversifying the economic base, which relies heavily on exports of sugar. Tourism income is also a major variable in the Fijian economy. The new plan emphasizes the need for an equitable distribution of income, a goal to be reached by a comprehensive system of regional planning. The crucial problem is one of skewed income distribution between rural and urban areas. Consequently, infrastructure investment needs to flow more to the rural hinterland. 10 percent of the total value of exports in Fiji emerges from seafood, and 9 percent from copra and coconut oil. Even so, Fiji has the most diversified industrial base of the Pacific Island nations. It is able to supply textiles, paper, chemicals, and metals to the domestic market.

The study of information-based economic activities in Fiji indicates that the supply and demand for telecommunications infrastructure is likely to increase with an increasing diversification of exports and imports. Since Fiji is basically an island economy, geographic isolation makes it necessary for telecommunication demand to be related to market concentration. As the export sector grows and reliance on imports increases, there will be a further expansion of telecommunication demand. However, there is a trend of concentrating telecommunications in metropolitan centers, further exacerbating the rural–urban dichotomy. The catalytic effect of telecommunications on living patterns may be lost to the rural dwellers who constitute the majority of the population in Fiji. Therefore, a modified version of Say's law is operating in Fiji, namely, that supply of telecommunication equipment is generating its own demand. Based on observed percentage change in telecommunications traffic between 1978 and 1980, as revealed from ITU's regional data base for 1980, the annual average growth rates for short-term demand were calculated. This reveals that international traffic of telephone calls will increase from 23 million paid minutes in 1985 to 155 million paid minutes in 2000. For rural demand, the telephone demand is likely to rise from 3.9 million minutes in 1985 to 5.2 million minutes in 2000.

Based on the 1976 I–O tables for Fiji, information workers as a percentage of total workers are identified as 10,976 workers, or 17.02 percent of the total work force. The total population of Fiji was 646,000 in 1981, and the total employment was 64,500 workers. This analysis has reconciled the *primary sector information matrices* with the activity classification into information and noninformation categories. In Fijian dollars, the *primary information sector* contributes 13 percent of GNP. The highest backward linkage effect is from a single sector, i.e., infrastructure. By implication, investment in Fiji would stimulate high growth of GNP if it were channeled into telecommunications infrastructure. Even for employment in Fiji, the three sectors that have the highest backward linkage are communications, education, and business services. For forward linkage, or supplying input to total output, advertising is among the top five highest sectors.

Fiji's economy is strengthening, domestically and in its relationship with other PINS (Pacific Island Nations). Its information sector would be considerably bigger if Intelsat offered the PINs subsidized tariffs for international communications. Scarce resources and their allocation become problematic when Intelsat requires standard specific earth stations for using its satellite facilities for voice, data, facsimile, and television. Even with the reduction in costs of hardware for earth stations, Fiji would have to import them and add these costs to the costs of linking the earth stations to telephone exchanges. With the University of the South Pacific stationed in Suva, and without the facility of using ATS-1, the potential for satellite-based education has become problematic for Fiji. The costs and benefits of telecommunication technology have to be evaluated constantly for investment decisions to be made in favor of increasing the flow of investment to telecommunications infrastructure.

The Information Sector in Papua New Guinea (PNG)

While the information sector analysis for PNG revealed a 12.3 percent value-added component of the GNP in 1976, indicating a growing trend in information activity, the analysis masks the dual nature of PNG's economy. In fact, the PNG study is a special case of rapidly advancing metropolitan sector and a stagnating, subsistence level rural sector (see Karunaratne, 1982). It is possible that the growth of telecommunications infrastructure in the urban areas may, in reality, be exacerbating the dualistic character of PNG's economy. This trend promotes the communication effects gap and emphasizes the center–periphery disparity.

Compared with India, another developing country, PNG has a higher telephone density—1.3 per 100 inhabitants, whereas India has 0.3. But the geographical distribution of the network is skewed in favor of Port Moresby, which has a density of 16 telephones per 100 inhabitants. This dichotomy exists because the telecommunication infrastructure was established to assist the colonial administration to protect its military interests. PNG received two loans from the World Bank in the 1970s, totaling $17 million, to modernize the trunk routes that connect Port Moresby with the copper mines and plantations. Eight urban centers have a sophisticated network using microwave tropospheric scatter systems and solar powered repeaters. While the rate of return on telecommunication assets is 14.2 percent, the revenues flow out of the country to multinational corporations and leave 85 percent of the total population without even basic telephone services. There is scope for cross-subsidization of low-income users, but this has not been done in PNG. At the time of this study, the dependence of PNG on Australia is substantial, and leakages of revenues through international trade exceed revenues.

The formal development plan for PNG focuses on rural development and the commercialization of subsistence agriculture towards greater cash-crop production. Copper mining is expected to provide employment, and, simultaneously, attempts are being made to reduce migration from the rural to the urban areas. The world market for copper is not favorable for providing PNG's three million people with a high per capita income, even though 42 percent of its copper is exported. The domestic markets are fragmented by lack of effective communication, so that regional markets cannot be integrated into a sizeable national market. Being a trade-oriented economy, PNG levies a single-column tariff on a series of nonessential imports, like automobiles and radios, and imposes protective duties on imports of chemicals, paper products, and barbed wire. Several agro-based resource processing industries generate employment, e.g., rice, copra, palm oil, coffee, and copper. The wage differential between Australia and PNG is 6:1, which attracts foreign investment with prospects of collaboration.

An analysis of the *primary information sector* of PNG shows that there is no single dominant information-based activity. Government bureaucracy and the services rank higher. There is also a lower degree of interdependence among information industries, which may be typical of a developing economy. It may be caused by the high degree of dependence on imports for technological resources. The country itself is unable to exercise autonomy over the structural development of its information economy. The control of importing enclaves influences the ratio of intermediate inputs of information to the value-added of total output. Therefore, the presence of the *primary information sector* in a sizeable form in PNG is misleading in its contribution to GNP growth. The reason is that the information sector is not endogenous. It is strongly motivated externally with links to foreign investment. It only serves to provide a market for the information commodities and services produced in Australia. When income and output are exogenously determined, the impact of the information sector on development cannot be assessed accurately. Both the income gap and the information gap continue to jeopardize the social and economic stability of the domestic economy. In terms of output, the primary information sector in

PNG accounted for 100.7 million kina, contributing 12.96 percent of total output of the country in 1972. This is somewhat higher than in the Philippines, though it is not endogenously generated. The main advantage at present is the fact that the primary information sector does contribute 13 percent to overall employment in PNG. In the Philippines only 5.7 percent of the work force is engaged in information-based activities, but they contributed 12 percent of the value-added. The interpretation of this result remains incomplete without an assessment of the secondary sector.

Decision makers in PNG are faced with the dilemma of a resource rich country, so far exploited by foreign investment. It provides a sizeable market for communication goods and services without reaping the gains from technology transfer. Planners in PNG will have to direct their investments to meet the twin goals of reducing dependence on foreign investment and the urban–rural dichotomy for telecommunication services.

The Information Sector in Malaysia

Slow growth is sabotaging Malaysia's domestic economic policies, called the "New Economic Policy" (NEP), because of its racial bias (see *The Economist,* August 11, 1984, pp. 70–71). Malaysia has 15 million people, 48 percent of whom are Malays, 34 percent Chinese, and 9 percent Indian. The Malays dominate political life, and the Chinese dominate business. Malaysia's NEP has made considerable progress, and indigenous Malays, or Bhumiputras, are running the two state-owned banks, the oil, gas, and tin mining industries. Poverty has declined to 17 percent below the poverty line from 49 percent in 1970, and the average income has risen by 186 percent. The economy grew by 7.9 percent a year through the 1970s, but prices of Malaysia's commodity exports like rubber, oil, and tin declined between 1980 and 1983, so that real GDP growth slumped in the 1980s to 5.9 percent. The government is, therefore, returning to privatization, and the entire telephone network will be gradually transferred to private ownership. At present, Malaysia has reasonable price stability and, being an open economy, it has a stable balance in its external account. The sectoral composition of output and employment changed over the last decade, and industrial products came to be diversified. Agriculture contributes 22.2 percent of GDP, while manufacturing has moved up its output from 13.4 percent to 20.5 percent of GDP over the last 10 years. The services sector makes a fairly large contribution of 45.1 percent. In foreign trade, Malaysia's export sector has increased, mainly due to an increase in manufactured exports. Its export base is well diversified, but the demand for its exports has declined because of world recession. As a result, fixed capital investment in the private sector has declined, but the services sector, even in 1982, represented the largest share of GDP, approximately 46.2 percent. The economy has exhibited a high savings ratio, a low rate of private consumption, and a relatively high rate of public consumption.

As a percentage of total value-added, Malaysia's primary information sector in 1975 was 16 percent, and, when looked at from final demand, it was 14.7 percent. If the contribution to GNP is calculated as a percentage of total output, the primary information sector made up 14.3 percent. Compared with Thailand, Philippines, and Papua New Guinea, the primary information sector in Malaysia can attract larger investment with greater benefits because of its contribution to GDP.

The Information Sector in Indonesia

Among the ASEAN countries, Indonesia's industrial development has been slowest. Only 10 percent of value-added to GNP is represented by the manufacturing sector. Value-added per worker in Singapore is almost 20 times that of Indonesia. Thailand's output per worker is three times that of Indonesia's. However, Indonesia has a large population base with high density in Java, and it has vast natural resources. Protectionist policies have been followed for several years, with a recent emphasis on export promotion (Kirby, 1984). Gross investment as a proportion of GNP rose duing the First Five Year Plan (1969–1974) from 12 percent to 19 percent, and inflation was gradually reduced. The Second Plan (1974–1978) continued to rehabilitate the economy, but growth was cut back due to depression.

Manufacturing has a large domestic market, and wages rose through 1976, due mainly to increased earnings from oil exports of about $14 billion, helping to transform the standard of living. The GDP's share from mining rose by 300 percent during the period 1953–1980, while the manufacturing contribution remained at 9 percent. This shows the importance of oil in Indonesia's economy. The Third Five Year Plan (1979–1983) set lower growth rate targets for the manufacturing sector. It emphasized income equalization and set out "eight roads to equality," viz: more equal access to subsistence needs, education, health, income distribution, equal access to employment and business, and equal access to justice. The planners decided to strengthen and coordinate forward and backward linkages between the sectors contributing to overall GDP. All foreign investments in Indonesia were to be on a joint venture basis. A Board for Coordinating Investments issues a scale of priorities and conditions for investment.

The use of microelectronics is still in a preliminary stage, with most use in the trading and services industries. The government offices are extensively equipped with computers, with a network between offices. Indonesian telecommunications is the biggest user of computer technology and is known as the Public Corporation for Telecommunications (PERUMTEL). Telecommunication investment rose by 12 percent to $1.2 billion in

1982–1983, with large amounts budgeted for the Palapa Satellite system (Alfian & Chu, 1982). Terrestial communications have been growing simultaneously. Private concession networks have sprung up for oil and gas producers, multinational companies, and trading enterprises. They have set up high quality microwave circuits for high speed communications (see Crawford, 1984). Digital switching of telephone exchanges was installed in 1984, with Siemans providing the equipment. Intercity satellite service is to be inaugurated under the "Packsatnet" system.

While the first Palapa A duo of satellites have served domestic communications for over 10 years, having been launched in 1975, the second duo of Palapa B has not had a successful beginning. Palapa B-1 was lost in orbit during the launch of June 1983, and subsequently recovered in 1984. The B system will be much bigger, with 24 transponders instead of 12, and excess transponders will be leased to other ASEAN countries for domestic and international communications. At present, there are 100 earth stations located throughout the islands connected with the Palapa system. Sixty new ones with smaller dishes are being constructed for the B systems, and can be used for television, radio, telex, telephone, and data services.

It becomes clear that Indonesia has made a significant investment in the information sector, relying on the most sophisticated technology. Not only has this investment resulted in skills formation within the labor force, it has also been instrumental in the launching of a national program on research and technology. Both LIPI (Institute of Sciences) and PUSPIPTEK (Center for Research, Science, and Technology) are aiming at applications of information technology to industrialization (*Far Eastern Economic Review,* August 18, 1983, p. 55). However, the microelectronics industry is in its infant stage in Indonesia, though the commitment to a high technology future is articulated in all its policies.

The primary sector of the information economy is contributing 19.2 percent in terms of output to the GDP. In size, therefore, it is almost the same as the informaon sector of Australia. Data for Indonesia pertains to 1975, and the results show that investment in Indonesia for that year was high in information production, processing, and distribution. The backward linkage for such activities in the Leontief inverse show a stronger trend than the forward linkage. The primary information sector contributed only 9 percent to national income, while agriculture contributed 48 percent, manufacturing 11 percent, and services 33 percent in 1975.

The Information Sector in Thailand

Colonial rule did not touch Thailand as it did Malaysia and Indonesia. The country has been both successful and progressive. Seventy-three percent of its work force is engaged in agriculture, and only 7 percent in manufacturing. The trade pattern reflects its agricultural base and its heavy reliance on industrial imports and oil. Telecommunications services have been meager in Thailand, despite the inflow of funds for the several UN agencies located in Bangkok. The operations of the UN agencies located in Bangkok would require basic local and long-distance telephone services, which have been inadequate. This situation is now to undergo major changes.

The Telephone Organization of Thailand (TOT) is planning to privatize its domestic telephone services and was to introduce international direct dialing by 1985 (*Far Eastern Economic Review,* September 6, 1984, p. 76). The introduction of international subscriber dialing will speed up communications with other countries and help to make Bangkok an improved regional business center. TOT is replacing old cross-bar telephone exchanges with electronic switching. The TOT has an arrangement with the Communications Authority of Thailand (CAT) for handling overseas calls. CAT is introducing a microwave network, high frequency radio transmission, and the leasing of Palapa for domestic television transmission. It provides international communication through INTELSAT and through the ASEAN cable network introduced in 1983.

The Ministry of Communications, in July 1984, contracted with Hughes Aircraft to conduct a feasibility study on the suitability of Thailand having its own communication satellite. The study was financed by Hughes at a cost of $1.5 million and was to be completed by the end of 1984. The Thai government contracted to purchase the rehabilitated Palapa satellite. The Thai government has also invested 44.4 percent of the total cost of the Singapore-Malaysia-Thailand submarine cable, and indicates the growing demand for telecommunications in Thailand. Despite these developments, telex services are inadequate for Thailand's expanding business sector. Even urban telephone services fall far short of demand. TOT has a 5-year plan, under which the telephone connections in Bangkok and the provinces will be increased by one million by the close of 1988.

TOT is planning to privatize a part of its domestic services to cope with rising demand. Bell Canada has submitted a proposal to TOT to enter the Thai market with premium services such as switched lines, dedicated lines, and mobile telephones. It calls for an investment of $500 million over a 10-year period. This plan will be implemented through a new public company called Telestar, in which Bell Canada will hold 15 percent of equity and TOT will hold 10 percent. The remaining 75 percent will be held by corporate investors.

With the increased investment and the intent to privatize telecommunication services, it is obvious that Thailand is expanding its primary information sector. From the I–O table constructed by our research team, based on 1975 data from Thailand, we find that, compared to other countries in the Pacific region, its information-related activities were the least significant. A description of the Thai economy, using the four-sector model and interindustry transaction tables, shows that the services sector has the highest growth. Both in terms of value-added and in terms of final demand, the services sector contributes well over 40 percent of GDP and is, therefore, ranked as the prime sector. In terms of output, the value-added by the tertiary sector is below that of the manufacturing sector. The contribution of the primary information sector to GDP is below 10 percent, which is relatively low compared with smaller economies like Fiji and Malaysia. Trends indicate that, in countries where there is political ferment, either internally, as in the Philippines, or on its borders, as in Thailand, the information sector is part of an interventionist policy. Consequently, its contribution, in terms of final demand and output, tends to become underestimated in a purely intersectoral, I–O approach. Perhaps, with greater liberalism and more reliance on the private sector, the value-added by the information sector will increase and match the growth trend of the services sector. However, the multiplier and linkage analysis shows a strong correlation between the information sector and the overall economy. The primary information sector accounted for only 10 percent of the national income in Thailand in 1975. The service sector contributed 42 percent, agriculture 25 percent, and manufacturing 22 percent to Thailand's national income in 1975.

Conclusion

Developed and developing countries in the region are consciously plunging their economies into the information age by deliberate policy decisions to expand their investments in the hardware and software of innovative communication technologies. Their differences in levels of achievement are the outcome of economic viability and capital availability. Prosperous countries like Singapore have invested in many types of sophisticated communication technology, ranging from digital telephone exchanges to videotext to cellular radio. Others, like Fiji, are using telecommunication technology to link centers of learning to and from the University of the South Pacific and outer Pacific islands. Malaysia and Papua New Guinea are endeavoring to make information services the key sector which will provide the leverage for all other sectors to grow in the future. Australia and New Zealand have large investments in telecommunication networks in their plan—Telecoms 2000. But some of their investments show up in the increases in value-added of their services sectors, rather than in their primary information sectors.

Analysis of the backward and forward multipliers and linkages for this group of Pacific Basin economies yields some interesting insights into the role of the primary information sector in each of the economies. It also indicates the potential benefits that increased investment in the primary information sector may bring about, either through derived demand for other goods and services produced in the economy or through lowered input costs for other sectors of the economy.

In most of the economies, it is a primary information sector that has the highest backward linkage effect. For both Fiji and PNG, it is the building of information infrastructure that has the highest backward linkage effect, while in Australia it is the printing and paper industry, and in the Philippines it is the cables and wires industry. What this implies is that, in these economies, investment in these industries would stimulate the biggest increases in overall demand for other sectors output. Overall, in terms of their backward multiplier/linkage effects on output, two of the top five sectors in Australia are primary information industries (printing/paper and infrastructure); in Fiji, it is one sector (infrastructure); in PNG, it is three of the top five (infrastructure, insurance, and miscellaneous); and in the Philippines, four of the top five (cables and wires, manufacture of inks, pencils, pens, etc., manufacture of precision instruments, and paper produciton) are primary information sectors.

In the area of forward multipliers and linkages, the primary information sector industries again appear as important agents in the stimulation of output and employment growth through increased availabilities of production inputs. In Australia, two of the top five sectors with respect to output, ranked by forward multiplier/linkage effects, are primary information industries: business services and banking; in Fiji, one of the top five is a primary information sector: advertising; in PNG, one of the top five is: office machinery and repair; and in the Philippines, one of the top five also is: paper production. In terms of forward employment effects, for Australia one of the top five is the primary information sector: education; for Fiji, all five of the top ranking sectors are information sectors: infrastructure, education, printing, advertising, and miscellaneous; and in PNG, four of the top five ranking sectors are information sectors: electronic equipment and repair, office machinery, education, and insurance. Thus, it can be seen that, in all the countries for which figures are available, education is among the most important in terms of its impact on the future employment growth.

In summary, then, the importance of the primary information sector for each of these economies is exemplified by the high backward and forward multipliers and linkages that result for primary information sector industries in each country. Investments in these industries will tend to result in increases in both output growth and employment growth, given other constraints which may exist in particular country settings. These results are guidelines for policy makers attempting to channel investment funds to productive ventures. *The Far Eastern Economic Review,* in its Special Focus supplement, declared that 1984, in a very real sense, "is year one of the long-heralded Information Age of which the communications industry will be the vital infrastructure linking men, computers, and a myriad of new products." Information is forecast as the basic commodity of the new era. In this framework, most countries of the Pacific region, led by Japan, are turning to privatization of their telecommunication services. Japan's large telecommunications agency, Nippon Telegraph and Telephone, when under Public ownership, will bring in effective decentralization of the telecommunications networks. Malaysia and Thailand are also planning to follow similar policies of decentralization. Likewise, greater availability of satellite communications makes it possible for the Pacific region to avail itself of the benefits of open skies. They provide more cost-effective and speedier networks than terrestrial systems. As part of a country's investment program, they contribute value-added growth to GNP.

Whether the high growth primary information sectors of the Pacific region countries create the "global village" forecast by Marshall McLuhen, or the self-sufficient, self-service economy, will remain debatable. The trends exhibited by this research study indicate that the countries studied are all moving towards increasing the volume and value of their primary information sectors, as measured in terms of linkages, multipliers, national income, output, and employment.

Table 1. Philippine GDP by Sector of Origin 1974

Sector	(1) Total Value-Added (P000s)	(2) Info Value-Added (P000s)	(2)/(1) % of Total
1. Agriculture and Fishing	28,088,088	n.a.*	n.a.
2. Mining and Quarrying	3,280,453	n.a.	n.a.
3. Manufacturing	24,705,882	1,128,141	4.57
4. Utilities	1,053,964	n.a.	n.a.
5. Construction	4,259,564	n.a.	n.a.
6. Commerce	16,011,611	920,878	5.75
7. Transportation and Storage	3,173,245	491,469	15.49
8. P.T.T.	667,828	667,828	100.00
9. Finance, Insurance and Real Estate	8,315,862	5,322,702	64.01
10. Recreation, Business, Cultural, and other services	6,638,069	2,895,324	43.62
11. Government	4,703,000	n.a.	n.a.
12. National Industry	(3,032,019)	n/a**	n/a
	97,865,547	11,426,342	11.68

*) Note: n.a. = not available; that is, not available from data sources utilized in this study.

**) Note: n/a = not applicable; this sector is a dummy sector designed to account for the imputed output of financial institutions. The figure in parentheses is negative in sign.

Table 2. The Contribution of the Primary Information Sector to GDP and Workforce

Region	Country	Year	% GDP	% Total Workforce
ASEAN	Indonesia	1975	10.6	6
	Malaysia	1975	14.3	11
Pacific	Philippines		12	5.7
	Singapore	1976	26	26
	Thailand	1975	9.9	9
PACIFIC	Fiji	1976	16.72	17.02
Region	New Zealand	1972	14.6	12
	P.N.G.	1972	12.96	13
O.E.C.D.	U.S.	1976	24	41
	W. Germany	1975	17	27
	Japan	1975	19	24
	Australia	1977	19	17
	U.K.	1975	22	33
	France	1976	19	28

References

Alfian, Chu, G. (1982). *Satellite television in Indonesia.* Honolulu, HI: East-West Center.

Arrow, K.J. (1962). "Economics of welfare and the allocation of resources for invention," *In The rate and direction of inventive activity: Economic and social factors,* (pp. 609–625). Princeton, NJ: Princeton University Press.

Arrow, K.J. (1974). Limited knowledge and economic analysis. *American Economic Review, 64,* 1–10.

Arrow, K.J. (1979). The economics of information." *In* M.L. Dertouzos and J. Moses (Eds.), *The computer age: A twenty year view.* Cambridge, MA: MIT Press.

Bell, D. (1973). *The coming of post-industrial society.* New York: Basic Books.

Boulding, K.E. (1963). "The Knowledge Industry," *Challenge,* 36–38.

Boulding, K.E. (1966). "The Economics of Knowledge and the Knowledge of Economics," *American Economic Review, 56* (2), 1–13.

Burck, G. (1966). Knowledge: The biggest growth industry of them all. *Fortune 70* (5), 128–131, 267–270.

Cheah, C.W. (1983). *An input-output analysis of the Singaporean primary information sector.* A paper presented to the Input-Output Workshop of the Regional Science Association, University of New England, Australia.

Cherry, C. (1978). *World communication: Threat or promise.* New York: John Wiley.

Crawford, M.M. (1984). *Information technology and industrialization policy in the Third World.* Cambridge, MA: Center for Information Policy Research, Harvard University.

Drucker, P. (1968). *The age of discontinuity.* New York: Harper and Row.

Galtung, J. (1980). *The true worlds: A transnational prespective.* New York: Free Press.

Hayek, F.A. (1949). *Individualism and economic order.* London: Routledge and Kegan Paul.

Hirshleifer, J., & Riley, J.A. (1979). The analytics of uncertainty and information—An expository survey. *Journal of Economic Literature, 17,* 1375–1421.

International Commission for Worldwide Telecommunications Development, (1984). *The Missing Link* (Maitland Report). Geneva: International Telecommunication Union.

International Commission for the Study of Communication Problems. (1980). *Many voices, one world* (MacBride Report). Paris: UNESCO.

Jussawalla, M. (1982). *Bulletin of Communication Research.* (Tokyo: Keio University), No. 19, pp. 3–29.

Jussawalla, M. (1983). The economics of telecommunications infrastructure. *In* O.H. Gandy, Jr., P. Espinosa, and J.A. Ordover (Eds.), Proceedings from the Tenth Annual Telecommunications Policy Research Conference, (pp. 309–320). Norwood, NJ: Ablex.

Jussawalla, M. & Cheah, C.W. (1983). The information economy of Singapore. *Information Economics and Policy, 1,* 161–176.

Jussawalla, M. & Dworak, S. (1983). The primary information sector of a developing economy: The case of the Philippines. Submitted for publication to *Information Economics and Policy.*

Karunaratne, N.D. (1982). Structural change, trade dynamics, and telecommunications in the Pacific island nations. A paper for the Public Service Satellite Consortium, mimeograph.

Karunaratne, N.D. (1984). Planning for the Australian information economy. *Information Economy and Policy, 1,* 365–367.

Karunaratne, N.D. & Cameron, A. (1980). Input-output analysis and the Australian information economy. *Information and Management,* 3, 191–206.

Komatsuzaki, S. & Tanimitsu, (1983). "Japan's Information Industry: A Structured Analysis," *Economic Eye,* March, pp. 12–15.

Krugman, P. (1983). New theories of trade among industrial countries. *American Economic Review, AEA Papers and Proceedings,* 73, 334–343.

Lamberton, D.M. (1977). Structure and growth of the communication industry. *In* K.A. Tucker (Ed.), *The service sector of the Australian economy.* London: Croom Helm.

Lamberton, D.M. (1981). The theoretical implications of measuring the communication sector. *In* M. Jussawalla and D.M. Lamberton (Eds.), *Communication economics and development.* New York: Pergamon.

Lange, O. & Rempp, M. (1977). *Qualitative and quantitative aspects of the information sector.* Karlsruhe: Federal Republic of Germany.

Machlup, F. (1962). *The production and distribution of knowledge in the United States.* Princeton, NJ: Princeton University Press.

Machlup, F. (1980). *Knowledge: Its creation, distribution, and economic significance.* Princeton, NJ: Princeton University Press.

Marschak, J. (1971). Economics of information systems. *Journal of the American Statistical Association, 66,* 192–219.

Newman, G. (1976). An institutional perspective on information. *International Social Science Journal,* 28, 466–492.

Nora, S. & Minc. A. (1980). *The computerization of society. A report to the President of France,* Cambridge, MA: MIT Press.

Patalinghug, E. (1983). *Discussion Paper on the Information Sector of the Philippines Economy,* (No. 83-14). Manila: University of the Philippines, College of Business.

Porat, M.U. (1976). *The information economy* (Vols. 1 and 2). Washington, DC: Department of Commerce, Office of Telecommunications.

Rogers, N. (1976). *Communication and development: Critical perspectives.* Beverly Hills, CA: Sage.

Rubin, M. & Taylor, E. (1981). The information sector and GNP: An input-output study. *Information Processing and Management,* 17, 163–194.

Saunders, R. (1981). Telecommunications in developing countries: Constraints on development. *In* M. Jussawalla and D.M. Lamberton (Eds.), *Communication Economics and Development.* New York: Pergamon.

Schiller, H.I. (1981). *Who Knows? Information in the Age of the Fortune 500.* Norwood, NJ: Ablex.

Schramm, W., & Lerner, D. (Eds.), (1976). *Communication and change: The last ten years and the next.* Honolulu, HI: East-West Center.

Streeten, P. (1981). Information gaps and suitability gaps, *In* M. Jussawalla and D.M. Lamberton (Eds.), *Communication economics and development,* (pp. 16–65). New York: Pergamon.

Kirby, S. (1984). *Towards the Pacific century: Economic development in the Pacific basin.* Special Report no: 137, the Economist Intelligence Unit, pp. 15–22.

Uno, K. (1982). The role of communication in economic development: The Japanese experience, *In* M. Jussawalla and D.M. Lamberton, (Eds.), *Communication economics and development,* New York: Pergamon.

Wall, S. (1977). *Four sector time series of the U.K. labor force,* 1841-1971. London: U.K. Post Office Long Range Studies Division.

PART II

METHODOLOGY

CHAPTER 4

Theoretical Aspects of the Measurement of the Information Sector

D. M. Lamberton

Introduction

In the chapters ahead, we have a statistical feast, and there is not to my knowledge any simple modern equivalent to the throat-tickling feather resorted to in Roman times. So I shall do my best to keep away from statistical detail and focus on conceptual problems in this chapter.

The Importance of Measuring Information Activities

Perhaps I can begin by asking, Why are we interested in information activities? There are many ways of answering this question. It was the late Joan Robinson who said it was the task of economics to explain why a banana cost three pence. So one way of answering our question would be to look to the ways in which information activities determine relative prices. Relevant information activities would include knowing how to grow bananas and when and where to sell them. These in turn would link to R & D, extension schemes, marketing systems, international communication of price data, knowledge of nutritional values, and a host of other matters.

There is, however, a more fundamental approach. We are really interested in decision making. Now, decisions involve information, views of the future, and related value systems. The view that these ingredients are inherently inscrutable because they are locked up inside some individual's skull should not be taken too seriously. For most of the important decisions are made by groups rather than by individuals, and the necessary communication within the group is observable. It is "observed" by sitting in on conversations, by asking questions of decision-makers, by studying the records kept and related background material. "The difficulty lies in making observation 'systematic'" (Hart, 1976, p. 232). Information economics, with its attempt to measure information sectors, provides one approach to such systematic observation of the necessary communication within the group or organization. It recognizes the role of information activities—of inquiring, communicating, deciding; of organizing—in the economy, and seeks its quantitative dimensions. And because economic activity is a process shaped by decisions, flows of information may be preconditions for later events, e.g., economic growth, and may have predictive value. It needs to be acknowledged that, in a pioneering study as early as 1960, this point was emphasized (Meier, 1960).

Information economics would seem to have grown and gained in respectability since it was officially recognized by the American Economic Association in 1976—by the award of a category in the Association's Classification System for Articles and Abstracts. In 1983, North-Holland initiated an international journal, *Information Economics and Policy;* the U.S. Council for World Communication Year selected Michael Rubin's book *Information Economics and Policy in the United States* as a significant publication; and, in the Netherlands, an important report (the "BIT" Report (Bordewijk and Arubak, 1983)) pinned great hopes on the role of information technology (IT) (De Witte, 1984). In 1984, Information Technology Month was observed, and Volume III of Fritz Machlup's monumental work on *Knowledge: Its Creation, Distribution and Economic Significance* was released by Princeton University Press, with the title *The Economics of Information and Human Capital.* Nineteen eighty-five was ushered in by publication of Kenneth Arrow's book, *The Economics of Information.* When interviewed in 1972 on the occasion of his Nobel Prize, Arrow stressed that standard economic theories have assumed a great deal of knowledge on the part of the individual economic actors. He was interested in the question of how their ability to plan rationally was constrained by the limitations of their knowledge. He saw the information differential between economic actors and the cost of acquiring information as very important. Organization was a response to the information-gathering need.

Information differentials, information cost, and cooperation in information-handling are not new. They are not peculiar to modern times, nor to the spectacular advent of intelligent electronics, with its greatly enhanced capacities for communication, computation, and control. All societies have been information societies and have employed IT; economists were not silent on these matters, as Machlup (1984) makes apparent. Now, however, on the technology front, it is the speed and pervasiveness of change that seems important. Within economics, the role being assigned to information in economic analysis has responded, not only to the use of computers and satellites, but also to the deficiencies of economic theory and failures of both government and business policies. Greater concern with the present and its problems, rather than long-run equilibrium, has led to information activities being seen as cause of disequilibrium and means to equilibrium, as endogenous rather than exogenous, as loss avoiding and potentially profitable. This shift of emphasis has been most obvious in the case of technology —perhaps the most important and potentially beneficial kind of information.

The Conflicting Perspectives on the Concept of Information

The preceding section refers to some very difficult problems of definition. A few comments are proffered to clarify rather than resolve the controversies about definitions. For starters, the word *information* is interpreted as an idea that "is precisely a reduction in uncertainty" (Arrow, 1979, p. 306). We are also told to regard information as data imbued with purpose. It is noted elsewhere that "meaning is always meaning to someone" (MacKay, 1969, p. 36), so the expected value of information depends upon "states of readiness" of those receiving it.

The above points are in sharp contrast with those of communication or information theory and cybernetics that sought an objective measure of information content: a measure that told nothing about the content, value, truthfulness, exclusiveness, history, or purpose of the information (Dunn, 1974, p. 27, fns. 1 and 46). I do not claim to understand the communication theory approach: I gather the information content of a message, to the communication theorist, is proportional only to the logarithm of the probability of that message being received. It appears to be possible that the economist's expected value measure and this communication theory measure move in the same direction, but this need not be so. An R & D manager who gave priority to projects with high information content and low profit prospects would be "sorely misguided" (Langlois 1983, p. 590, fn.11).

If we can reject this cybernetic approach and adopt instead an economic approach to the value of information, there are some important implications. First, we should perhaps play down the idea of uncertainty reduction and accept that information can add to uncertainty and that order can come out of chaos (Prigogene & Stengers, 1984). Second, the expected value depends upon the state of readiness of the recipient—a form of capital. It has been argued that capital is processing capacity—which would include information processing capacity (Ramos, 1981, p. 170).

As to the word *organization,* it is useful to quote the following explanation:

> Rather the concept is really a primitive term in a system, its significance being revealed by assumptions and their consequences. . .the term, "organization" should be interpreted quite broadly. Formal organizations, firms, labor

> unions, universities, or government, are not the only kind. Ethical codes and the market system itself are to be interpreted as organizations; the market system, indeed, has elaborate methods for communication and joint decision-making. As this example makes clear, the participants in organizations may be themselves organizations as well as individuals. Furthermore, it is important to note that individuals typically belong to many organizations. (Arrow, 1974, p. 32).

The Link Between Organization and Information Economics

A decade ago, those interested in information matters still emphasized the need to incorporate a role for information in economic models because of its bearing upon market performance. Pioneers like Jacob Marschak and Fritz Machlup had already done much to shape the pattern of development of information economics. Marschak had initited true theoretical work and established a link with the study of organization as an information-handling decision system (Marschak, 1974). Machlup had provided a detailed statistical account of information activities (Machlup, 1984). The radical thought that is only now emerging with increasing clarity is that organizational change, as well as technological change, is fundamentally important and can be analyzed in economic terms.

Information and the information-handling mechanisms we call organizations are now to be treated as resources. But it seems that generations will have passed before the full implications are understood. Put in the simplest terms possible, organization is now to be a variable, as the product was made a variable in the exciting days of imperfect and monpolistic competition theory. This provides a link between the Marschak and Machlup contributions. The decision theory framework of Marschak gives a role to information which, depending upon the costs of information, shape the pattern of information activities recorded in such rich detail by Machlup and his followers.

There can be great advantages in cooperating with others in information handling, i.e., forming an organization. This calls for creation of information channels, the building up of a stock of information, and the creation of an "organization" language that may limit access to nonmembers. The technical characteristics of these "resources" (uncertainty, indivisibility, and capital intensity) have two major implications: first, random events can have considerable importance; and, second, the more successful the pursuit of efficiency, the more rigid and unresponsive the organization may become (Arrow, 1974, p. 49). This line of thought leads to an understanding that decision makers may become locked into their information systems just as easily as into stocks of buildings and machines. Organizational obsolescence is in this way given an economic rationale.

Propositions Central to Information Economics

The subject matter of information economics is, of course, neither more nor less than that of economics itself, because all decision makers, except those in economics textbooks, are involved in choosing which information to acquire and use. Even rational (consistent) expectations theory must recognize that there is a wide range of procedures that economic actors use to cope with uncertainty. When circumstances dictate that reliance upon these procedures is important, as in the dynamic conditions of new technologies and new markets, the theorist is once more in need of a theory of the decision-making process (Simon, 1983, p. 486).

It is, however, possible to single out some of the important economic characteristics of information, and to emphasize some propositions central to information economics:

1. There is a difference between personal and group or organizational use of information. It has been argued that the division of information gathering is perhaps the most fundamental form of the division of labor (Arrow, 1979, p. 310).
2. The cost of producing information is independent of the scale on which it is used, e.g., the cost of producing the formula for a metal alloy.
3. The greater part of the cost of information is the cost incurred by the recipient, i.e., the user cost.
4. The stock of information and the organizations created to handle information have the characteristics of capital.
5. The complexity of information activities makes information as a resource difficult to contain within the traditional production function analysis.
6. The limitations on information as a commodity dictate resort to organization as an alternative to markets.

Research, both theoretical and empirical, continues on a wide front, and publication regularly reaches to every category in the entire American Economic Association classification.

Measurement of the Information Sector and its Significance

A major effort on the empirical front has been to measure and examine the structure of the information sector, which embraces all information activities. Just as food activity would require farming, transportation, agents, wholesalers, retailers, grocers, fast-food shops, and manufacturers of stoves, refrigerators, and the like, so information activity requires a wide range of production and service inputs: education, the media, advertising, consulting, finance and brokerage, and the production and operation of such information machines as computers, telephones, and television sets.

The information sector divides into two sub-sectors. The primary sector includes all information goods and services sold in markets. But comparable activities are conducted in-house in both the private and public sectors. Such in-house information activities make up the secondary information sector. Table 1 provides a classification of information occupations for those who work in the information sector. Figure 1 shows the share of economically active population in some OECD countries accounted for by these information occupations. The level is high and the trend upward. For comparative purposes, note that the Australian percentages were 39.4 in 1971 and 41.5 in 1981 (Lamberton, 1984).

An alternative approach is to measure the component goods and services of the primary information sector as a percentage of GDP at factor cost. This is done for some countries in Table 2.

Disaggregation of these statistics could prove useful. Consider the category of market search and coordination. The occupation statistics show that Australia and the United Kingdom reduced the share of the work force devoted to these activities. In sharp contrast, Japan revealed a very considerable increase (almost a trebling). This could be of much practical significance if the Meier thesis (Meier, 1960) holds good. That thesis implies that changes in information flows precede changes in trade patterns and structural adjustments, and can possibly have useful predictive value.

Table 1. Typology of Information Occupations

— *INFORMATION PRODUCERS*
Scientific and Technical Workers (components)
Market Search and Coordination Specialists
Information Gatherers
Consultative Services
— *INFORMATION PROCESSORS*
Administrative and Managerial
Process Control and Supervisory
Clerical and Related (components)
— *INFORMATION DISTRIBUTORS*
Educators
Communication Workers
— *INFORMATION INFRASTRUCTURE OCCUPATIONS*
Information Machine Workers
Postal and Telecommunication

Source: (Organization for Economic Cooperation and Development, 1981, p. 24).

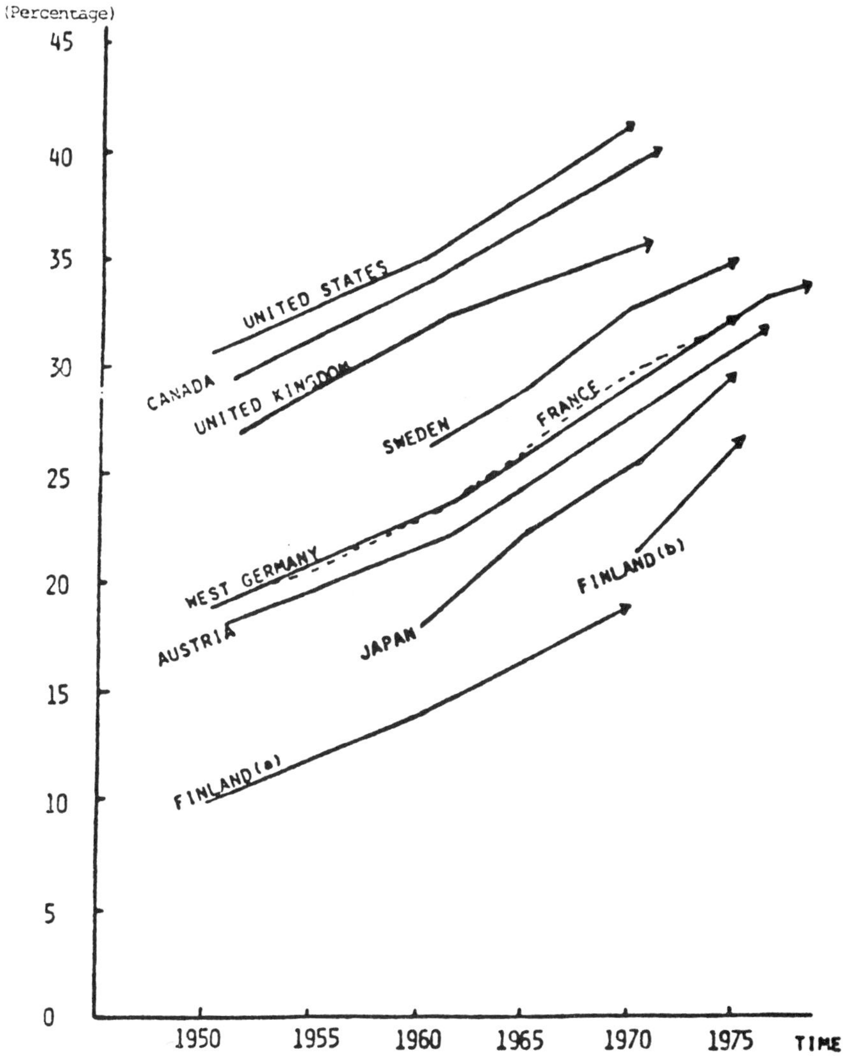

Source: Organization for Economic Cooperation and Development, 1981, p. 25).

Figure 1. Information Occupations as Percentage of Economically Active Persons

Consideration of information sector statistics should remind us that standard economic theory "assumes no constraints on man's information gathering, processing, communicating, deciding, and agreeing capabilities" (Nelson, 1981, p. 95). Given that constraints do exist, whatever adjustment process take place, "it cannot achieve an allocation of resources that would

Table 2. Size of the Primary Information Sectors as of % GDP (Factor Cost)* 1970s

Country	%
Australia	25
U.S.	24
Singapore	24
U.K.	22
France	19
Japan	19
N.Z.	19
Sweden	17
Fiji	17
Malaysia	16
Philippines	13
Papua New Guinea	11
Venezuela	10
Thailand	10

(* N.B.: Data do not relate to the same year, so furnish only a broad comparison.)

Sources: For Australia, see Lamberton, (1984). Venezuela: Michael Rubin (private communication). Data for other countries (i.e., Singapore, New Zealand, Fiji, Malaysia, Philippines, P.N.G., and Thailand) have been provided by a joint East-West Center/University of Queensland project, with the work directed by Meheroo Jussawalla, Neil Karunaratne, and D.M. Lamberton.

be optimal in the absence of information costs'' (Arrow, 1979, p. 315). The available statistics give reason to think that those information costs are major costs.

The Growth of Information—Was It a Revolution or Xerox Effect?

''Information (the collection, transmission, processing, storage and retrieval, and analysis of data, the communication of orders or other signals, and the feedback necessary for the evaluation of decisions taken as a result of the signals) is a necessary input into every aspect of economic decision-making. The larger the number of participants in the economic process, the greater the division of labor, the more complex the technological processes, and the wider the assortment of goods and services an economic system produces, the more information intensive the economic process becomes'' (Neuberger, 1966, pp. 132–133). Naturally, there is an international dimension: trade in information and international communication grow with greater international specialization and with the frequency of structural changes.

If we think of capital as processing capacity, we should ask, What is being processed? To answer this question, we might distinguish between the production task and the information-handling task in the economy (Jonscher, 1983, pp. 14–15). The production task was to produce goods and services, given the limited labor and material resources, and it was the dominant task. Capital was the capability to process those materials. The information-handling task is one of managing, organizing, coordinating, and developing. It now challenges the production task in importance. The capital now sought is the capability to process information. The R & D effort and innovation generally can be viewed as complementing the dominant task. It was directed to production and sought there the productivity gains that gave bigger profits and higher incomes. Some would say that was the industrial revolution. As the balance shifted towards the information-handling task, R & D and innovation were redirected and yielded IT. Some now call this the information revolution. This view is generally optimistic.

A less optimistic view is based on the "Xerox effect"—a label we adopted for situations where consequential cost increases outweighed such of the planned cost reductions as were in fact realized when new technology was introduced (Lamberton et al., 1982). Similar reasoning about what has been called the "cost disease" has been presented elsewhere (Baumol & Blackman, 1983). The analysis builds on the changing ratio of hardware/software costs. Some of this work suggests that information activities can be both labor absorbing and capital absorbing.

One can list the shortcomings of a typical modern economy: protection, subsidies, tax disincentives, bad allocation of investment, and a too-complicated wage determination system. Although one could perceive the advantages of removing those distortions, one cannot at all be confident that they will be removed by action through direct governmental policy. If that is so, is there an alternative approach? It is suggested that we look to the informational efficiency of the economy, that we try to tackle the problem of organizational obsolescence—even if that problem may have come about largely as a result of a long-sustained high level of protection.

Informational Efficiency and Trade Policy

It is a complex problem to ask how informational efficiency is affected by the operation of tariffs, but it is a problem that underlies the world debate about the costs of protectionism. The new "technology intensity" approach to trade analysis has reinterpreted the notion of comparative advantage and, after assigning a role to imperfect competition and economies of scale, has recognized the potential role or technological competition (Krugman, 1983). Some contributors have begun to integrate welfare analysis of trade with industrial policy under oligopoly (Dixit, 1984; Eaton & Grossman, 1983). Others have noted that there are significant costs to develop knowledge, and have sought to treat R & D capital as a quasi-fixed factor (Bernstein & Nadiri, 1983). These approaches have yet to recognize the comprehensiveness of the role of information. R & D is only part of the overall information process, which includes monitoring of rivals' behavior and markets. For example, recently it has been reported that Mitsubishi has some 650–800 employees in New York whose main task is gathering information about American rivals and their markets (*The Economist,* June 23, 1984, p. 63). Informational efficiency must be viewed in this broader fashion when the effects of protection on the innovation process are to be analyzed. Consider the characteristics of information and the central propositions of information economics mentioned earlier.

1. Information activities can be divided into: (a) R & D as conventionally defined, and (b) non-R & D. The latter category would appear to need close association with the experience of the firm. In these activities, it has been argued, "every organization must learn largely on its own, in a somewhat idiosyncratic and inimitable way" (Nelson, 1980, p. 95). Insofar as the restriction of trade leads to local production on a small scale, it would seem to impair the informational efficiency of both R & D and non-R & D activities. The benefits of the most fundamental form of the division of labor are denied.
2. If the cost of producing information is independent of the scale on which it is used, small scale production inevitably suffers a disadvantage. Gathering information is one way of creating awareness of technology, and trade restriction must reduce the opportunities for observation and learning, and the scope for imitation.
3. To the extent that the recipient bears the greater part of information cost, once again small scale, local production is placed at a disadvantage.
4. The capital nature of information and organizational capacity, in circumstances of uncertainty and indivisibility, lead to obsolescence, with a continuing incentive to rely on old information capital.
5. The limitations of the conventional production function analysis are relevant because the input–output relationships depend upon complex information infrastructures ("states of readiness") that may be impaired by long-sustained protection policies. The form taken by those policies can be important: frequent changes in duties can raise uncertainty and information costs incurred in coping with that uncertainty.
6. Quite inadequate researching of the problems of optimal design of organization means that little can be said on this aspect. Perhaps the basic fact is that resort to organization paves the way for organizational obsolescence. Most certainly, we hear little about organizational innovation.

The Information Sector Approach—A Solution to Some Unresolved Trade Issues?

There are several additional aspects to be noted. First, foreign investment behind trade barriers raises the usual questions about the effectiveness of transfer of technology. Second, while a patent system can facilitate access to information about technology, patents can enable action to restrict the entry of competitive goods covered by the same patent from elsewhere.

In broad terms, information activities are important in both the *domestic* and the *international* economy. Protection policies can hamper informational efficiency, and yet analysis must leave room for the equivalent of an "infant industry" argument in relation to the development of comparative advantage in information handling.

The real problem would seem to be clarification of the nature of comparative advantage in relation to technological capacity. I do not find this clarification in the literature, and I have no ready answer for how it is to be achieved. Let me, however, mention two research findings:

1. In Australia, Welch (1983) studied the firm's first international transaction. He found that there was a complex sequence of information activities that preceded that first transaction.
2. Teubal (1983) has looked at "hi-tech" investment in developing countries and was led to put heavy emphasis upon "the accumulation of intangibles" as a precondition of success.

Such results suggest that intervention in the system might well be directed to the organizational aspects of the economy, as a way of getting new items on the agenda. In conclusion, it is submitted that information sector analysis is a promising approach to the study of these aspects.

References

Arrow, K.J. (1974). *The limits of organization.* New York: Norton.

Arrow, K.J. (1979). The economics of information, *In* M.L. Dertouzos and J. Moses (Eds.), *The computer age: A twenty-year view,* (pp. 306–317).Cambridge, MA: MIT Press.

Arrow, K.J. (1985). *Collected works, Vol. 4, The economics of information.* Oxford, England: Blackwell.

Baumol, W.J., & Blackman, S.A.B. (1983). Electronics, the cost disease, and the operation of libraries. *Journal of the American Society for Information Science, 34,* 181–191.

Bernstein, J.I., & Nadiri, M.I. (1983). *Does knowledge intensity matter? A dynamic analysis of research and development capital utilization and labor require-*

ments. (NBER Working Paper 1238.) Cambridge, Mass.: National Bureau of Economic Research.

Bordewijk, J.L., & Arnbak J.C. (1983). (BIT) Report on Policy on Communication and Information Systems. Netherlands Ministries of Education and Science and of Economic Affairs.

De Witte, H. (1984). Some order in information chaos. *Science Policy in the Netherlands*, 6, (2), 15–16.

Dixit, A. (1984). International trade policy for oligopolistic industries. *Economic Journal.* Conference Papers Supplement to Vol. 94, pp. 1–16.

Dunn, E.S., Jr. (1974). *Social information processing and statistical systems — change and reform.* New York: John Wiley.

Eaton, J., & Grossman, G.M. (1983). *Optimal trade and industrial policy under oligopoly.* (NBER Working Paper 1236.) Washington, DC: National Bureau of Economic Research.

Hart, A.G. (1976). The multiple futures. *In* M. Pfaff (Ed.), *Frontiers in social thought: Essays in honor of Kenneth E. Boulding,* (pp. 231–263). Amsterdam: North-Holland.

Jonscher, C. (1983). Information resources and economic productivity. *Information Economics and Policy, 1,* 13–35.

Krugman, P. (1983). New theories of trade among industrial countries. *American Economic Review, 73,* 343–347.

Lamberton, D.M. (1984). Information age economics. *In* A.W. Goldsworthy (Ed.), *Technological Change — Impact of Information Technology, 1984,* pp. 3–12. Canberra: National Information Technology Committee.

Lamberton, D.M., Macdonald, S., & Mandeville, T.D. (1982). Productivity and technological change. *Canberra Bulletin of Public Administration, 9,* (2), 23–30.

Langlois, R.N. (1983). Systems theory, knowledge, and the social sciences. *In* F. Machlup and U. Mansfield (Eds.), *The study of information: Interdisciplinary messages.* (pp. 581–600). New York: John Wiley.

Machlup, F. (1984). *Knowledge: Its creation, distribution, and economic significance, Vol. III, The economics of information and human capital.* Princeton, NJ: Princeton University Press.

MacKay, D.M. (1969). *Information, mechanism and meaning.* Cambridge, MA: MIT Press.

Marschak, J. (1974). *Economic information, decision and prediction: Selected essays, Vol. II.* Boston, MA: Reidel.

Meier, R.L. (1960). Information, resource use, and economic growth. *In* J.S. Spengler (Ed.), *Natural resources and economic growth.* Washington, DC: Resources for the Future.

Nelson, R.R. (1980). Production sets, technological knowledge, and R & D: Fragile and overworked constructs for analysis of productivity growth? *American Economic Review, 70,* 62–67.

Nelson, R.R. (1981). Assessing private enterprise: An exegesis of tangled doctrine. *Bell Journal of Economics, 12,* 93–111.

Neuberger, E. (1966). Libermanism, computopia and visible hand: The question of informational efficiency. *American Economic Review, 56,* 131–144.

Organization for Economic Cooperation and Development. (1981). *Information activities, electronics and telecommunications technologies: Impact on employment, growth and trade, Vol. 1.* Paris: Organization for Economic Cooperation and Development.

Prigogene, I. & Stengers, I. (1984). *Order out of chaos.* London: Heinemann.

Ramos, A.G. (1981). *The new science of organizations: A reconceptualization of the wealth of nations.* Toronto: University of Toronto Press.

Simon, H.A. (1983). Rational decision making in business organizations. *In* H.A. Simon, *Models of bounded rationality,* (Vol. 1, pp. 474–494). Cambridge, MA: MIT Press.

Teubal, M. (1983). The accumulation of intangibles by high-technology firms. In S. Macdonald, D.M. Lamberton, and T.D. Mandeville, (Eds.), The trouble with technology (pp. 56–74). London: Frances Pinter.

Welch, L.S. (1983). The technology transfer process in foreign licensing agreements. *In* S. Macdonald, D.M. Lamberton, and T.D. Mandeville, (Eds.), The trouble with technology (pp. 155–168). London: Frances Pinter.

CHAPTER 5

An Input–Output Approach to the Measurement of the Information Economy

Neil D. Karunaratne

Introduction

Many trendy cliches blare the impending changes that new information technologies will bring about in the economies of the world. Phrases such as "post-industrial society," "technetronic era," "telematic society," and "compunications" conjure up visions of an information revolution. Reams of theorizing and policy prescriptions have been published about the societal and economic implications of the information revolution. Nevertheless, it is fair to claim that the basic parameters of the size, structure, economic performance, and sectoral interdependencies of the information economy remain an under-researched, empirical subject in many countries. National data bases, current techniques of national income accounting, and input–output statistics hardly provide any revelations about the latent potential, let alone identify the broad contours of the information economy. The main purpose of this chapter is to devise an operational methodology to quantify in an objective manner the magnitude and structure of a country's latent information economy using input–output techniques.

Benchmark data on the composition and potential of the information economy is vital for rational decision making. The intention of this study is to unravel the hidden parameters of a country's information economy in a consistent manner, using the Leontief I–O framework. The procedure for computing the information intensity of economic activity is detailed. A methodology for quantifying the nature and the size of marketed or primary information activities is enunciated. Techniques for imputing values to the nonmarketed information transactions by the vast public and private bureaucracies or secondary information sectors are presented. Together, the generation of the primary and secondary information sectors provide, against the backdrop of a given macroeconomy, the salient structural characteristics of the emergent information economy of any given country. An algebraic stylization of the methodologies to generate the information sectors, and the plausibility of the underlying assumptions of the Input–Output modelling used, are reviewed. Consistent multipliers and linkages of the information sectors are calculated to provide insights on the structural characteristics inherent in a given macro economy. Finally, the methods devised are empirically validated using Australian data bases, thus confirming their practicability and usefulness.

Information Intensity and Generation of the Information Economy

The Generation of the Information Economy has been accomplished by amalgamation of a procedure to generate the primary and secondary information sectors, designated as the Generation of the Primary Information Economy, and the Generation of the Secondary Information Economy, respectively. The methodology is depicted in Flow Chart 1. The sectoral information intensity coefficients that are crucial to the methodology have been estimated from the valuation of production of information commodities as disclosed by the latest available Census and Surveys of production. A catalogue of primary information commodities has been compiled from the International Standard Industrial Classification (ISIC). The OECD has also prepared a catalogue (Organization for Economic Cooperation and Development, 1981), which can be used for the purpose. The use matrix of an Input–Output (I–O) table which details the commodity by industry classification, when used in conjunction with the catalogued values of primary information commodities and noninformation commodities for each sector, enables the estimation of the primary information intensity coefficient for the ith sector, p_i:

$$p_i = \left[\frac{\text{Value of primary information commodity output of } i^{th} \text{ sector}}{\text{Total value of all commodities produced by the } i^{th} \text{ sector}} \right]$$

The complement of the primary information intensity coefficient defines the noninformation intensity of the ith sector, i.e., $1 - p_i$.

The primary information intensity coefficient enables the identification of the primary information economy that is obscured in the conventional presentations of national accounts and I–O tables. The four steps that generate the primary information economy have been abbreviated as dichotomization, homogenization, condensation, and structurization, as depicted in Flow Chart 1.

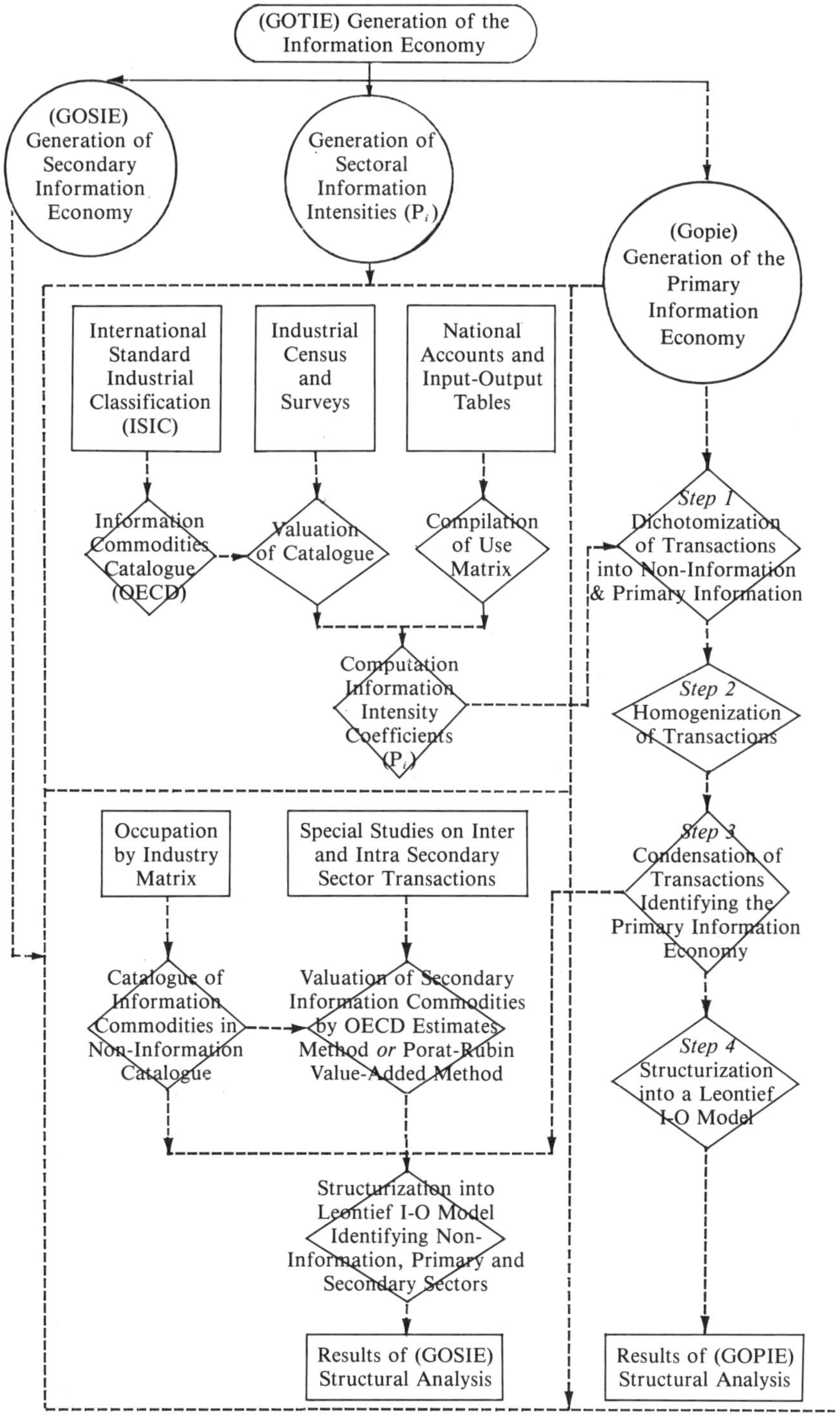
(GOTIE) Generation of the Information Economy
(GOSIE) Generation of Secondary Information Economy
Generation of Sectoral Information Intensities (P_i)
(Gopie) Generation of the Primary Information Economy
International Standard Industrial Classification (ISIC)
Industrial Census and Surveys
National Accounts and Input-Output Tables
Information Commodities Catalogue (OECD)
Valuation of Catalogue
Compilation of Use Matrix
Computation Information Intensity Coefficients (P_i)
Step 1 Dichotomization of Transactions into Non-Information & Primary Information
Step 2 Homogenization of Transactions
Step 3 Condensation of Transactions Identifying the Primary Information Economy
Step 4 Structurization into a Leontief I-O Model
Occupation by Industry Matrix
Special Studies on Inter and Intra Secondary Sector Transactions
Catalogue of Information Commodities in Non-Information Catalogue
Valuation of Secondary Information Commodities by OECD Estimates Method or Porat-Rubin Value-Added Method
Structurization into Leontief I-O Model Identifying Non-Information, Primary and Secondary Sectors
Results of (GOSIE) Structural Analysis
Results of (GOPIE) Structural Analysis

Flow Chart 1

How the Primary Sector is Generated

The identification of the primary information economy, from a conventional presentation of the fundamental equilibrium relationship between demand and supply, can be explained using a simple bi-sector economy, where notation:

X_{ij}: refers to intermediate sales from sector i to sector j.
F_i: refers to final demand of the ith sector.
X_i: refers to gross output or supply of the ith sector.
V_i: refers to value-added or income of the ith sector.
$i = 1, 2$.

A Bi-sector Economy

Intermediate demand			Final Demand		Gross Output
X_{11}	X_{12}	+	F_1	=	X_1
X_{21}	X_{22}		F_2		X_2

Value Added	V_1	V_2

In *Step 1* of the methodology, the transactions of the bi-sector economy are divided into noninformation (N) and primary information (P) components using the information intensity coefficients (p_i). The division of the ij^{th} intermediate transaction yields a four-fold partitioning on the basis of input–output interdependence logic as depicted in Tree Diagram 1 below. Here, the inner pair of subscripts describe the interindustry location, and the outer pair of subscripts provide noninformation, primary information address:

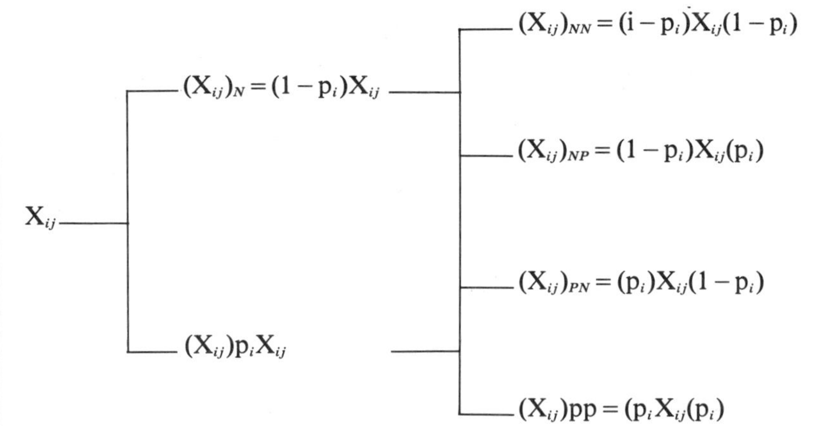

TREE DIAGRAM 1

The new bi-sector economy has 16 intermediate transactions and has the following format, where outer subscripts N and P refer to noninformation and primary information sectors.

		Sector 1 N	Sector 1 P	Sector 2 N	Sector 2 P				
Sector 1	N	$(X_{11})_{NN}$	$(X_{11})_{NP}$	$(X_{12})_{NN}$	$(X_{12})_{NP}$		F_{1N}		X_{1N}
	P	$(X_{11})_{PN}$	$(X_{11})_{PP}$	$(X_{12})_{PN}$	$(X_{12})_{PP}$	+	F_{1P}	=	X_{1P}
Sector 2	N	$(X_{21})_{NN}$	$(X_{21})_{NP}$	$(X_{22})_{NN}$	$(X_{22})_{NP}$		F_{2N}		X_{2N}
	P	$(X_{21})_{PN}$	$(X_{21})_{PP}$	$(X_{22})_{PN}$	$(X_{22})_{PP}$		F_{2P}		X_{2P}
Value-added		V_{1N}	V_{1P}	V_{2N}	V_{2P}				

In *Step 2* of the methodology, homogenization is implemented by re-arranging in a proximate manner similar transactions of noninformation (N) and primary information (P), leading to the following result for the bi-sector economy:

		N	P	N	P				
	N	$(X_{11})_{NN}$	$(X_{12})_{NN}$	$(X_{11})_{NP}$	$(X_{12})_{NP}$		F_{1N}		X_{1N}
		$(X_{21})_{NN}$	$(X_{22})_{NN}$	$(X_{21})_{NP}$	$(X_{22})_{NP}$	+	F_{2N}	=	X_{2N}
	P	$(X_{11})_{PN}$	$(X_{12})_{PN}$	$(X_{11})_{PP}$	$(X_{12})_{PP}$		F_{1P}		X_{1P}
		$(X_{21})_{PN}$	$(X_{22})_{PN}$	$(X_{21})_{PP}$	$(X_{22})_{PP}$		F_{2P}		X_{2P}
Value-added		V_{1N}	V_{2N}	V_{1P}	V_{2P}				

In *Step 3*, the homogeneous transactions are aggregated or a condensation of like transactions is effected clearly identifying separately the non-information and primary information activities of the bi-sector economy thus:

	N	P				
N	X_{NN}	X_{NP}	+	F_N	=	X_N
P	X_{PN}	X_{PP}		F_P		X_P
	V_N	V_P				

In *Step 4*, the bi-sector transactions are restructurized in terms of Leontief fixed coefficients to facilitate further structural analysis of the information economy, yielding the following:

	Intermediate Demand			Final Demand		Gross Output
Noninformation	$A_{NN}X_N$ +	$A_{NP}X_P$	+	F_N	=	X_N
Primary Information Sectors	$A_{PN}X_N$ +	$A_{PP}X_P$		F_P		X_P
Value-added	V_N	V_P				

Generation of the Secondary Information Sector

The planning, coordinating, managerial, and organizational functions of public and private bureaucracies are not marketed; they are in-house transactions. The current national accounts, or I–O statistics, do not, therefore, reflect the contribution to national income of these informational activities of bureaucracies. In every noninformation sector, there are a bureaucracy and a support infrastructure that generate information commodities. If the noninformation sectors can be dichotomized into information and noninformation sub-sectors, we would define the information sub-sector as the secondary information sector. This would comprise quasi firms engaged in informational tasks. The valuation of the national income generated by the secondary information sector can be achieved by either the Rubin-Porat technique (Porat, 1977) or the OECD ratio technique (Organization for Economic Cooperation and Development, 1981).

The Porat-Rubin technique uses a catalogue of information workers in noninformation industries to identify information workers in an occupation by industry matrix. A matrix of occupation by industry or sectors (0/OXS) is compiled from the latest available demographic census. Average wages or workers' compensation of information workers by sector (W/SX1), and average proprietors' income by sector (P/SX1), are estimated. The capital depreciation of information machines by sector is also collated from published sources for each sector (K/SX1). The employee compensation, proprietary incomes, and capital depreciation allowances, when added, proxy the national income generated by the secondary information sector, thus:

$$V_s = \underset{1XS}{i} (\underset{SX1}{W} + \underset{SX1}{P} + \underset{SX1}{K})$$

The final demand of the secondary information sector (F_S) comprises of two items: (a) export of royalties and managerial fees, and (b) sale of R&D contracts to the government. These final demand transactions could be evaluated from published statistics.

The transactions matrix generated by the Primary Information Economy could now be augmented with estimated secondary information sector transactions to give a complete picture of a trichotomized economy, clearly identifying the noninformation (N), primary information (P), and secondary information (S) economies. In a simplified representation, only four types of transactions have to be empirically validated to generate the secondary information economy. They are the intra-industry transactions X_{SN} and X_{SS}, final demand F_S, and the value-added V_S, according to methods described earlier. At least three submatrices are rendered null by definition or assumption. The final upshot could be picturized as follows:

Intermediate Transactions				Final Demand		Output
X_{NN}	X_{NP}	ϕ		F_N		X_N
ϕ	X_{PP}	X_{PS} $(=X_{PN})$	+	F_P	=	X_P
X_{SN}	ϕ	X_{SS}		F_S		X_S

V_N	V_P	V_S

The first four submatrices provide the same information given by GOPIE. $X_{PS} = X_{PN}$, comprise sale of primary information industries to the secondary information sector, and are valued at cost of goods sold. X_{PN} is is rendered a null matrix, as noninformation firms do not have any use for information inputs by definition. By assumption, secondary information sectors transact only a negligible amount of royalties, and can often be regarded as null.

The diagonal matrix X_{SN} represent intrafirm sales of informational services. They are substantial, and are evaluated at going prices for similar services in the primary information sector. The diagonal matrix X_{SS} refers to intraindustry royalty payments, and accounts for royalties on processes or patents sold by one firm to another, e.g., BHP to Utah.

The Structural Analytics of the Information Economy

The economy trichotomized into noninformation (N), primary information (P), and secondary information (S) can be used for structural analysis through the computation of linkages and multipliers. The total linkage L^T, and their additive constituents of backward linkage L^B and forward linkage

L^F, take account of sectoral interdependencies and provide insights on the potential capacities and bottlenecks prevailing in a given economy. The multipliers, on the other hand, quantify the responsiveness of the economy to an exogenously induced shock, usually an expansion of demand. Type I and Type II multipliers are calculated using the open and closed Leontief inverse. The closed inverse endogenizes the household income and final demand components, and reckons their induced effects. Therefore, the Type II multipliers are analogous to the Keynesian multiplier concepts.

Consistent linkages can be computed using the partitioned inverse of the general solution. Total linkage has been defined in the consistent linkage approach as the difference between the actual and hypothetical general solution which freezes intereconomic transactions in the trichotomized model (Cella, 1984).

The actual general solution is:

$$\begin{bmatrix} X_N \\ X_P \\ X_S \end{bmatrix} = \begin{bmatrix} (I - A_{NN}) & -A_{NP} & -A_{NS} \\ -A_{PN} & (I - A_{PP}) & -A_{PS} \\ -A_{SN} & -A_{SP} & (I - A_{SS}) \end{bmatrix}^{-1} \begin{bmatrix} F_N \\ F_P \\ F_S \end{bmatrix}$$

or, equivalently by partitioned inversion, the actual general solution can be represented as:

$$\begin{bmatrix} X_N \\ X_P \\ X_S \end{bmatrix} = \begin{bmatrix} \gamma_{11} & \gamma_{12} & \gamma_{13} \\ \gamma_{21} & \gamma_{22} & \gamma_{23} \\ \gamma_{31} & \gamma_{32} & \gamma_{33} \end{bmatrix} \begin{bmatrix} F_N \\ F_P \\ F_S \end{bmatrix}$$

(Note: the Greek letter γ represents submatrices).

The hypothetical solution freezing intersectoral transactions renders all the off-diagonal matrices in the Leontief inverse of the actual general solution into null matrices. Further, if we define: $B_{JJ} = (I - A_{JJ})^{-1}$ for any J, by partitioned inversion we could obtain the hypothetical general solution, notated with a bar on top as:

$$\begin{bmatrix} X_N \\ X_P \\ X_S \end{bmatrix} = \begin{bmatrix} B_{NN} & \phi & \phi \\ \phi & B_{PP} & \phi \\ \phi & \phi & B_{SS} \end{bmatrix} \begin{bmatrix} F_N \\ F_P \\ F_S \end{bmatrix}$$

The consistent total linkages defined using the differences between actual and hypothetical solutions are:

$\Delta X_J = (X_J - X_J)$, for any J.

$$\begin{bmatrix} \Delta X_N \\ \Delta X_P \\ \Delta X_S \end{bmatrix} = \begin{bmatrix} (\gamma_{11} - B_{NN}) & \gamma_{12} & \gamma_{13} \\ \gamma_{21} & (\gamma_{22} - B_{PP}) & \gamma_{23} \\ \gamma_{31} & \gamma_{32} & (\gamma_{33} - B_{SS}) \end{bmatrix} \begin{bmatrix} F_N \\ F_P \\ F_S \end{bmatrix}$$

Total linkage $L^T = (L^B) + (L^F)$, or, equivalently, it is the scalar:

$$L^T = [i_N'\{(\gamma_{11} - B_{NN}) + \gamma_{21} + \gamma_{31}\}F_N] + [i_p'\{\gamma_{12} + (\gamma_{22} - B_{PP}) + i_S'\{\gamma_{13} + \gamma_{23} + (\gamma_{33} - B_{SS})F_S]$$

The first component in the above summation is the measure of the backward linkage L^B and is analogous to the conventional backward linkage (Rasmussen, 1958). It measures the total direct and indirect inputs needed to support the final demand expansion: F_N. Note that the intraeconomic transactions B_{NN}, are rightly excluded in this measure. The remainder $|L^T - L^B| = L^F$ is the magnitude of the forward linkage which describes the gross outputs required from the noninformation economy N to support the demand expansions on sectors P and S.

By substituting for the unit output expansion (vector i), household income, and employment (vectors V^H and e, respectively), consistent linkages in terms of income and employment can be derived.

Consistent multipliers of various types can be derived on the basis of responsiveness per unit of initial effects (West & Jensen, 1980). Type I multipliers are based on the open inverse $Z = I - A)^{-1}$, where A refers to the direct technical coefficients of the trichotomized economy. Type II multipliers are calculated using the closed inverse $Z^* = (I - A)^{-1}$. Z^* refers to the inverse coefficients truncating the household sector. In closing the system, the household sector has been endogenised. The different types of West-Jensen consistent income multipliers, where V^H is the vector of household income coefficients, is tabulated below, where T denotes transpose and the circumflex (^) denotes the diagonalization operators respectively.

Type	Income (V) Multiplier	Description
IA	$V^T(I + A)\hat{V}^{-1}$	(Initial + First Round ÷ (Initial)
IB	$V^T(\ Z\ )\hat{V}^{-1}$	(Initial + Production Induced) ÷ (Initial)
IIA	$V^T(\ Z\ )\hat{V}^{-1}$	(Initial + Production Induced + Consumption Induced) ÷ (Initial)
IBB	$V^T(Z^* - I)\hat{V}^{-1}$	(Flow-ons) ÷ (Initial)

By substituting i^T and e^T, a sum vector and an employment coefficients vector for V^T, the corresponding consistent output and employment multipliers can be derived.

Conclusion

This study presents a set of value-free techniques to identify the components of the emerging information economy of a nation. The basic input–output models have been modified to generate the primary and secondary information economies in a comprehensive manner. The methodology is logical and holistically accurate. It can be empirically validated for any country that has published national income, census, and input–output statistics. Cross-country comparisons of the latent information structures will provide valuable insights into the process of informatization or the information revolution that is sweeping the world. The benchmark statistics on the information economies that can be derived by the techniques enunciated herein would aid our understanding of the complexities of the new world information order that is replacing the old industrial order.

References

Cella, G. (1984). The input-output measurement of inter-industry linkages. *Oxford Bulletin of Economics and Statistics, 46,* (1).

Organization for Economic Cooperation and Development. (1981). *Information activities, electronics and telecommunication technologies.* (Vol. I and Vol. II). Paris: Organization for Economic Cooperation and Development.

Porat, M.U. (1977). *The information economy.* (9 Vols.) Washington, DC: Government Printing Office.

Rasmussen, D.N. (1958). *Studies in intersectoral relations.* Amsterdam: North-Holland.

West, G.R. & Jensen, R.C. (1980). Some reflections on input-output multipliers. *Annals of Regional Science, 14*(2).

CHAPTER 6

Information Inputs and Outputs in Firms and Quasi-Firms

Yale M. Braunstein

Introduction

This chapter describes the ways in which production processes involving information have been modeled, and, after discussing some of the shortcomings with these efforts, explores new approaches to the modeling problem. Firms use information that is produced externally (by other firms and organizations) and internally (by its employees). A model is developed which includes both purchases of information services and the employment of information (nonproduction) workers as inputs, and then estimates its parameters using econometric methods. The results show that this approach allows us to obtain insights both into the production process and about the contributions of information services and information workers to the economy.

The Information Firm

Due to the similarities in manufacturing certain information products (e.g., typewriters) and noninformation products (e.g., small appliances), the more restrictive definition of information industries utilized elsewhere (Hayes & Erickson, 1982) has been used here. Specifically, only the providers of information services—industries 14 through 23 in Table 1—have been included.

These information firms are generally characterized by economies of scale and scope. This is due to the presence of the relatively high fixed and set-up costs in the information business (commonly referred to as "first-

Table 1. The Information Sectors of the Economy

Sector Rubin #	Number BEA #	SIC #	Sector Name
Products:			
1	11*	15-17*	Information Buildings
2	23*	252-3*	Office Furniture
3	24*	262-4*	Paper
4	26*	27*	Printing and Publishing
5	48*	355*	Printing and Paper Machinery
6	51	357	Office, Computing and Accounting Machines
7	53*	3581	Electronic Components
8	56	365-6	Radio, TV and Communications Equipment
9	57	367	Electronic Components
10	58*	3693	Misc. Electronic Instruments
11	62*	38*	Mechanical Instruments
12	63*	383,6	Photographic Equipment
13	64*	395,9	Advertising Signs and Misc.
Services:			
14	66	48*	Telecommunications
15	67	483	Radio and TV Broadcasting
16	69*	—	Information Trade Margin (wholesale & retail trade)
17	70*	61-4,7	Finance and Insurance
18	71*	65-6*	Real Estate
19	72.02	72*	Repair of Information Products
20	73*	73,81,9	Misc. Business Information Services (incl. advertising)
21	76*	78-9	Motion Pictures
22	77*	80*	Medical and Educational Services
23	78*	4311	Postal Services

Note: *After additions or deletions. Source: Rubin and Sapp (1981)

copy costs") and the opportunities for a variety of products from a common base of inputs. To put the presence of economies of scope into a broader perspective, one can use a special framework (Bailey & Friedlaender, 1982). There are five situations in which economies of scope are likely to arise:

1. sharing tangible factor(s) of production, such as sheep in the production of mutton and wool;
2. flexibility in production technology coupled with the presence of fixed factors of production, such as that which arises from the use of robotics on the factory floor;
3. networking in which coordination leads to cost savings, as in airline routing and telecommunications switching and transmission;
4. reusing an input by multiple outputs, such as in publishing a database in printed and magnetic versions; and
5. sharing of intangible assets, such as research activities.

Figure 1
Firm in the Primary Information Sector

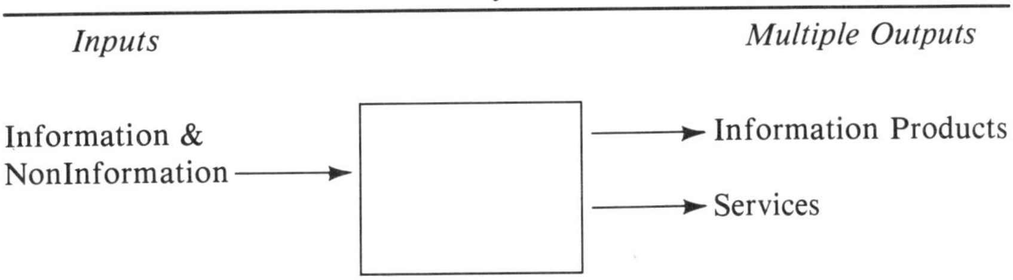

It is frequently the case that the operations of an information firm fit into one or more of these situations. Many of the efforts at modeling firms in information industries have explicitly or implicitly utilized the concepts of economies of scale and scope. The multi-product production process for an information firm is illustrated in Figure 1. Examples from information and communications industries, where the production process has been modeled and the multi-product nature of the output recognized explicitly include journal publishing (Baumol & Braunstein, 1977), abstracting and indexing services (Pulley & Braunstein, 1984), and telephone companies (Fuss & Waverman, 1981).

The Noninformation Firm

The many econometric models of production and cost functions at the level of the (noninformation) firm have been described in several review articles (Bailey & Friedlaender 1982; Johnston, 1960; Walters, 1963). Of interest to this study are those models where informaiton is an identifiable factor in determining the size and scope of the firm, or where information is an explicit input into the production process.

Models in the first category use a Coasian approach to the theory of the firm: the firm exists because it is often economical to perform certain transactions inside one organization rather than to rely on explicit contracts or external markets (Coase, 1937). These studies have focused on the high costs of obtaining information and the problems in transferring information and know-how (Arrow, 1974; Teece, 1980; Williamson, 1975). Porat used the term "quasi-information firm" to describe the information activities inside noninformation firms (Porat, 1977). When aggregated, the activities of these quasi-information firms constitute the "secondary information sector."

Because of the difficulties in obtaining data on information flows at the level of the firm or the industry, there are few studies that explicitly model

Figure 2
Non-Information Firm

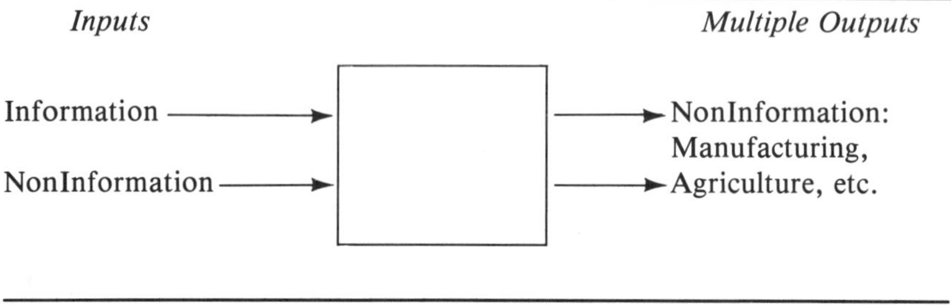

information as an input into the production process itself. Two studies (Hayes & Erickson, 1982; Braunstein, 1985) have used the Porat-Rubin input–output data from U.S. manufacturing industries. These data sets for 1967 and 1972 include the value of shipments from each information industry to each of the other industries in the economy. This allows information to be treated much like any other input, such as labor or intermediate goods and services. The problems of measuring capital stocks versus flows and of obtaining physical units for the inputs remain, but, conceptually, information is treated as just one of several identifiable inputs (see Figure 2).

The Quasi-Information Firm

There are three major problems with the approaches to modeling the contribution of information to the economy as described above:

1. information is produced by both firms in information industries and firms in other (noninformation) industries, and models of the former may not be suitable for the latter;
2. information may be an input, an intermediate product, and an output of noninformation firms, and models that focus on only one of these roles may not accurately reflect how information is produced and used in the economy;
3. the use of aggregate economy-wide data, in the absence of firm or industry data, may prevent one from being able to reflect adequately the complexities of information production and use.

Jonscher has avoided the first two of these problems by developing a macroeconomic framework for analyzing the productivity in the (noninformation, nonextraction) production sector and in the information sector (Jonscher, 1982, 1983). His two-sector approach explicitly classifies "the

Figure 3
Combined NonInformation Firm & Quasi-Information Firm

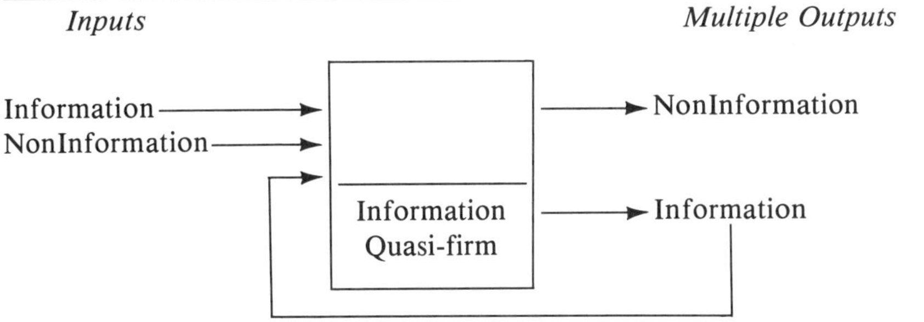

activity of all individuals whose primary function is to create, process, and handle information'' into an information sector (Jonscher, 1983, p. 16).

In other words, the information sector as defined by Jonscher contains the activity of all information workers, regardless of whether they are employed in the primary or secondary information sector. Jonscher then measures aggregate outputs, value added, and productivity for his information and production sectors, but he makes no effort to disaggregate his results to the firm or industry level.

Another approach would be to model the production process to incorporate explicitly the various information inputs—purchased information services and the effort of information workers. The firm would be viewed conceptually as being like the model in Figure 3.

The econometric analysis could proceed by dividing the labor input into information and noninformation employment, and generalizing the production function to include the additional inputs. This requires obtaining data that are not available in either Porat's original published works or the data tapes that were made available at that time. The work published by Porat and Rubin contained data on total compensation of information and noninformation workers by industry, but they did not make available the components to enable one to develop data on the number of information and noninformation employees by industry. Conceivably, it is possible to use data from an unpublished Bureau of Labor Statistics Occupation-by-Industry matrix for 1970 that would be consistent with the Porat-Rubin compensation totals. (For more on this procedure, see Porat, 1977, v. 7, p. 2).

An alternative source of data is a 1978 Bureau of Economic Analysis staff paper which provides 1967 employment data for production and nonproduction workers for all of the industries as defined for the 1967 input-output tables (Coughlin, 1978). These data use the Census of Manufactures definition of production workers, rather than the Porat breakdown by job classification. In addition, employees of "central administrative offices" are included (originally, they were included by the Census in mineral industries, but excluded from the manufacturing data), and there are minor changes to reflect corrections made since the release of the original Census data.

Six alternative versions, having from two to four inputs, of the Cobb-Douglas specification of the production function were estimated (see equations 2-1 through 2-6 in Table 2). The general forms of these equations are:

$\ln V = a_0 + a_1 \ln K + a_2 \ln L + a_3 \ln I$ and

$\ln V = b_0 + b_1 \ln K + b_2 \ln Lp + b_3 \ln Li + b_4 \ln I$

where:

K = capital; the sum of gross book value of fixed assets, from 1968-1969 Annual Survey of Manufactures, and inventory, from 1967 Census of Manufactures;

L = total employment (see text);

Lp = number of production workers (see text);

Li = number of non-production workers (see text);

I = information services; the purchases from ten information service sectors (see Table 1), as calculated by Porat (1977).

The results indicate that purchases of information services from the information sector are an important input (see equation 2-2)[1], and that it is useful to disaggregate total employment into production and non-production workers (see equations 2-3 through 2-5). However, when both information purchases and the disaggregated labor variables are used as explanatory variables, the presence of multicollinearity causes one of the coefficients to no longer be statistically significant.

The marginal products of the information and labor inputs, calculated at the mean values of the variables, are also presented in Table 2. The estimates of the marginal product of information are all close to the value of 2.37 calculated by Hayes and Erickson using 1967 data (Hayes & Erickson, 1982, p. 325). With one exception, the marginal products of the labor variables indicate that nonproduction workers have marginal products two to three times that of productions workers. The one exception is equation 2-6, which has the coefficients whose accuracy is suspect because of the presence of multi-collinearity.

It is interesting to compare these calculated marginal products with the actual average payments of wages and salaries to employees in manufacturing industries. The Bureau of Economic Analysis data include total wages paid to production workers and total wages and salaries paid to all workers

[1] The results in equation 2-2 are similar to those of Hayes and Erickson (1982). However, as they use different data for total employment, the estimated coefficients are not identical.

Table 2. Regression Results: Cobb-Douglas Production Functions (1967 Data)

Independent Variable	Coefficient	2-1	2-2	2-3	2-4	2-5	2-6
ln K	b_1	.509	.347	.355	.400	.444	.341
(capital)		(10.3)	(6.88)	(7.09)	(6.19)	(8.01)	(6.67)
ln L		.451	.353	—	—	—	—
(total empl.)		(7.77)	(7.05)	—	—	—	—
ln Lp	b_2	—	—	.287	—	.232	.260
(pdn. workers)				(7.02)		(4.20)	(5.62)
ln Li	b_3	—	—	—	.269	.276	.0844
(nonpdn. workers)					(3.45)	(4.16)	(1.23)
ln I	b_4	—	.275	.336	.245	—	.290
(inf. services)			(5.22)	(6.69)	(3.07)		(4.66)
Constant	b_0	1.34	1.62	1.66	2.19	2.00	1.83
R^2		.955	.972	.972	.954	.960	.973
F		503.	532.	530.	316.	365.	402.
Calculated Values:	**MP: Marginal Products**						
MP_L		5.24	4.10	—	—	—	—
MP_{Lp}		—	—	4.67	—	3.77	4.23
MP_{Li}		—	—	—	10.9	11.2	3.42
MP_I		—	2.23	2.73	1.99	—	2.35

Note: For each regression coefficient, the entry is: Coefficient
(t-statistic)

in these industries (Coughlin, 1978, p. 23). (Supplements are not disaggregated by employment category, so it is necessary to use wage and salary data rather than total compensation). As shown in Table 3, the estimates of the marginal products of both total employment and the two categories from equations 2-1 through 2-5 are quite close to the average earnings of each group. One interesting result is that the nonproduction workers have marginal products slightly above their average earnings in these industries, while the reverse is true for the production workers and for all workers combined.

The second set of equations uses the translog specification of the production function. The specific form of these equations is:

$$\ln V = b_0 + b_1 \ln K + b_2 \ln Lp + b_3 \ln Li + b_4 \ln I + c_1 (\ln K)^2 + c_2(\ln Lp)^2 + c_3 (\ln Li)^2 + c_4 (\ln I)^{2s} d_1 (\ln K)(\ln Lp) + \ldots + d_6(\ln Li)(\ln I).$$

This is a general second-order approximation to any production function (Christensen, Jorgenson, & Lau, 1973). Unlike the Cobb-Douglas assumption of unitary, constant elasticities of substitution, the flexibility of the translog allows the pairwise elasticities of substitution between the inputs to vary.

Table 3. Calculated Marginal Products and Average Wages and Salaries Data (1967 Data in thousands of dollars)

Worker Type	2-1	2-2	2-3	2-4	Equation 2-5	2-6	Actual Wages & Salaries
All workers	5.24	4.10	—	—	—	—	6.90
Production Workers	—	—	4.67	—	3.77	4.23	5.83
Nonproduction Workers	—	—	—	10.9	11.2	3.42	9.53

Translog equations with different subsets of the explanatory variable were estimated; three equations (4-1 through 4-3) with all coefficients statistically significant are shown in Table 4.

Each of these equations includes a different set of explanatory variables and has slightly different coefficient estimates. Nevertheless, the estimated values of the marginal products of information and the two types of labor are consistent within the set and, with one exception, consistent with the Cobb-Douglas estimates. The exception is the marginal product of nonproduction workers—the estimated values from translog equations 4-2 and 4-3 are 3.13 and 1.95, respectively. These estimates are considerably less than two of the three Cobb-Douglas estimates (see equations 2-4 and 2-5). Although the estimates of the marginal products from the translog equations are similar to those from equation 2-6, again the presence of multicollinearity in these equations casts doubt on the accuracy of the parameter estimates.

Conclusion

Although the data used for this analysis are at the industry level and are from only one cross-section, the regression results show that it may be possible to identify separately the contributions of information and labor inputs to value-added in manufacturing. The evidence indicates that both the purchases of information services (external information) and the employment of information workers (internal information) make substantial contributions to the productivity of U.S. manufacturing industries.

More detailed data at a less aggregated level, and/or data from additional years, are needed to refine this analysis. By obtaining and analyzing additional data, it should be possible to estimate the elasticities of substitu-

Table 4. Regression Results: Translog Production (1967 Data)

Independent Variable	Coefficient	4-1	4-2	4-3
ln K	b_1	1.18	1.01	—
(capital)		(5.17)	(4.01)	
ln Lp	b_2	.283	.262	.257
(pdn. workers)		(7.10)	(6.04)	(6.12)
ln Li	b_3	—	.452	1.06
(non-pdn. workers)			(3.87)	(5.99)
ln I	b_4	—	—	—
(inf. services)				
$(\ln K)^2$	c_1	−.0478	—	—
		(−3.46)		
$(\ln Li)^2$	c_3	—	.133	.178
			2.76	3.39
$(\ln I)^2$	c_4	.0248	—	−.161
		(6.53)		−4.52
(ln Li)(ln K)	d_2	—	−.187	−.309
			(−3.63)	(4.29)
(ln K)(ln I)	d_3	—	.0309	.275
			(4.32)	(5.26)
Constant	b_o	−.717	−.878	2.04
R^2		.974	.978	.979
F		418.	313.	337.
Calculated values:		**MP: Marginal Product**		
Mp_{Lp}		4.60	4.26	4.18
MP_{Li}		—	3.13	1.95
Mp_I		2.54	2.18	2.91

Note: For each regression coefficient, the entry is: Coefficient
(t-statistic)

tion between internal and external information and between production and information workers. This will shed light on questions of whether these inputs are substitutes or complements and will add to our knowledge of the roles of the primary and secondary information sectors in the economy.

References

Arrow, K.J. (1974). *Limits of organization.* New York: Norton.

Bailey, E.E., & Friedlaender, A.F. (1982). Market structure and multiproduct industries. *Journal of Economic Literature, 20,* 1024–1048.

Baumol, W.J., & Braunstein, Y.M., (1977). Empirical study of scale economies and product complementarity: The case of journal publication. *Journal of Political Economy, 85,* 1037–1048.

Braunstein, Y.M. (1985). Information as a factor of production: Substitutability and productivity. *The Information Society,* 3, 261–273.

Christensen, L.R., Jorgenson, D.W., & Lau, L.J. (1973). Transcendental logarithmic production frontiers. *Review of Economics and Statistics, 55,* 28–45.

Coase, R.H. (1937). The nature of the firm. *Economica* N.S., *4,* 386–405.

Coughlin, P.E. (1978). *Employment and employee compensation in the 1967 input-output study.* (BEA Staff Paper No. 31). Washington, DC: Bureau of Economic Analysis.

Fuss, M.A., & Waverman L. (1981). Regulation of the multiproduct firm: The case of telecommunications in Canada. In G. Fromm (Ed.), *Studies in public regulation.* Cambridge, MA: MIT Press.

Hayes, R.M., & Erickson, T. (1982). Added value as a function of purchases of information services. *Information Society, 1,* 307–338.

Johnston, J. (1960). *Statistical cost analysis.* New York: McGraw-Hill.

Jonscher, C. (1982). Aggregate measurement of information resources in the economy. (Mimeo.) Cambridge, MA: Sloan School of Management, Massachusetts Institute of Technology.

Jonscher, C. (1983). Information resources and economic productivity. *Information Economics and Policy, 1,* 13–35.

Porat, M.U. (1977). *The information economy.* Washington, DC: Department of Commerce, Office of Telecommunications.

Pulley, L.B. & Braunstein, Y.M. (1984). Scope and scale augmenting technological change: An application in the information sector. *In* M. Jussawalla and H. Ebenfield (Eds.), *Communications and information economics: New perspectives,* New York: Elsevier.

Rubin, M.R., & Sapp, M.E. (1981). Selected roles of information goods and services in the U.S. national economy. *Information Processing and Management, 17,* 195–213.

Teece, D.J. (1980). Economies of scope and the scope of the enterprise. *Journal of Economic Behavior and Organization, 1,* 223–247.

Walters, A.A. (1963). Production and cost functions: An econometric survey. *Econometrica, 31,* 1–66.

Williamson, O.E. (1975). *Markets and hierarchies: Analysis and antitrust implications.* New York: Free Press.

CHAPTER 7

Sectoral Interdependencies Within An Information Economy

Chee-Wah Cheah

I. Introduction

The size of an economy's primary information sector can be quantified in terms of the aggregate value added originating from the production or distribution of information goods and services, or in terms of the number of workers engaged in information-related occupations. The former approach is facilitated by the availability of factor income components, which are conveniently derived from an input–output (IO) accounting scheme (Cheah, 1983; Karunaratne, 1983). Even though IO methods suffer from certain restrictive assumptions, there are advantages to be gained, since IO models are amenable to dealing with questions of economic dependencies.

The present chapter is motivated, in part, by a recognition that the IO approach to information sector analysis is but a special case of a general class of IO models.[1] Its main purpose is to extend the analysis of sectoral interdependencies within the information economy, through an intensive application of IO techniques. The point of departure for the proposed exercise is the Leontief inverse. Although conventional output multipliers derived from the Leontief inverse are useful in denoting total demand-generating effects, it is felt that certain inherent properties of intersectoral as well as intrasectoral industrial relationships have been unnecessarily neglected (Kanunaratne & Cameron, 1980, 1981; Jussawalla & Dworak, 1983).

Section II establishes the conceptual premise of sectoral submultipliers within an IO framework. In particular, the disjoined effects of these multi-

[1] The general class of IO models referred to are those which separate industries within an economy into two or more groups of research or policy interest. Familiar examples include interregional IO models and other IO models which distinguish between sectors subject to capacity limitations and sectors with ample capacity.

pliers are made explicit through the solution of an IO system formulated in terms of partitioned martrices. The usefulness of the submiltiplier concept is then demonstrated in an empirical study of sectoral interdependencies in the Singaporean information economy. The empirical results are summarized and discussed in Section III. Finally, Section IV concludes the paper with some brief remarks on the methodological and policy implications of submultiplier analysis.

II. Sectoral Interdependencies and Submultipliers

Consider the IO system of an information economy with n industries. It is assumed that these industries are prearranged in such a manner that the first p industries (where $p<n$) constitute the primary information sector, while the remaining q industries (where $q=n-p$) make up the rest of the economy (i.e., the noninformation sector). The IO system of the overall economy is conveniently summarized by the matrix expression

$$X=AX+F \tag{1}$$

where X is an (nxl) column vector of output levels, A is an n-square matrix of input coefficients, and F is an (nxl) column vector of final demand. The solution of X in (1) leads to the standard (open) input- output model

$$X=(I-A)^{-1}F \tag{2}$$

where $(I-A)^{-1}$ is the familiar Leontief inverse or multiplier matrix. It is well known that elements of the Leontief inverse can be summed vertically (i.e., column-wise) and horizontally (i.e., row-wise) to yield coefficients of backward and forward multipliers, respectively. Although these multipliers convey useful information about the direct and indirect effects of variations in final demand on industry production levels, pertinent information about economic interdependencies at a subaggregate level is often overlooked.

The relevant sectoral subaggregates of an information economy are, of course, the primary information and non-information sectors.[2] Conceptually, the distinct identity of these two sectors can be maintained in the framework of a segregated economy with corresponding IO relationships expressed as

$$X_i=BX_i+B_oX_g+F_i \tag{3a}$$

$$X_g=C_oX_i+CS_g+F_g \tag{3b}$$

[2] For convenience, subsequent discussion in the text makes use of the letters "i" and "g" to denote references to the primary information sector and noninformation sector, respectively.

where X_i, X_g are output vectors, and F_i, F_g are final demand vectors of the i and g sectors respectively; B, C are square matrices of intrasectoral input coefficients with dimensions (pxp) and (qxq) respectively, and B_o, C_o are rectangular matrices of intersectoral input coefficients with dimensions (pxq) and (qxp) respectively.

Let X* and F* be partitioned column vectors such that $X^{*\prime} = \{X_i' \mid X_g'\}$ and $\mathbf{F}^{*\prime} = \{F_i' \mid F_g'\}$. Furthermore, let **A*** be a partitioned matrix which is define

$$A^* = \left[\begin{array}{c|c} B & B_o \\ \hline C_o & C \end{array}\right] \tag{4}$$

By analogy to (1), the IO system of (3a) and (3b) can be rewritten as

$$x^* = A^*X^* + F^* \tag{5}$$

This can be solved for X* by inverting the partitioned matrix

$$(I - A^*) = \left[\begin{array}{c|c} (I-B) & -B_o \\ \hline -C_o & (I-C) \end{array}\right] \tag{6}$$

where it is understood that the identity matrices I are of conformable order. Note that (I – A*) in (6) is a disjoined version of the original technical coefficients matrix (I – A). In general, (I – A*) has a nonnegative inverse, since there is no a priori reason why the original technical coefficients matrix should violate the Hawkins-Simon conditions.

It is simple but tedious to show that $(I - A^*)^{-1}$ can be obtained by solving

$$(I - A^*)\,(I^* - A^*)^{-1} = (I - A^*)^{-1}\,(I - A^*) = I^* \tag{7}$$

where the unit matrix I* has been partitioned conformably. This amounts to solving a system of simultaneous equations involving submatrices. The solution to (7) may be expressed as

$$\left[\begin{array}{c|c} \{P + (PB_o)(RQ)(C_oP)\} & (PB_o)(RQ) \\ \hline (RQ)(C_oP) & (RQ) \end{array}\right] \tag{8a}$$

$$= \left[\begin{array}{c|c} (SP) & (SP)(B_oQ) \\ \hline (QC_o)(SP) & \{(Q + QC_o)(SP)(B_o)\} \end{array}\right] \tag{8b}$$

where

$$P = (I - B)^{-1} \tag{9}$$

$$Q = (I - C)^{-1} \tag{10}$$

$$R = \{I - (QC_o)(PB_o)\}^{-1} \tag{11}$$

and $$S = \{I - (PB_o)(QC_o)\}^{-1} \tag{12}$$

The analytic advantage of (8) is that it provides details about the "composition" of conventional multiplier effects. It is interesting to note that the diagonal submatrix expressions in (8) suggest an equivalence between the additive and multiplicative forms of multiplier effects originating from intrasectoral activities. In particular,

$$P + (PB_o)(RQ)(C_oP) = SP \tag{13}$$

and

$$Q + (QC_o)(SP)(B_oQ) = RQ \tag{14}$$

The economic meanings of P and Q are relatively straightforward. P and Q are submultipliers internal to the i and g sector respectively since each of these matrices are defined upon sector-specific input coefficients.

The products of internal submultipliers (i.e., P or Q) and intersectoral input requirements (viz., B_o and C_o) yield coefficients of intersectoral effects on production. Thus, PB_o denotes the extent to which production within the i sector is induced by the use of i goods in the g sector, while QC_o denotes the use of g goods in the i sector induced by multiplier effects internal to the i sector, and B_oQ denotes similar effects from the standpoint of the g sector.

These intersectoral relationships enter into the definitions of R and S (see 11 and 12). In other words, R and S are essentially submultipliers derived from intersectoral coefficients of induced effects on production. Thus, for any given sector (i or g), these submultipliers indicate roundabout repercussions of productive activities within the other sector. Since the inducement effects originate from an "external" source, R and S can be interpreted as "external" submultipliers. For example, S is an external submultiplier of the i sector because it is derived from its own sectoral coefficients of induced effects (i.e., PB_o) weighted by similar inducement effects originating from an external source (i.e., QC_o).

Thus, the submultiplier analysis from the standpoint of the i sector can be summarized as follows. The multiplier effects arising from intrasectoral activities within the i sector itself are due to an internal component P and an external component S, or, as indicated in (13), intrasectoral multipliers are the sum of direct and indirect submultipliers. Similarly, multipliers arising from intersectoral activities are due to two submultiplier components. The first of these components are coefficients of intersectoral induced effects on production (viz., PB_o and C_oP). These coefficients matrices are either pre- or postmultiplied by the matrix of aggregate intrasectoral multipliers within the g sector (viz., RQ).

III. An Empirical Application

The extended multiplier analysis developed above is applied to the case of Singapore's information economy (Jussawalla & Cheah, 1983; Cheah, 1983). In particular, the analysis is based on an IO system with 25 industries, which has been defined in such a manner that the first 17 industries (i.e., $p = 17$) constitute the primary information sector i. The remaining 8 industries (i.e., $q = 8$) make up the noninformation sector.[3] In view of (4), the technical coefficients matrix for this IO system is partitioned into four submatrices with dimensions conforming to the predetermined values of p and q. The submultiplier matrices of relevance are computed according to equations (9) through (12).

The pattern of intrasectoral submultipliers is summarized by column and row totals of the internal (P) and external (S) submultiplier matrices for the 17 industries within the i sector. The results are presented in Table 1. It can be seen that the column totals of P exceed those of S in all industries. This is also true of the row totals, with the exception of sector 7. The average magnitude of the internal submultiplier is 1.095. According to equation (13),

Table 1. Internal and External Submultipliers of the Information Sector

	Column Totals		Row Totals	
Sector	Internal (P)	External (S)	Internal (P)	External (S)
1	1.015	1.013	1.002	1.000
2	1.078	1.015	1.028	1.001
3	1.046	1.010	1.010	1.000
4	1.032	1.005	1.047	1.003
5	1.092	1.014	1.059	1.000
6	1.055	1.011	1.002	1.000
7	1.164	1.014	1.140	1.151
8	1.185	1.026	1.026	1.008
9	1.095	1.057	1.035	1.012
10	1.039	1.014	1.052	1.007
11	1.140	1.026	1.419	1.052
12	1.164	1.010	1.282	1.021
13	1.026	1.007	1.018	1.003
14	1.120	1.002	1.000	1.000
15	1.189	1.017	1.135	1.003
16	1.059	1.011	1.282	1.031
17	1.108	1.024	1.028	1.005
Average	1.095	1.016	1.085	1.016

[3] Data for the present empirical exercise are drawn from Singapore's IO table for the year 1978 (see Singapore, 1983).

this would evoke a roundabout external repercussion via the g sector's industrial activities. The average size of this external effect is 1.016, or about 7 percent of the aggregate multiplier effect associated with intrasectoral industrial activities. This results suggests that the i sector's dependence on g's activities is rather minimal.

The nature of intersectoral relationships can be inferred from coefficients of intersectoral inducement effects. These coefficients are summarized in terms of column and row totals of four submultiplier matrices. Table 2 presents the inducement effects on production in one sector which are due to the other sector's input activity. For instance, the use of i goods in the g sector (as indicated by the input coefficients matrix B_o) will induce output effects within the i sector (via the internal submultipliers P_o). The row totals of PB_o show the size of the inducement effect "received" by industries within the i sector, while the column totals measure the extent of "in-

Table 2. Intersectoral Submultiplier Analysis: Inducement to Production Per Unit of Cross-sectoral Input

Sector	Industry Inducing	Industry Receiving
Information	(Column Sum QC_o)	(Row Sum PB_o)
1	.287	.0
2	.231	.001
3	.108	.0
4	.089	.008
5	.188	.0
6	.188	.0
7	.115	.0
8	.198	.140
9	.431	.015
10	.236	.013
11	.226	.089
12	.103	.030
13	.148	.092
14	.182	.0
15	.161	.005
16	.098	.044
17	.184	.014
Average	.187	.027
Noninformation	(Column Sum PB_o)	(Row Sum QC_o)
18	.020	.803
19	.168	1.296
20	.098	.530
21	.022	.005
22	.038	.002
23	.096	.003
24	.011	.374
25	.011	.164
Average	.058	.164

ducible power'' associated with unit changes in the input requirements of industries within the g sector. The column and row totals of QC_o give the obverse of these relationships from the standpoint of the g sector.

From Table 2 it can be seen that the average inducible power of the i sector is more than twice that of the g sector. At the same time, the average induced effects received by the g sector is more than 10 times of those received by the i sector. This finding is consistent with the earlier conclusion that the i sector's expansion does not depend heavily on g activities. On the whole, Table 2 suggests that the g sector will receive measureable benefits via the intersectoral production processes as a result of stimulative investment programs in the i sector.

This observation is strengthened by an analysis of the submultiplier matrices C_oP and B_oQ in Table 3. These submultipliers show the extent of inducement to input in one sector resulting from the internal submultiplier

Table 3. Intersectoral Submultiplier Analysis:
Inducement to Cross-sectoral Input Activity Due to Internal Multiplier Effect

Sector	Industry Inducing	Industry Receiving
Information	(Column Sum C_oP)	(Row Sum B_{oq})
1	.23	.001
2	.203	.001
3	.093	.0
4	.077	.010
5	.168	.0
6	.165	.0
7	.111	.190
8	.181	.017
9	.319	.019
10	.189	.014
11	.200	.096
12	.100	.032
13	.125	.109
14	.158	.0
15	.152	.005
16	.085	.043
17	.160	.016
Average	.162	.033
Noninformation	(Column Sum B_oQ)	(Row Sum C_oP)
18	.025	.578
19	.171	.172
20	.108	.510
21	.035	.001
22	.045	.0
23	.133	.0
24	.014	.359
25	.020	.140
Average	.069	.345

effects in the other sector. For instance, the internal propagation of multiplier effects in i (as measured by P) will create inducements to input activities in the g sector (as per the input coefficients matrix C_o). The row of totals of C_oP gives the size of these inducements received by industries in the g sector, while the column totals represent the inducible power associated with the output submultipliers of the i sector. Of course, the column and row totals of B_oQ measure the obverse relationships from the standpoint of the g sector (see Table 3). On average, the differential pattern displayed by these multiplier-induced intersectoral input activities is similar to that observed for the cases of PB_o and QC_o in Table 2.

Conclusion

The policy relevance of IO-based structural analysis stems from the information it provides about the essential elements of structural change which accompany economic development. In this regard, the analysis of multipliers at the subaggregate level can be considered useful. In particular, it provides information by which the inducible power of one sector (or an industry within a particular sector) on another can be ascertained. The results from the Singapore example indicate that, even though the i sector does not rely heavily on the g sector, the i sector does generate substantial inducement effects on the production activities of the g sector. On the basis of an understanding of intrasector relationships, policymakers should be well equipped in determining priorities for sectoral allocation of resources.

The methodological usefulness of an extended analysis of sectoral interdependencies via submultipliers can be gauged from a short discourse on the standard approaches to structural analyses. The simplest approach is based on an examination of ratios of intermediate to total transactions (Hirschman, 1961). For instance, the distribution of sectoral purchases by origin, expressed as percentages of total supply, provides linkage indicators of the extent to which a given industry draws on its economic environment. These indicators for the case of Singapore are presented in Table 4. The self-sufficient nature of the i sector is apparent from the observation that only two out of 17 i industries in Table 4 (viz., sectors 1 and 9) purchase more than 20% of their inputs from the g sector.

The finding is consistent with the results of Section III. However, the indicators in Table 4 are only useful in denoting direct production effects as measured within the technical coefficients matrix. This drawback can be overcome by using the Leontief inverse. Aside from the derivation of multipliers, coefficients of power of dispersion (or backward linkages) and sensitivity to dispersion (or forward linkages) can be computed from the Leontief inverse via column and row sums which are standardized by the

Table 4. Sectoral Purchases by Origin (%)*

Sector	Information Sector	Noninformation Sector	Primary Inputs	Imports
1	1.3	23.1	32.8	42.8
2	7.0	19.3	28.0	45.8
3	4.3	8.7	37.0	50.0
4	3.0	7.4	26.5	63.1
5	8.4	15.5	38.1	38.1
6	4.5	15.0	50.0	25.0
7	14.6	9.1	72.1	4.2
8	16.5	15.7	63.8	4.1
9	8.6	34.2	36.3	20.9
10	3.4	18.3	75.2	3.0
11	12.7	18.1	52.2	17.1
12	14.3	8.3	42.5	34.9
13	2.4	12.2	55.3	30.1
14	10.5	14.3	69.7	5.5
15	16.2	12.7	60.0	11.1
16	5.3	7.8	83.2	3.7
17	9.7	14.6	70.0	5.8
18	1.8	13.8	19.4	65.0
19	14.6	22.1	42.5	20.8
20	8.7	18.1	63.9	9.3
21	2.1	37.0	43.6	17.3
22	3.5	13.9	60.2	22.5
23	9.1	32.4	42.0	16.5
24	1.0	24.2	54.2	21.0
25	1.0	27.1	42.5	29.4

* Row entries may not sum at 100%, due to rounding errors.

grand mean of all elements in the inverse matrix (Rasmussen, 1956). The values and relative ranks of Singapore's output multipliers (M) and backward and forward linkages (L_b and L_f respectively) are shown in Table 5. It can be seen that five of the top ten sectors ranked by size of M and L_b are industries within the i sector.

There is no denying that such information is of great value in exercises of key sector identification. However, since the level of analysis is still being conducted at a somewhat gross or aggregate level, details about sectoral variations and subsequent reactions in an interdependent system of industrial activities are unavailable. In light of this, the analysis in Section III should be considered a supplementary rather than a substitute approach to IO-based structural analysis. As mentioned earlier, the advantage of the submultiplier approach lies in its provision of more refined information of policy relevance. Finally, it is possible that more intensive multiplier analysis of the information economy can be devised in terms of the "segregated IO model" in Section II by appropriate partitioning of important economic

Table 5. Sectoral Multipliers and Linkages Ranked by Size

Sector	M	L_B	Sector	L_F
9	1.6159	1.2065	18	2.2681
23	1.6117	1.2034	19	2.2297
19	1.5080	1.1260	20	1.3721
21	1.4817	1.1063	11	1.1898
8	1.4483	1.0814	24	1.1302
11	1.4238	1.0631	7	1.1285
15	1.4061	1.0499	16	1.0275
20	1.3722	1.0245	12	1.0056
14	1.3484	1.0068	23	0.9515
25	1.3473	1.0059	25	0.9290
2	1.3419	1.0019	15	0.8548
17	1.3404	1.0008	13	0.8451
7	1.3236	0.9883	8	0.8194
1	1.3229	0.9877	10	0.8044
5	1.3153	0.9821	9	0.7978
24	1.3068	0.9757	4	0.7930
12	1.3013	0.9717	5	0.7915
10	1.2671	0.9461	2	0.7694
22	1.2283	0.9171	21	0.7587
18	1.1980	0.8945	3	0.7548
13	1.1867	0.8860	22	0.7506
16	1.1806	0.8815	1	0.7494
3	1.1744	0.8769	6	0.7481
4	1.1318	0.8450	14	0.7467

aggregates such as trade balance, employment and income (value added) distribution. Research along these directions will be of much relevance for further and more robust studies of information economies.

References

Cheah, C.W. (1983). *Further evidence on the size and structure of Singapore's primary information sector.* Paper presented at the Input-Output Workshop, Eighth Annual Meeting of the Regional Science Association, University of New England, Armidale, Australia.

Hirschman, A.O. (1961). *The strategy of economic development.* New Haven, CT: Yale University Press.

Jussawalla, M. & Cheah, C.W. (1983). Towards an information economy: The case of Singapore. *Information Economics and Policy, 1,* pp. 161–176.

Jussawalla, M. & Dworak, S. (1983). *The primary information sector of a developing country: The case of the Philippines.* Unpublished manuscript, East-West Communication Institute, Honolulu, Hawaii.

Karunaratne, N.D. (1983). *The information economy and a methodology for its identification.* Unpublished manuscript, East-West Center-University of Queensland Collaborative Project, Honolulu, Hawaii.

Karunaratne, N.D., & Cameron, A.D. (1980). Input output analysis and the Australian information economy. *Information and Management, 3,* 191–206.

Karunaratne, N.D., & Cameron, A.D. (1981). A comparative analysis of the "Information Economy" in developed and developing countries. *Journal of Information Science, 3,* 113–127.

Rasmussen, P.N. (1956). *Studies in inter-sectoral relations.* Amsterdam: North-Holland.

Singapore, Department of Statistics, (1983). *Singapore input-output tables, 1978.* Singapore: Department of Statistics.

CHAPTER 8

Secondary Sector Analysis: Methods and Data Requirements

D. McL. Lamberton

Introduction

Let me begin this Chapter by reproducing a short section from a recent study (Organization for Economic Cooperation and Development, 1981, pp. 21–22).

> The "Primary Information Sector" (PIS) is a proportion of total GDP, with this sector including goods and services which intrinsically convey information (such as books), or which are directly useful in its production, processing or distribution (such as computers). Further, these goods and services must be transacted on established markets for inclusion in the IS. The PIS provides the technical infrastructure for a variety of information processing and transmission activities as well as offering information goods and services for sale directly as a commodity (as with software consultants). Put another way, the PIS is the productive focus of an information-based economy. The *entire* value added[1] in providing such goods and services will be attributed to the Primary Information Sector.
>
> The "Secondary Information Sector" (SIS) is a proportion of total GDP, with this sector recording the value added by "information activities"[2] used up on producing *non-information* goods and services.
>
> The "Primary Information Sector" accounts, by omitting non-market transactions, understate the true contribution of "information" goods and services

[1] That is, resulting from *both* information and noninformation activities as factor input.

[2] Principally, employee compensation of information workers and depreciation on information equipment.

> to GDP. For instance, non-information principal products use information inputs in their production and these would only have been included in the PIS accounts IF they had been purchased on established markets. Suppose the pharmaceuticals industry hired chartered accountants in preparing financial statements, such consultative activity would have appeared in the PIS under ISIC 8322 as a professional service. However, if the pharmaceuticals industry had used its own accountancy section (should such exist) then this non-market "information" activity would *not* have been measured within the Primary Information Sector. The Secondary Information Sector helps in this respect by recording the value added by all information "services" produced for *internal consumption* within those parts of the public sector and private industry which do not belong to the Primary Information Sector. It includes the costs of organizing departments and firms, maintaining and regulating markets, developing and transmitting prices, the monitoring of performance and the making and enforcing of policy.

"Nonmarket" is used in a restricted sense. If I walk to work, or prepare my own tax returns rather than employ a consultant, these are nonmarket activities but they are not comparable to the pharmaceutical firm using its own accountancy section. In information sector analysis, "nonmarket" seems to be restricted to those nonmarket activities engaged in, in connection with other market activities. Where the noninformation goods and services are not marketed, as may be the case in the public sector, the other market activity may be confined to the labor market. I emphasize this as a reminder of the importance of convention and market orientation in national income accounting.

The Magnitude of the Secondary Information Sector

How important is this secondary sector? Table 1 shows a comparison for Japan, U.K., and the U.S.

If we view the primary and secondary sectors as additive, and take the latest available year in each case, the totals range from 35 percent (Japan, in 1970) to approximately 49 percent for U.S. Of course, we lack such secondary sector statistics for all but a few countries. What can we deduce about the secondary sector from knowledge of the primary sector magnitude and other statistics such as those for employment and foriegn trade? Rubin's study of the Venezuelan information economy suggests an approach (Rubin, 1982). Lacking the more detailed analysis that use of an input–output matrix would make possible, he argued that employment and foreign trade conditions indicated a pent-up demand not currently satisfied by local production. A quarter of the workforce was employed in information activities, but the primary information sector accounted for only 10 percent of

Table 1. Secondary Information Sector (as % of GDP at Factor Cost)

Country	Year	PIS	SIS
Japan	1965	14.4	21.8
	1970	18.8	16.2
U.K.	1963	16.0	13.8
	1972	22.0	10.9
U.S.A.	1958	19.6	23.1
	1967	23.8	24.7
	1972	24.8	—
	1974	—	24.4

Source: (Organization for Economic Cooperation and Development, 1981, pp. 35–39).

GDP. Information sector imports equalled 20 percent of the total production of the primary information sector. In terms of consumption, imports of information goods represented 18 percent of the national total. He reasoned that the whole information sector must be somewhere between 20 and 25 percent of GDP, so that the SIS must be in the range 10–15 percent. If the calculations are accepted, it is possible to go on to consider the PIS/SIS balance and the overall informational efficiency of the economy.

Relative Importance of Secondary vis-a-vis Primary Information Sector

These matters are, of course, difficult to separate from the changes in the IS (Information Sector) contribution to GDP and in the relative importance of the primary and secondary sectors. The U.S. statistics may be suggestive of stable growth. The available statistics for Japan and the U.K. indicate that PIS (Primary Information Sector) growth may have occurred at the expenses of the SIS (Secondary Information Sector)—in both cases, declines were recorded. This tends to be interpreted simply as a shift from in-house activity to purchased services (or goods), and viewed favorably as likely to be beneficial because it can bring gains from specialization. I suggest that this is a superficial interpretation.

1. It focuses on the most-market-oriented part of the system, and ignores the public sector aspect.
2. It does not consider the possibility that, in contrast to a simple shifting from in-house to market, there has been a change in the composition of activities. In-house R & D may have declined while purchased advertising services have expanded. This brings in questions about the impact of economic fluctuations and the relevance of business concentration.

3. The assumed beneficial results must be questioned. Even if, in the case of R & D, a simple shift were involved, the weakening of in-house capacity may well lead to less innovation. Nevertheless, some analysts have stressed the role of in-house R & D capacity in successful industrial innovation.

Of the countries listed in Table 1, Japan may well be the most interesting, but my comments are brief because the statistical comparison is so limited and I have too little background in the Japanese economy. Despite this recorded decline in the SIS, Japan would appear to have expanded considerably the resources devoted to market search and coordination. A case emerges for disaggregation.

Turning to the U.K., it may be important to appreciate the kind of structural changes that have been occurring. The growth trend in business services in the British economy during recent decades "has been little short of dramatic" (Mathias, 1983, p. 32). Over the last 30 years, the most rapidly expanding large occupational group has been "financial, business, professional and scientific services," increasing as a share of the working population from 9.3 percent to 18.1 percent between 1954 and 1977. This change has been reflected in the balance of payments, continuing the long-established trend by which net surpluses earned by services offset deficits in the balance of commodity trade. International banking, insurance, aviation, shipbroking, international metal exchanges and commodity markets, retailing, merchanting, property companies, construction firms, auctioneering, accountancy, and medical professional, and academic expertise have held or achieved competitive advantage.

Such change obviously affects the recorded contribution of the information sector and the PIS/SIS balance. As that sector incorporates infrastructure activity, it is of interest to note what has been happening and is expected to happen in the U.K. in respect of the adoption of IT. Recent research (Barras, 1984) at the Technical Change Centre, London, has shown that investment in IT has been led by financial and business services. While the findings imply some doubt about net benefits in the short term (0–5 years), a better prospect of productivity gains is reported for the longer term (5–10 years). It would, of course, be foolish to project the IT adoption experiences to other industries that are not experiencing similar growth success.

Some Results from an Australian Study

It may be of interest to add some results we obtained recently in the Australian case. In the course of a regional information economy study (Mandeville, Macdonald, Thompson, & Lamberton, 1984) for the State of Queensland, we analyzed the composition of and change in the workforce, using the information occupation classification employed in the OECD study. Table 2 illustrates the large diversity among industries in terms of their occupational information intensity. Of the total employment growth in the decade 1971–1981, the top-ranking industries were those of greatest information intensity and the lowest were those that are least information intensive (construction, manufacturing, and mining).

We supplemented the employment analysis with a survey of private firms, and included questions about contracting out of information services. The responses are shown in Table 3.

Table 2. Information Intensity of Queensland Industries, 1981

Industry	Labor Force[a]	Information Workers	Percent Information Workers
Finance, insurance, business services	74,555	53,753	72.1
Community services	130,604	68,078	52.1
Public administration and defense	54,124	25,540	47.2
Wholesale, retail	173,955	67,431	38.8
Electricity, gas, water	15,331	5,746	37.5
Communication	20,558	6,960	33.9
Transport and storage	57,534	18,367	31.8
Recreation and personal services	52,182	15,758	30.2
Construction	71,341	18,249	25.6
Manufacturing	123,355	31,152	25.3
Mining	19,183	4,451	23.7
Agriculture	76,061	2,132	2.8

[a] Adequately described labor force.
Sources: (Australian Bureau of Statistics, 1981 Census, Table 22; Mandeville et al., 1984, p. 19).

Table 3. Information Services Contracted Out In Whole Or In Part (Percentage of Respondents, 1973–1983)

Occupation/Year	1973	1978	1983
Accountancy	35.4	34.5	34.0
Technical research and development	10.7	11.2	15.2
Computer/data processing	12.0	19.1	17.8
Software development	10.7	12.7	34.2
Staff training	22.0	26.5	31.6
Recruitment services	24.9	31.5	33.9
Management services	7.2	11.1	14.7
Photocopying	15.5	13.9	14.3
Drafting services	16.0	18.5	21.2
Market research	11.0	14.0	18.3
Advertising	37.1	42.1	47.5
Public relations	5.8	9.1	12.2

Source: (Mandeville et al., 1984, p. 68).

Many firms contract out all of part of the work required for their information services, and the practice seems to have become more common over the last decade (Table 3). Only accountancy and photocopying are exceptions to the trend, the latter presumably because photocopying has come to be used so extensively that the service is needed instantly. Contracting out of information services presents hazards for those who seek to measure changes in the gross size of the three traditional sectors of the economy. As long as manufacturing industry, for example, performs its information services in-house, that activity is part of secondary sector activity. But as soon as the work is contracted out, exactly the same activity becomes part of primary sector activity. Increased contracting out, or the formation of subsidiary firms to perform a service function, thus swells the size of the primary sector. Though activity within the whole economy is unchanged, it may seem as if the agricultural and manufacturing sectors are shrinking and the tertiary sector expanding. This is, of course, occurring—Table 3 amply presents evidence of the demand for service sector activity—but perhaps not at quite the pace an initial reading of national sectoral statistics suggests. However, it would be a mistake to assume that service sector growth springs mainly from the real goods sectors. The Queensland study illustrates the primacy of new demand, compared with propensity to contract out. Much of this new demand, and much contracting out, arises from within the non-manufacturing sector itself.

Forces Influencing the Growth of the Information Sector

The question of what forces influence the growth of the IS and the relative sizes of the PIS and SIS is of special interest in the Australian case. The latest available statistics[3] (Lamberton, 1984a, pp. 7–8) suggest that the primary information sector as a percentage of GDP at factor cost increased from 24.79 percent in 1968–1969 to 36.11 percent in 1977–1978. Unless there had been a substantial decline in the SIS, Australia might well have become the most information-intensive economy in the world. Of course, the 1977–1978 PIS figure represents such a sharp increase that one is led to question its accuracy.[4]

From all this, I wish to emphasize that the simple shift interpretation of the decline in the SIS—and, for that matter, of the growth of the PIS—is

[3] These statistics were prepared by the Australian Bureau of Statistics for inclusion in the updated version of the statistical tables of OECD 1981 now in preparation.

[4] Correspondence indicates that ABS calculation of the SIS for 1968–1969 and 1977–1978 produced figures of 5.84 percent and −2.38 percent. While this is consistent with the decline suggested above, it throws serious doubt upon the methods used and this in turn may help explain the high level of the PIS reached in 1977–1978.

inadequate. Disaggregation is clearly called for, as is consideration of the impact of technological change. While economies of scale, scope, and growth might dictate specialization, there are complex pressures leading to organizational rather than market solutions (Arrow, 1974; Wildavsky, 1983; McNulty, 1984; Lamberton, 1984b). And especially in the case of developing economies, the restricted meaning attached to "nonmarket" must be borne in mind, because the changes observed may reflect a shifting boundary between market and nonmarket activity as monetization and commercialization of economic activity occur.

References

Arrow, K.J. (1974). *The limits of organization.* New York: Norton.

Australian Bureau of Statistics, *1981 Census,* Table 22. Canberra, Australia Government Publishing Service.

Barras, R. (1984). *Information technology and economic perspectives: The case of office based services.* Paris: Organization for Economic Cooperation and Development.

Lamberton, D.M. (1984a). Information age economics. *In* A. Goldsworthy (Ed.), *Technology change: Impact of information technology,* 1984, (pp. 3–12). Canberra: National Information Technology Committee.

Lamberton, D.M. (1984b). The economics of information and organization. *Annual Review of Information Science and Technology, 19,* 3–30.

McNulty, P.J. (1984). On the nature and theory of economic organization: The role of the firm reconsidered. *History of Political Economy, 16,* 233–253.

Mandeville, T., Macdonald, S., Thompson, B., & Lamberton, D.M. (1984). *Technology, employment and the Queensland information economy.* Brisbane, Australia: Information Research Unit, University of Queensland.

Mathias, P. (1983). The machine: Icon of economic growth. S. Macdonald, D. McL. Lamberton, and T.D. Mandeville, (Eds.), The Trouble with Technology, (pp. 11–25). New York: St. Martin's Press.

Organization for Economic Cooperation and Development (1981). *Information Activities, Electronics and Telecommunications Technologies,* Vol. 1. Paris: Organization for Economic Cooperation and Development.

Rubin, M. (1982). The information sector in the Venezuelan economy: Toward definition and measurement. Caracas: Intergovernmental Bureau for Informatics.

Wildavsky, A. (1983). Information as an organizational problem. *Journal of Management Studies,* 20, 29–40.

CHAPTER 9

The Secondary Information Sector: Its Meaning, Measurement, and Importance

Michael R. Rubin

Introduction

The concept of the secondary information sector was first introduced in a nine-volume report published by the United States Department of Commerce entitled *The Information Economy*. (Porat and Rubin, 1977) That report, authored in part by Marc U. Porat, and in part by Michael R. Rubin, built upon earlier work by Machlup (Machlup, 1962) and others on the measurement of the role of the production and distribution of knowledge in the nation's Gross National Product (GNP). However, where Machlup had measured only the total cost of output of the "knowledge industry," Porat and Rubin sought to measure "primary" and "secondary" information sectors.

The industries which make up the primary information sector as defined in *The Information Economy* are shown in Table 1. In concept, these are the industries which participate directly in the marketplace for information goods and services. In contrast, the industries which make up the secondary information sector represent information activities which take place outside of the marketplace, as an adjunct to the manufacturing process for noninformation products. For example, the activities of businesses which provide legal services to the general public are counted in the primary information sector. In contrast, the "in house" legal counsel to a company which manufactures, for example, ball bearings, is a part of the secondary information sector.

Table 1. Detailed Typology of the Primary Information Sector*

Abstracts for Information
Knowledge Production and Inventive Industries

R & D and Inventive Industries
- (7391) Commercial Research and Development Laboratories
- (7397) Commercial Testing Laboratories
- (8921) Nonprofit Education and Scientific Research Agencies

Private Information Services
- (6281) Services Allied with the Exchange of Securities of Commodities
- (6611) Combinations of Real Estate, Insurance, Loans, and Law Offices
- (7392) Business, Management, Administrative, and Consulting Services
- (8111) Legal Services
- (8911) Engineering and Architectural Services
- (8901) Accounting, Auditing, and Bookkeeping Services
- (8999) Services, Not Elsewhere Classified

Information Distribution and Communication Industries

Education
- (8211) Elementary and Secondary Schools
- (8221) Colleges, Universities, and Professional Schools
- (8222) Junior Colleges and Technical Institutes
- (8241) Correspondence Schools
- (8242) Vocational Schools, Except Vocational High Schools
- (8299) Schools and Educational Services, Not Elsewhere Classified

Public Information Services
- (8231) Libraries and Information Centers

Regulated Communication Media
- (4832) Radio Broadcasting
- (4833) Television Broadcasting

Unregulated Communication Media
- (2711) Newspapers: Publishing, Publishing and Printing
- (2721) Periodicals: Publishing, Publishing and Printing
- (2731) Books: Publishing, Publishing and Printing
- (2741) Miscellaneous Publishing
- (7351) News Syndicates
- (7813) Motion Picture Production, Except for Television
- (7814) Motion Picture and Tape Production for Television
- (7815) Production of Still and Slide Films
- (7816) Motion Picture Film Exchange
- (7817) Film or Tape Distribution for Television
- (7821) Motion Picture Service Industries
- (7822) Theatrical Producers (Except Motion Picture) and Miscellaneous Theatrical Services

Information in Markets

Search and Coordination Industries

Search and Nonspeculative Brokerage Industries
- (6052) Foreign Exchange Establishments
- (6053) Check Cashing Agencies and Currency Exchanges
- (6055) Clearing House Associations
- (6161) Loan Correspondents and Brokers
- (6231) Security and Commodity Exchanges
- (6411) Insurance Agents, Brokers, and Service
- (6531) Agents, Brokers, and Managers

Table 1. Continued

(6541) Title Abstract Companies
(7313) Radio, Television, and Publishers' Advertising Representatives
(7321) Consumer Credit Reporting Agencies, Mercantile Reporting Agencies, and Adjustments and Collection Agencies
(7361) Private Employment Agencies
(7390) Temporary Help Supply Services
(7018) Services Allied to Motion Picture Distribution

Advertising Industries
(3993) Signs and Advertising Displays
(7311) Advertising Agencies
(7312) Outdoor Advertising Services
(7319) Miscellaneous Advertising
(7331) Direct Mail Advertising Services

Nonmarket Coordinating Institutions
(8611) Business Associations
(8621) Professional Membership Organizations
(8631) Labor Unions and Similar Labor Organizations
(8651) Political Organizations

RISK Management Industries

Insurance Industries (Components Only)
(63) Life, Accident, Fire, and Casualty
(636) Title Insurance

Finance Industries (Components Only)
(60) Commercial, Savings Banks, and Related Institutions
(61) Credit Institutions

Speculative Brokers (Components Only)
(62) Security Brokers and Commodity Contractors
(63) Patent Owners and Lessors

Information Infrastructure

Information Processing and Transmission Services

Nonelectronic-Based Processing

Fixed Costs:
(2753) Engraving and Plate Printing
(2791) Typesetting
(2793) Photoengraving
(2794) Electrotyping and Stereotyping

Variable Costs:
(2732) Book Printing
(2751) Commercial Printing, Except Lithographic
(2752) Commercial Printing, Lithographic
(2789) Bookbinding and Related Work
(7221) Photographic Studios, Including Commercial Photography
(7332) Blueprinting and Photocopying Services
(7339) Stenographic Services; and Duplicating Services, Not Elsewhere Classified
(7395) Photofinishing Laboratories

Electronic Based Processing
(7392) Pure Data Processing Services

Telecommunication Infrastructure
(4811) Telephone Communication (Wire or Radio)
(4821) Telegraph Communication (Wire or Radio)
(4899) Communication Services, Not Elsewhere Classified

(continued)

Table 1. Continued

Information Goods Manufacturing Industries

Nonelectronic Consumption or Intermediate Goods

(2621) Paper Mills, Except Building Paper Mills
(2642) Envelopes
(2761) Manifold Business Forms
(2782) Blankbooks, Loose Leaf Binders and Devices
(2893) Printing Ink
(2895) Carbon Black
(3861) Photographic Equipment and Supplies
(3951) Pens, Pen Points, Fountain Pens, Ball Point Pens, and Mechanical Pencils and Parts
(3952) Lead Pencils, Crayons, and Artists' Materials
(3953) Marking Devices
(3955) Carbon Paper and Ink Ribbons

Nonelectronic Investment Goods

(3554) Paper Industries Machinery
(3555) Printing Trades Machinery and Equipment
(3574) Calculating and Accounting Machines, Except Electronic Computing Equipment
(3576) Scales and Balances, Except Laboratory
(3579) Office Machines, Not Elsewhere Classified
(3821) Mechanical Measuring and Controlling Instruments, Except Automatic Temperature Controls
(3822) Automatic Temperature Controls
(3821) Optical Instruments and Lenses

Electronic Consumption or Intermediate Goods

(3852) Phonograph Records
(3671) Radio and Television Receiving Type Electron Tubes, Except Cathode Ray
(3672) Cathode Ray Picture Tubes
(3673) Transmitting, Industrial and Special Purpose Electron Tubes
(3674) Semiconductors and Related Devices
(3679) Electronic Components and Accessories, Not Elsewhere Classified
(5065) Electronic Parts and Equipment

Electronic Investment Goods

(3573) Electronic Computing Equipment
(3611) Electric Measuring Instruments and Test Equipment
(3651) Radio and Televison Receiving Sets, Except Communication Types
(3661) Telephone and Telegraph Apparatus
(3662) Radio and Television Transmitting, Signalling, and Detection Equipment and Apparatus
(3693) Radiographic X-ray, Fluoroscopic X-ray, Therapeutic X-ray, and other X-ray Apparatus and Tubes; Electromedical and Electrotherapeutic Apparatus
(3811) Engineering, Laboratory, and Scientific and Research Instruments and Associated Equipment

Wholesale and Retail Trade in Information Goods

Household Investment Goods

(5732) Radio and Television Stores
(5996) Camera and Photographic Supply Stores
Hand Calculators

Consumption Goods

(5942) Book Stores
(5994) News Dealers and Newsstands

Table 1. Continued

(7832)	Motion Picture Theaters, Except Drive-in
(7833)	Drive-in Motion Picture Theaters
Support Facilities for Informational Activities	
(15)	Contract Construction of Office, School, Communications Buildings
(65)	Rentals of Information Structure
(25)	Furnishings for Office Buildings

* Source: Organization for Economic Cooperation and Development, 1981.

Definition of the Secondary Information Sector

The objective in measuring the secondary information sector is to account for information activities which would otherwise be "hidden" in noninformation industries. The secondary information sector is difficult to measure, since the measurement requires dividing "noninformation" firms and industries into two parts, one of which does "pure" noninformation activities, while the other does "pure" information activities. Conceptually, each firm is divided into two "quasi-firms," one of which does information activities, while the other does no such activities. The various quasi-firms which conduct information activities comprise the secondary information sector. Taking the ball-bearing industry as an example, the measurement of the secondary information sector requires, conceptually, that each ball-bearing firm be broken into two parts. One part, or quasi-firm, produces purely ball-bearings, while the other part is an information company providing management, legal, and accounting services to the first. The second quasi-firm is part of the secondary information sector.

The challenge is to convert this simple scheme to real life. Statistics on a national economy are rarely available to the researcher in enough detail for the conceptual cleave between information and noninformation actually to be carried out. The next section of this paper describes the techniques used by Porat and Rubin to accomplish this task.

Techniques for Measurement of the Secondary Information Sector

Two methods are described in *The Information Economy* for the measurement of the secondary information sector. Each method uses indirect means to approximate the output of those information producing quasi-firms which are a part of the activities of noninformation firms. Specifically, the value added generated by firms outside of the information sector is broken into two parts by dividing those firms' labor inputs between their information and noninformation components.

The validity of this procedure rests upon the assumption that the nature of the output of a firm or of an industry will be proportional to the nature of the labor inputs used by that industry. This assumption bridges two very wide chasms of doubt. First, it ignores the possibility that capital expenditures will make the labor input of one class of workers more productive than the labor of another class of workers. Second, and perhaps more profound, it begs the question of whether a unit of "noninformation" output can legitimately be treated partially as an "information" output if its production required some input of information labor. Criticisms of this assumption are substantial, and are described in the third section of this paper.

The Secondary Information Sector Contribution by National Income Method

The first step in a detailed description of the computation of the GNP generated by the secondary information sector is to remind ourselves of the components of GNP as measured from the value-added perspective. Gross National Product, of course, may be measured from two points of view: (a) from the perspective of income generated by all economic activity, (Value Added approach); or (b) from the perspective of expenditures for products and services which will be for consumption, (Final Demand approach). As noted earlier, Porat and Rubin measured the contribution of the secondary information sector to GNP by using the value added approach.

Table 2, below, presents a comparison of the components of GNP under the final demand and value added approaches to its computation. Within this schema, Porat and Rubin assigned three elements of GNP, as measured in the value added approach, to the secondary information sector. These were (a) employee compensation of information workers, (b) the labor income of proprietors and unpaid family workers performing informational tasks, and (c) capital consumption allowances taken on information machines. By assumption, all other elements of GNP under the value added approach were allocated to noninformation activities. (Porat, and Rubin, 1977, v. 1, pp. 153–154).

Table 2. The Components of Gross National Product

Value-Added	Final Demand
Compensation of employees	Personal Consumption expenditures
Rental income of persons	Gross private domestic investment
Corporate profits and inventory change	Net exports of goods and services
Net interest	Government purchases of goods and services
Business transfer payments	
Indirect business taxes	
Capital consumption allowances	

Measurement of Employee Compensation and Proprietors' Income

In measuring the secondary information sector, data on the compensation of employees and the income of proprietors were derived by Porat and Rubin from statistics originally compiled by the Bureau of the Census. For the year 1970, Census had published a matrix showing the detailed composition of the labor force, by occupation, for each of some 200 industries. These statistics, which reported upon some 422 separate occupations, had been a special tabulation for the 1970 Decennial Census. Each cell in the matrix showed how many people in a particular occupation were employed in a particular industry. One cell, for example, might show the number of lawyers employed in the ball-bearing industry, and another cell the number of welders employed in the automobile industry.

A matrix of 200 rows and 422 columns, or over 80,000 separate observations, the Census industry-by-occupation table was a remarkable and unique source of information about the employment pattern within particular industries in the United States in 1970. Besides its breakouts of data by industry and occupation, the matrix was essentially three dimensional, offering separate "layers" of data, by industry and occupation, about the number of employees, the number of sole proprietors, and the number of unpaid family workers in the national workforce. In truth a matrix that was 3 by 200 by 422, it contained over 240,000 separate observations!

The first step that Porat and Rubin undertook was to convert this detailed "people" matrix into a matrix of employee compensation. While the techniques they used are described briefly below, a more detailed description of the process required to create the so-called "wage" matrix may be found in Volume 6 of *The Information Economy* (Porat and Rubin, 1977). In this new matrix, each cell represented the total income of all people of a particular occupation employed in a particular industry. Using again the examples described above, a cell of this new matrix might report upon the total wages of all lawyers employed in the ball-bearing industry, or the total wages of all welders employed by the automobile industry. The matrix was created by multiplying each cell (number of people) in the matrix by the average wage (dollars) earned by the corresponding occupation. The average wage vector was weighted to correct for the substantial earnings differences between males and females. The resulting matrix was then scaled so that the total of all wages, economy wide, was equal to the amount reported in the national income accounts for the year 1967. (The underlying data from the Census Bureau was available only for the year 1970. Since all other statistical elements of the Porat-Rubin study were benchmarked to 1967, the assumption was made that the structure of the workforce, and the distribution of wages, was identical for the years 1967 and 1970.)

A separate matrix showing proprietors' income was also produced by Porat and Rubin, using the same techniques.

The matrices of employee compensation and proprietors' income contain all the information required to compute the corresponding elements of the secondary information sector's contribution to value added. The one hundred odd "information" occupations contained in the matrices were identified for each noninformation industry, and summed. This total was then added to similar totals for all other noninformation industries. The result, when added to the capital consumption allowances for information machines reported by the Commerce Department, was the value-added generated by the secondary information sector of the United States economy for the year 1967.

This technique for measuring the secondary information sector was an essentially "once in a lifetime" effort. The data to accomplish it was not available for any earlier year, and has become available since only for the year 1980. Either data on the secondary information sector was destined to remain extremely sparse, or a more simple means of calculation was required.

The Ratio Method of Measuring the Secondary Information Sector

A second, shorthand method of calculating the size of the secondary information sector was also described by Porat and Rubin. In short, the percentage of national income enjoyed by the information sector was assumed to be equal to the percentage of information workers in the total national work force. Once this amount was known, the size of the secondary information sector was equal to the residual after the primary information sector was subtracted out. Thus:

$$NS = NT\,(LI/LT) - NP$$

Where NS = secondary sector national income
NT = total national income
NP = primary sector national income
LI = total information labor force
LT = total labor force

Under this technique, the number of information workers in the labor force was determined from published statistics. The primary information sector could be calculated from published sources, leaving only the size of the secondary information sector to be calculated. For example, were the hypothetical size of the information labor force equal to 40 percent of a nation's total work force, the total size of the primary and secondary information sectors in that economy would also equal 40 percent of national income and GNP. If the primary information sector amounted to 25 percent of GNP, the secondary information sector would equal 15 percent of GNP.

This technique was used by the Organization for Economic Cooperation and Development (OECD) to estimate the size of the secondary sectors of Japan and the United Kingdom (Organization for Economic Cooperation and Development, 1981, pp. 55–59).

The Importance and Reservations on Measuring the Secondary Information Sector

The concept of the secondary information sector, the way it was measured, and some of the uses that have been made of the results of that measurement have each contributed in some small way to casting the entire exercise into a certain degree of disrepute. These problems should not, however, be allowed to overwhelm the valuable knowledge which the secondary information sector imparts.

Perhaps the most severe criticism of the secondary information sector should be reserved to the author. *The Information Economy* made fashionable the statistic that 46 percent of GNP in the United States in 1967 could be attributed to the production and distribution of knowledge. This figure in turn was the product of the summation of the contribution of the primary information sector, 25.1 percent of GNP, and the secondary information sector, 21.1 percent of GNP. Porat asserted that these latter two figures were directly comparable, and could be legitimately summed to arrive at a total figure for the role of information in GNP (Porat, and Rubin, 1977, v. 1, p. 1).

This calculation was based on false premises, and served to substantially overstate the true contribution of the information sector to GNP. As we have seen in the preceding section, the secondary information sector was calculated by prorating the output of noninformation activities according to the nature of the labor input to that product. In essence, a given unit of noninformation output was, by decree, converted into a unit of *information* output.

Unfortunately, the calculation of the primary information sector, and the 25.1 percent figure, included not only information labor input but also the input of noninformation labor. Had the primary sector been computed just with information labor as inputs, the results would have been more than 20 percent lower, and the size of the primary information sector would have been of the order of 18 to 20 percent of GNP. This number could have been added to that of the secondary information sector, giving a grand total of roughly 40 percent instead of the widely reported 46.2 percent of GNP.

Conclusion

The totals for the primary and secondary sectors are not directly comparable, and indeed amount to the proverbial mixing "of apples and oranges." However, this should not obscure the fact that treated independently, the calculation of the primary and secondary information sectors are internally correct.

Similar criticisms of the secondary information sector were also made by Fritz Machlup, who argued that the measurement of employment in information industries, which he dubbed the "occupation approach," should be kept separate from the measurement of the information goods and services in the national economy. Machlup stated that *The Information Economy* method "mixes information *inputs* in industries outside the information sector with *outputs* of industries in the information sector." (Machlup, 1980, p. 240).

The concept of the secondary information sector, however, is not without its redeeming features. It is, by definition, a measurement of the bureaucratization of the production process. As such, it has substantial implications for both productivity growth and the rate of inflation.

References

Machlup, F. (1980). *Knowledge and knowledge production.* Princeton, NJ: Princeton University Press.

Machlup, F. (1962). *The production and distribution of knowledge in the United States.* Princeton, NJ: Princeton University Press.

Organization for Economic Cooperation and Development. (1981). *Information activities, electronics and telecommunication technologies.* Paris: Organization for Economic Cooperation and Development.

Porat, M.U., & Rubin, M.R. (1977). *The information economy.* (9 vol.). Washington, DC: Department of Commerce, Office of Telecommunications.

Porat, M.U. (1977). Definition and measurement. In *The Information Economy* (Vol. 1, pp. 153–154). Washington, DC: Department of Commerce, Office of Telecommunications.

PART III

COUNTRY STUDIES

CHAPTER 10

The Information Revolution in Australia and Her Developing Neighbors

Neil D. Karunaratne

Identification and Measurement of the Information Sector

The importance of the information economy or sector, as perceived from growth and development angles, dictates its measurement and structural analysis as an aid to policy formulation. Available national income and input–output statistics are impervious to the importance of the information economy, as they have been designed to address macro-economic stabilization and growth problems of a fading industrial age. Although the data bases are admirably suited to study the structural transformation from a predominantly agrarian to a post-industrial society, they provide no insights on the magnitude or the inter-links of the information sector with the macro-economy.

A nonsurvey method to tease out the information sector by using secondary data from census and sample surveys has been devised (Karunaratne, 1983a,b). This methodology identifies, using an OECD classification (Organization for Economic Cooperation and Development, 1981) and supplementary country records, the information activities that are embodied in each conventional sector of an input–output table. These input–output tables show the information sector's interrelationship to the conventional sectors.

The information sector in this study is defined as the quarternary sector, and covers only marketed or the primary information goods and services. The quarternary or primary information sector is the hub of the growing information economy. There also exist secondary or nonmarket information activities which have been glossed over in this study. The secondary information activities emanate from the in-house transactions of the private and public sector bureaucracies.

The output of the quarternary or the primary information sector consists of commodities that intrinsically convey information or are used for distribution of information through the market.

An interindustry transaction in an input–output table may have embedded in it an information component. The goods and services that comprise the transaction can be indentified as informational or noninformational using the OECD classification of information commodities (Organization for Economic Cooperation and Development, 1981). Using country-specific census and survey data, values could be imputed to information transactions, thus determining their relative importance in each sector's gross output. The dichotimization of sectoral transactions to noninformation and information results in a four-way partitioning of each transaction, preserving the dictates of input–output logic thus:

	Pre-Dichotomization	*Post-Dichotomization*
(Original transaction) =	Non-information into Non-information	Non-information into Information
	Information into Non-information	Information into Non-information

All similar components are rearranged clearly, distinguishing noninformation, cross-transactions, and information transactions. Thereafter, the detailed sectoral picture of the macro-economy could be reaggregated and condensed to any level desired. In this study, a highly aggregated four sector economy was generated for all economies reviewed, with agriculture (primary), manufacturing (secondary), and services (tertiary) as the three non-information sectors. The information sector is the fourth (quarternary) sector.

A comparative study of macro-economic magnitudes such as value-added, final demand, and output reveal that Australia and her neighboring economies under review are either predominantly service or are industrial in character. The top ranking modal sector was the service sector followed by manufacturing (see Table 3). Australia was also a pre-eminent service economy, with the service sector generating 49 percent of the total value-added, 61 percent of the total final demand, and 41 percent of the total output. The comparable figures for the Australian information sectors are 25, 16, and 19 percent of the total value-added, final demand, and output, respectively (see Appendix A). In the cross-country sample of economies reviewed, the

Table 1. Macro-economic Magnitude (Sectoral Rankings)

Macro Criterion	Value-Added (Ranking)				Final Demand (Ranking)				Output (Ranking)			
Australia	(4)	(3)	(1)	(2)	(4)	(2)	(1)	(3)	(4)	(2)	(1)	(3)
Fiji	(2)	(4)	(1)	(3)	(4)	(2)	(1)	(3)	(3)	(2)	(1)	(4)
New Zealand	(4)	(2)	(1)	(3)	(4)	(2)	(1)	(3)	(4)	(2)	(1)	(3)
Papua New Guinea	(1)	(4)	(2)	(3)	(1)	(3)	(2)	(4)	(2)	(3)	(1)	(4)
Indonesia	(1)	(4)	(2)	(3)	(2)	(3)	(1)	(4)	(1)	(3)	(2)	(4)
Malaysia	(3)	(2)	(1)	(4)	(4)	(1)	(2)	(3)	(3)	(1)	(2)	(4)
Philippines	(2)	(3)	(1)	(4)	(4)	(2)	(1)	(3)	(3)	(1)	(2)	(4)
Singapore	(4)	(2)	(1)	(3)	(4)	(2)	(1)	(3)	(4)	(2)	(1)	(3)
Thailand	(2)	(3)	(1)	(4)	(4)	(2)	(1)	(3)	(3)	(1)	(2)	(4)
Mode	(4)	(3) or (4)	(1)	(3)	(4)	(2)	(1)	(3)	(3)	(2)	(1)	(4)

Source: Appendix A.
Sector Code: 1 Primary or Agriculture
2 Secondary or Manufacturing
3 Tertiary or Service
4 Quarternary or Information

information sector frequently ranked a notch above the bottom-ranking agricultural sector. The economies under focus were low in information intensity, and clearly a long way off from the promised land of the information era.

Structural Analysis Using Linkages and Multipliers

The structure of the macro-economy can be probed for productivity prospects at sector level using linkage and multiplier criteria. These criteria are based on sectoral interdependencies prevalent in a given macro-economy as captured by the statistical Leontief input–output table snapshot. The backward linkages show, on the basis of potential bottlenecks in intermediate input demands, the attractiveness of sectors from a growth perspective. The forward linkages show how an excess supply of intermediate inputs can provide inducements to establish industries based on excess supply conditions. These input shortages due to excess demand or input over-supply trigger unbalanced growth in the context of an endemic shortage of investible resources in developing economies (Hirschman, 1958). In the economies under review, the sector that qualifies for special treatment on the basis of backward linkage is the manufacturing sector. This is the top-ranking modal sector. In the case of forward linkage, the topmost modal sector is the service sector, for the sample of countries under study. Australia's top-ranking sector for backward linkage was the manufacturing sector, showing a compatibility with the modal rankings of the neighbouring economies (see Table 4).

The spread indices monitor the potential for maximal diversification due to sectoral expansion, and have an affinity with balanced growth strategies (Myrdal, 1957). For the cross-country sample of economies, the first position was earned by manufacturing on the basis of both the backward and forward spread indices. In the case of Australia, the agricultural sector qualified as the topmost sector with forward spread effects. Overall, for Australia and her neighbors, the linkages and spread criteria did not accord the information sector a star billing. On the contrary, often it was relegated to a slot just above the bottom ranking agricultural sector (See Table 2).

Several multipliers covering output and income were calculated to gain further insights about the nature of the information sector. Various income multipliers, excluding the endogenizing the household sector, were calculated. The service and the information sectors ranked first and second modal sectors from the standpoint of output multipliers for the sample of economies under study. Australia's output multiplier rankings were consistent with the modal rankings of her neighbors. The modal sectoral ranking from the standpoint of income multipliers were manufacturing and agriculture, in that order of importance. Australia's sectoral ranking for income multipliers was compatible with the modal rankings for her neighbors (see Table 3).

The linkages indicate the attractiveness of sectors for development if marginal changes are effected by allocating resources to sectors with high linkage sectors. The multipliers, on the other hand, demonstrate the responsiveness of sectors on the basis of output or income criteria as a result of exogenous changes. Both linkage and multiplier criteria are basically static measures that sort out the growth potential of a given economic structure as captured by the Leontief input–output tables. In the predominantly noninformation economic structures prevailing in Australia and her neighboring economies, therefore, it is not surprising that the information sector did not emerge as a sector with much development potential. The analysis highlights the danger of using static criteria based on existing economic structures to program for the harnessing of the productivity of a sector that is still emerging. The use of these linkage and multiplier criteria for policy formulations to usher in the information revolution in Australia and her neighbors would be, therefore, quite misleading.

The Conceptualization of the Relationship Between the Information Economy and Development

The disappointing results yielded by sector programming criteria (linkages and multipliers) for examining the structure and nature of informatization

Table 2. Linkage and Spread Effects

Criterion / Country	Backward Linkage (Ranking)				Forward Linkage (Ranking)				Backward Spread (Ranking)				Forward Spread (Ranking)			
Sector Code	**1**	**2**	**3**	**4**	**1**	**2**	**3**	**4**	**1**	**2**	**3**	**4**	**1**	**2**	**3**	**4**
1 Australia	(3)	(1)	(2)	(4)	(4)	(1)	(3)	(2)	(1)	(3)	(2)	(4)	(4)	(1)	(2)	(3)
2 Fiji	(4)	(1)	(2)	(3)	(2)	(3)	(1)	(4)	(2)	(1)	(4)	(3)	(1)	(3)	(2)	(4)
3 Papua New Guinea	(4)	(2)	(1)	(3)	(4)	(2)	(1)	(3)	(3)	(1)	(4)	(2)	(1)	(3)	(4)	(2)
4 New Zealand	(2)	(1)	(3)	(4)	(3)	(2)	(1)	(4)	(2)	(1)	(4)	(3)	(3)	(2)	(1)	(4)
5 Indonesia	(4)	(1)	(2)	(3)	(1)	(2)	(3)	(4)	(1)	(4)	(3)	(2)	(4)	(3)	(2)	(1)
6 Malaysia	(4)	(1)	(2)	(3)	(4)	(2)	(1)	(3)	(4)	(2)	(3)	(1)	(2)	(1)	(3)	(4)
7 Philippines	(4)	(1)	(2)	(3)	(4)	(1)	(2)	(3)	(4)	(1)	(2)	(3)	(1)	(2)	(3)	(4)
8 Thailand	(4)	(1)	(2)	(3)	(4)	(1)	(2)	(3)	(4)	(1)	(2)	(3)	(2)	(1)	(3)	(4)
9 Singapore	(4)	(2)	(1)	(3)	(4)	(3)	(1)	(2)	(4)	(3)	(1)	(2)	(2)	(1)	(4)	(3)
Mode	(4)	(1)	(2)	(3)	(4)	(2)	(1)	(3)	(4)	(1)	(2) and (4)	(3)	(1) and (2)	(1)	(2) and (3)	(4)

Source: Appendix B; Appendix C for Methodology for linkages and spreads.

Table 3. **Multiplier Analysis**

Criterion / Country	Output Multiplier (Ranking) (Ranking)				Income Multiplier —Type IA (Ranking)				Income Multiplier —Type IB (Ranking)				Income Multiplier —Type IIA (Ranking)				Income Multiplier —Type IIB			
Sector Code	**1**	**2**	**3**	**4**	**1**	**2**	**3**	**4**	**1**	**2**	**3**	**4**	**1**	**2**	**3**	**4**	**1**	**2**	**3**	**4**
Australia	(4)	(3)	(1)	(2)	(4)	(3)	(1)	(2)	(2)	(1)	(3)	(4)	(2)	(1)	(3)	(4)	(2)	(1)	(3)	(4)
Fiji	(4)	(3)	(2)	(1)	(3)	(1)	(2)	(4)	(3)	(1)	(2)	(4)	(3)	(1)	(2)	(4)	(3)	(1)	(2)	(4)
New Zealand	(4)	(2)	(3)	(1)	(1)	(2)	(3)	(4)	(1)	(2)	(3)	(4)	(1)	(2)	(3)	(4)	(1)	(2)	(3)	(4)
Papua New Guinea	(4)	(3)	(1)	(2)	(2)	(1)	(3)	(4)	(2)	(1)	(3)	(4)	(2)	(1)	(3)	(4)	(2)	(1)	(3)	(4)
Indonesia	(4)	(2)	(1)	(3)	(2)	(1)	(3)	(4)	(2)	(1)	(3)	(4)	(2)	(1)	(3)	(4)	(4)	(1)	(3)	(2)
Malaysia	(4)	(3)	(1)	(2)	(2)	(1)	(3)	(4)	(2)	(1)	(4)	(3)	(4)	(1)	(3)	(2)	(2)	(1)	(4)	(3)
Philippines	(4)	(2)	(1)	(3)	(4)	(1)	(3)	(2)	(4)	(1)	(3)	(2)	(4)	(1)	(3)	(2)	(4)	(1)	(3)	(2)
Singapore	(4)	(3)	(2)	(1)	(2)	(1)	(4)	(3)	(2)	(1)	(4)	(3)	(2)	(1)	(4)	(3)	(2)	(1)	(4)	(3)
Thailand	(4)	(2)	(1)	(3)	(4)	(2)	(1)	(3)	(2)	(1)	(3)	(4)	(2)	(1)	(3)	(4)	(2)	(1)	(3)	(4)
Mode	(4)	(3)	(1)	(2)	(2)	(1)	(3)	(4)	(2)	(1)	(3)	(4)	(2)	(1)	(3)	(4)	(2)	(1)	(3)	(4)

Sources: Appendix B; Appendix C gives definitions of multipliers.

lead us to review briefly whether any mileage could be gained by the neoclassical aggregate production function for planning purposes. The main contribution of this section, however, is the conceptualization of the interrelationship or the nexus that prevails between informatization and macroeconomic variables. Such modelling will provide insights into the complex structure and nature of the interactions between informatization and development in Australia and her neighboring economies.

The neoclassical model that attempts to measure the contribution of the information sector to growth is plagued by several deficiencies. First, the contribution of the information sector to growth is derived in a residual manner, after accounting for the weighted growth rates of factor inputs. This neutrino or residual is an amalgam of stochastic error and total factor productivity, and has been labelled as "technical progress" (Solow, 1957), "advances in knowledge" (Denison, 1981), and "total factor productivity" (Kendrick & Grossman, 1980), and we refer to it here as the contribution of the information sector. The residual or tail is the parameter that signifies a shift in the neoclassical production function. It has become so large that it has been observed that the tail now wags the neoclassical dog (paradigm) (Nelson & Winter, 1982, p. 205). Second, it is alleged that the neoclassical paradigm, with its rigid foundation of competitive equilibrium mechanics, is inappropriate to capture the disequilibria that characterize the development process (Chenery, 1983, p. 857). Third, the meager empirical research that has explored the nexus between value-added and investment in the information sector, using Cobb-Douglas production functions (Hayes & Erickson, 1982) or the two-sector models analyzing growth and investment in information technology (Jonscher, 1983) have been partial equilibrium approaches. Moreover, they posit a one-way casual relationship between information sector and growth. However, many macro-economic policy reports have perceived the two-way relationship that prevails between growth and the informatization of the economy (Nora & Minc, 1978; Canada, Department of Communications, 1978; Japan, Ministry of International Trade & Industry.

There is an unequivocal case to conceptualize a model that will overcome some of the limitations of the neoclassical paradigm. The magnitude of the information sector can be measured directly, as described by the methodology in Section 2 of this study. The disequilibria and interactions that occur in the development process can be conceptualized by an electric simultaneous equation model:

$$G_i = f(Y_i, Q_i, T_i) \quad \ldots\ldots\ldots\ldots\ldots \quad \text{I}$$
$$Q_i = f(G_i, S_i, D_i) \quad \ldots\ldots\ldots\ldots\ldots \quad \text{II}$$
$$S_i = f(Q_i, T_i, X_i) \quad \ldots\ldots\ldots\ldots\ldots \quad \text{III}$$
$$T_i = f(Q_i, P_i, \Pi_i) \quad \ldots\ldots\ldots\ldots\ldots \quad \text{IV}$$

where subscript:	i = ith country of macro-economy;
and endogenous variables:	G_i = Growth rate of per capita GNP.
	Q_i = Size of the information sector as % of GNP or informatization.
	S_i = Size of manufacturing sector as % of GNP or industrialization.
	T_i = Trade performance indicator or exports as % of total trade (exports plus imports); and
predetermined variables:	Y_i = Per capita GNP.
	D_i = Tele-density or telephone/100 people.
	X_i = Rate of growth of exports.
	P_i = Unit export price index.
	Π_i = Rate of growth of inflation.

It could be hypothesized, as in equation I, that rate of growth of the macro-economy (G) depends on the prevailing institutional modes and market orientation as proxied by per capita income (Y), the size of the information sector (Q), and the country's trade performance or revealed comparative advantage as depicted by (T). The sample of economies under scrutiny in this particular case are constrained by an institutional malaise, small information sectors, and poor trade performance. Hence a priori, we cannot expect a strong nexus between growth and the explanatory variables in this equation.

Equation II of the model endogonizes the information sector (Q) and explicates it by growth (G), the magnitude of the manufacturing sector (S), and the importance of telematics as shown by the surrogate tele-density (D). A priori, we could anticipate that growth and telematics will contribute significantly to informatization, while manufacturing will decrease as informatization accelerates, due to macro-economic restructurization. Equations I and II also depict the simultaneous interaction between growth and informatization, and vice-versa—a phenomenon ignored in the neoclassical single equation approach.

In equation III, we postulate that the size of the manufacturing sector (S) depnds on the size of the information sector (Q), trade performance (T), and the rate of growth of exports (X). The radiant dynamics of the manufacturing sector in industrializing economies covered by the sample will be significantly explained by informatization and growth of exports. Poor trade performance may hinder the manufacturing sector, while a healthy trade performance may give it a shot in the arm.

The trade performance indicator (T) depicted in equation IV is explained by informatization (Q), the international competitiveness proxied by export price index (P), and domestic cost structures represented by the surrogate inflation rate (Π). A priori, the poor trade performance captured in the trade performance indicator (T) may be inversely related to informatization and competitiveness, and directly related to domestic cost structures.

The four equation model, which describes the interaction between informatization and crucial aspects of macro-economic development, comprises nine variables, four of which are endogenous and the remaining five are predetermined variables. The identification rules decree that all equations are overidentified. The simultaneity bias that prevails in the model equations can be rectified by estimating the model parameters by the two-stage least squares (2SLS) technique. The empirical basis and the results of validation of the model are shown in Table 4 and Table 5, respectively. A linear and log version of the model have been fitted; the latter version has the advantage of yielding elasticity interpretations for estimates of the regression coefficients.

Table 4. Sample Data Base for Simultaneous Equation Modelling

Country \ Macro-Variable	(1) G_i	(2) Y_i	(3) Q_i	(4) S_i	(5) T_i	(6) X_i	(7) P_i	(8) Π_i	(9) D_i
Australia	2.8	5641	25	18	47	1.8	66.8	11.7	52.6
Fiji	6.0	915	17	11	45	1.7	73.0	7.8	7.3
New Zealand	1.9	1932	19	20	61	2.6	54.6	12.3	56.8
Papua New Guinea	2.8	375	11	11	62	1.6	43.4	9.5	1.6
Indonesia	4.1	244	9	11	56	2.4	40.9	20.3	0.3
Malaysia	4.0	683	16	25	47	3.1	58.7	7.3	4.4
Philippines	2.6	374	13	18	38	2.2	78.4	13.3	1.1
Singapore	7.4	2153	24	32	43	3.2	62.0	5.5	35.0
Thailand	4.6	408	10	20	41	3.9	66.2	9.5	1.1

Explanatory notes on model variables:

G_i: Per capita growth rate of GNP (%) (1960–1979).
Source: World Development Report 1981, The World Bank.

Y_i: Value-added or Income per capita (1975) in USS.
Source: Input-output tables used in the study.

Q_i: Value-added or Income (1975) generated by the quarternary sector.
Source: Input-output tables used in the study.

S_i: Value-added or Income (1975) generated by the secondary sector.
Source: Input-output tables used in the study.

T_i: $T_i = \frac{X_i}{X_i + M_i}$
where X_i = Value of exports and M_i = Value of imports (1975).
Source: Input-output tables used in the study.

X_i: Average annual rate of growth of exports (%) (1975–1980).
Source, IMF, *Financial Statistics,* Yearbook, 1983.

P_i: Unit price of exports (1975).
Source: International Monetary Fund, *Financial Statistics,* Yearbook, 1983.

Π_i: Rate of inflation or AAGR of CPI (1970–1978).
Source: International Monetary Fund. *Financial Statistics,* Yearbook 1983.

D_i: Tele-density or telephones per 100 persons.
Source: AT&T, *The World Telephones,* 1980, 1981, 1982.

Table 5. Regression Results of 2SLS Estimation of the Model

Endogenous Variable \ Pre-determined Variable	Linear Version									
	Constant	G	Q	S	T	Y	X	π	P	D	Statistics
G	5.02 (0.87)		(0.17) (0.63)			−0.0006 (−0.69)					S = 2.04 R^2 = 0.18 F = 0.36
Q	1.63 (0.34)	4.83 (2.23)*		−0.59 (−1.54)						0.33 (4.11)•	S = 2.84 R^2 = 0.85 F = 9.69*
S	−0.94 (−0.59)		0.68 (2.29)*		0.002 0.011	(2.90)*	6.59				S = 4.59 R^2 = 0.73 F = 4.63
T	7.25 (5.45)*		0.43 (1.09)					0.22 (0.44)	−0.62 (−3.78)*		S = 5.29 R^2 = 0.77 F = 5.57*

Table 5. Continued

Endogenous Variable \ Pre-determined Variable	Constant	G	Q	S	T	Y	X	π	P	D	Statistics
					Log Version						
G	4.36 (0.91)		0.99 (0.47)		−0.86 (−0.79)	−0.36 (−0.49)					S = 0.49 R^2 = 0.20 F = 0.43
Q	2.45 (5.42)•	0.20 (1.56)*		−0.11 (0.56)						0.20 (5.92)•	S = 0.14 R^2 = 0.92 F = 18.0•
S	1.00 (0.50)		0.59 (3.00)*		−0.14 (0.32)		0.92 (3.77)•				S = 0.20 R^2 = 0.83 F = 8.35*
T	6.22 (8.16)•		0.20 (1.85)					0.09 (0.86)	−0.76 4.57•		S = 0.09 R^2 = 0.83 F = 8.01*

Notes: (t-statistic in parenthesis); * Significant at 5% level; • Significant at 1% level.

Empirical Validation of the Information Economy and Development

The sample results for the growth function (Equation I) gave a disappointing fit. Institutional modes, informatization, and poor trade performance emerged as significant explanatory variables. Together, they explained only 18 percent of the overall variation in growth and proved to be jointly nonsignificant. The results corroborate that institutional modes, the low status of the information sector, and trade performance constrain growth by not contributing to it in a manner discernible in advanced information economies.

The information function (Equation II) was significantly and positively explained by growth and telematic activity. Industrialization, surprisingly, showed a negative bearing on informatization. The explanatory variables were jointly significant and explained nearly 85 percent of the variation of the information sector.

The size of the manufacturing sector (Equation III) was explained in a significant manner by the contribution of informatization and rate of growth of exports. The prevailing comparative advantage or trade performance indicator hardly made any impact on industrialization. Jointly, the explanatory variables explained 73 percent of the variation in industrialization. One could suspect that multicollinearity is the culprit that renders trade performance effects on growth insignificant.

Trade performance (Equation IV) was not related to informatization in a significant manner; the poor performance simulated by the variable was positively related to inflation, albeit insignificantly. It was negatively and significantly related to international competitiveness, which has been proxied by unit export price indices. Jointly, the variables explain nearly 77 percent of the variation in trade performance (see Table 5).

The log-version of the empirical results broadly support the conclusions derived from the linearized version above (see Table 5). The results, based on a small cross-country sample, are not definitive. They are, nevertheless, indicative of the need for more theoretical and empirical research on the complex process that links informatization and development. Such research is imperative to provide meaningful insights to policymakers who formulate goals and strategies for long terms macro-economic development.

Conclusion

There has been much canvassing of the benefits of the information revolution both in Australia and her developing neighbors. This study reviews the promise of the information revolution against the backdrop of the structure and magnitude of informatization prevalent in a sample of neighboring macro-economies. The linkage, spread multiplier criteria clearly revealed that noninformation sectors, such as service and manufacturing, were the most attractive for development, given the makeup of these economies. Even the interrelationships prevailing in the economies between informatization and macro-economic variables hint that the information and development nexus was shaky and imperceptible.

The empirical insights gained by applying static mainstream planning criteria, although disappointing to the pushers of rapid informatization panaceas, are not surprising, given the fact that the economies under the spotlight are basically industrial or service in character. The linkages and multipliers indicate that, in promoting short term maximal growth, industrial and service sectors of the economy will be the favored candidates, if the status quo is to be preserved.

However, informatization of Austrailia and her developing neighbors presupposes massive structural changes and an ushering in of a new economic ethos based on the resource information, rather than on industrial raw materials and energy. Therefore, the guidelines for growth and development proffered by static marginal criteria are misdirected. New dynamic linkages, spreads, and comparative advantage have to be created. These dynamic linkages, although latent in the economies under scrutiny, have yet to surface. Information economies, such as Japan, ushered the information era by rejecting the guidelines given by static mainstream paradigms (Scott, 1984). The same message is valid for Australia and her neighbors, if the aim is to harness the rewards of informatization for rapid growth and development.

The attempt to detect signals and devise blueprints to implement a rapid informatization strategy by analyzing empirical data bases and interconnections existing in preinformation economies may be a futile exercise. It may be as counterproductive as the blind man's attempts to look for a black cat in a dark room that is not there. Nevertheless, both in Australia and her neighboring economies, those who call the shots or decision makers persist, with obsolete techniques and myths, trying to foster the information economy using industrial criteria (Lamberton, 1984).

The way to informatize is to create or innovate dynamic linkages, multipliers, and comparative advantage. A range of interventionist and market-oriented policies may have to be evolved to foster dynamic linkages and dynamic comparative advantage. The rapid diffusion of the new information order will see that Australia and her neighbors collectively fall behind their competitors, if timely policies for the informatization of their economies are not evolved. In the past, the pursuit of neoprotectionist policies have generated much trade friction between Australia and her ASEAN neighbors, with heavy economic and foreign policy costs to all parties (Garnaut & Anderson, 1980). The promise of the information revolution can be harvested by eschewing the narrow nationalistic policies of the past and adopting, instead, policies for horizontal cooperation to identify and promote projects in the emergent information sector in Australia and the neighboring countries.

References

American Telephone and Telegraph Company (1980, 1981, 1982). *The World Telephones.* New York.

Canada. Department of Communications. Consultative Committee on the Implications of Telecommunications for Canadian Sovereignty. (1978). *Report in Telecommunications and Canada.* (Clyne Report). Canadian Department of Communications, Ottawa.

Chenery, H.B. (1983). Interaction between theory and observation in development. *World Development, 11,* 853–861.

Denison, E.F. (1981). *Accounting for slower economic growth.* Washington, DC: Brookings Institution.

Garnaut, R. & Anderson, K. (1980). ASEAN export specialisation and the evolution of comparative advantage in the Western Pacific region. *In* R. Garnaut (Ed.), *ASEAN in a changing Pacific and world economy.* (pp. 374–420). Canberra: Australian National University Press.

Hayes, R.M. & Erickson, T. (1982). Added value as a function of purchases of information services. *Information Society, 1,* 307–338.

Hirschman, A.O. (1958). *The strategy of economic development.* New Haven, CT: Yale University Press.

International Monetary Fund (1983). *Financial Statistics Yearbook.* Washington, D.C.

Jonan (1980), Ministry of International Trade & Industry.

Jonscher, C. (1983). Information resources and economic productivity. *Information Economics and Policy, 1,* 13–35.

Karunaratne, N.D. (1983a), *The information economy and a methodology for its identification.* Unpublished paper based on *East-West Center University of Queensland Project.*

Karunaratne, N.D. (1983b). *Programming for the Australian information economy.* Paper presented to the Input-Output Workshop, *Regional Science Conference,* University of New England, Armidale.

Karunaratne, N.D. & Cameron, A.D. (1980). Input output analysis and the Australian information economy. *Information and Management, 3,* 191–206.

Kendrick, J.W. & Grossman, E.S. (1980). *Productivity in the United States. Trends and cycles.* Baltimore, MD: John Hopkins University Press.

Lamberton, D.M. (1984). Australia as an information society: Who calls the shots? *Search, 15,* 101–103.

Macdonald, S. & Mandeville, T. (1984). *Telecommunications in ASEAN and Australia* (Economic Paper No. 5), ASEAN-Australia Joint Research Project, Kuala Lumpur and Canberra.

Myrdal, G. (1957). *Economic theory and Under-developed Regions.* London: Duckworth.

Nelson, R.R. & Winter, S.G. (1982). *An evolutionary theory of economic change.* Cambridge, MA: Belknap Press of Harvard University Press.

Nora, S. & Minc, A. (1980). *The computerization of society: A report to the President of France.* Cambridge, MA: MIT Press.

Organization for Economic Cooperation and Development, (1981). Information activities, electronics and telecommunication technologies. Paris: Organization for Economic Cooperation and Development.

Scott, B.R. (1984). National strategy for stronger U.S. competitiveness. *Harvard Business Review,* 84, (March–April), 77–91.

Solow, R. (1957). Technical change and aggregate production function. *Review of Economics and Statistics, 39,* 312–320.

Tokyo, Ministry of International Trade and Industry (1980). *The visions of MITI policies in the 1980s.*

West, G.R. & Jensen, R.C. (1980). Some reflections on input–output multipliers. *Annals of Regional Science, 14,* (2) 77–89.

World Bank (1981). *The World Development Report.* Washington, D.C.

Appendix A: Macro-economic Magnitudes

Country	Sector	Value-added	%	(Rank)	Final Demand	%	(Rank)	Output	%	(Rank)
AUSTRALIA	1	7.44	8.4	(4)	4.24	4.8	(4)	13.40	7.7	(4)
(1977–78)	2	16.25	18.5	(3)	16.40	18.7	(2)	56.65	32.3	(2)
	3	42.74	48.6	(1)	53.20	60.7	(1)	80.96	40.8	(1)
(A$ billion)	4	21.59	24.5	(2)	13.78	15.7	(3)	32.97	19.2	(3)
Total		88.02	100.0		87.62	100.0		174.00	100.0	
FIJI	1	137.49	22.7	(2)	62.61	10.5	(4)	187.04	16.9	(3)
(1977)	2	66.96	11.3	(4)	137.56	23.2	(2)	300.16	27.1	(2)
	3	292.54	49.3	(1)	303.98	51.2	(1)	476.48	43.0	(1)
(F$ million)	4	99.23	16.7	(3)	89.36	15.1	(3)	143.94	13.0	(4)
Total		593.52	100.0		593.51	100.0		1107.62	100.0	
NEW ZEALAND	1	864.8	12.9	(4)	399.3	6.0	(4)	1540.4	12.1	(4)
(1972)	2	1354.6	20.2	(2)	1914.3	28.6	(2)	3885.0	30.4	(2)
	3	3229.2	48.2	(1)	3421.7	51.1	(1)	5478.9	42.9	(1)
(NZ$ million)	4	1247.1	18.6	(3)	960.3	14.3	(3)	1855.1	14.5	(3)
Total		6695.8	100.0		6695.5	100.0		12759.4	100.0	

Appendix A: Macro-economic Magnitudes (Continued)

Country	Sector	Value-added	%	(Rank)	Final Demand	%	(Rank)	Output	%	(Rank)
PAPUA NEW GUINEA	1	588.05	43.9	(1)	652.25	48.0	(1)	785.31	34.1	(2)
(1976–77)	2	147.78	10.6	(4)	135.36	9.8	(3)	313.27	13.6	(3)
	3	459.87	34.3	(2)	444.63	32.7	(2)	983.93	42.7	(1)
(Kina million)	4	150.28	11.2	(3)	127.71	9.4	(4)	222.38	9.6	(4)
Total		1339.98	100.0		1359.95	100.0		2304.89	100.0	
INDONESIA	1	6545.0	47.8	(1)	5099.9	37.3	(2)	8276.0	7.7	(1)
(1975)	2	1459.0	10.6	(4)	2128.2	15.5	(3)	6720.1	32.3	(3)
	3	4477.3	32.7	(2)	5427.3	39.6	(1)	7099.0	40.8	(2)
(Rupiah billion)	4	1212.9	8.9	(3)	1038.7	7.6	(4)	2033.1	19.2	(4)
Total		13695.1	100.0		13694.1	100.0		24128.2	100.0	
MALAYASIA	1	4.55	23.2	(3)	0.1	0.5	(4)	7.14	15.9	(3)
(1975)	2	4.91	25.1	(2)	8.42	43.0	(1)	20.18	44.9	(1)
	3	7.00	35.7	(1)	8.18	41.8	(2)	11.22	24.9	(2)
(M$ million)	4	3.13	16.0	(4)	2.87	14.7	(3)	6.41	14.3	(4)
Total		19.59	100.0		19.57	100.0		44.95	100.0	

(continued)

Appendix A: Macro-economic Magnitudes (Continued)

Country	Sector	Value-added	%	(Rank)	Final Demand	%	(Rank)	Output	%	(Rank)
PHILLIPPINES	1	34.11	29.8	(2)	11.25	9.8	(4)	51.37	20.71	(3)
(1975)	2	21.24	18.6	(3)	40.20	35.2	(2)	102.99	41.6	(1)
	3	44.49	38.8	(1)	50.37	44.1	(1)	70.16	28.3	(2)
(Pesos million)	4	14.71	12.8	(4)	12.41	10.9	(3)	23.15	9.4	(4)
Total		114.55	100.0		114.23	100.0		247.77	100.0	
SINGAPORE	1	343.0	2.6	(4)	−4392.3	−33.4	(4)	5978.4	11.8	(4)
(1975)	2	4240.5	32.3	(2)	6114.8	46.5	(2)	25718.0	50.9	(2)
	3	5453.4	41.5	(1)	8183.4	62.3	(1)	10837.4	21.4	(1)
(S$ million)	4	3108.0	23.6	(3)	3238.1	24.6	(3)	8027.8	15.9	(3)
Total		13144.9	100.0		13143.7	100.0		50561.6	100.0	
THAILAND	1	89.48	25.7	(2)	31.13	8.9	(4)	128.01	18.3	(3)
(1975)	2	76.57	22.0	(3)	113.79	32.7	(2)	291.59	41.6	(1)
	3	147.83	42.4	(1)	171.67	49.3	(1)	51.19	7.3	(4)
(Baht million)	4	34.59	9.9	(4)	31.86	9.1	(3)	51.19	7.3	(4)
Total		348.47	100.0		348.45	100.0		701.14	100.0	

Appendix B:

Linkages and Spread Criteria

Sector	Country	L_jB	(Rank)	L_iF	(Rank)	S_jB	(Rank)	S_iF	(Rank)
1	AUSTRALIA	0.97	(3)	0.80	(4)	0.86	(1)	1.14	(4)
2		1.67	(1)	1.26	(1)	1.03	(3)	0.91	(1)
3		0.99	(2)	0.96	(3)	0.95	(2)	0.96	(2)
4		0.88	(4)	0.98	(2)	1.15	(4)	0.97	(3)
1	FIJI	0.91	(4)	1.06	(2)	1.05	(2)	0.87	(1)
2		1.14	(1)	0.91	(3)	0.82	(1)	1.09	(3)
3		1.04	(2)	1.17	(1)	1.08	(4)	0.90	(2)
4		0.92	(3)	0.86	(4)	1.05	(3)	1.14	(4)
1	NEW ZEALAND	1.02	(2)	0.99	(3)	0.98	(2)	1.05	(3)
2		1.13	(1)	1.03	(2)	0.86	(1)	0.98	(2)
3		0.97	(3)	1.12	(1)	1.09	(4)	0.87	(1)
4		0.88	(4)	0.85	(4)	1.07	(3)	1.06	(4)
1	PAPUA NEW GUINEA	0.85	(4)	0.80	(4)	1.06	(3)	0.80	(1)
2		1.11	(2)	0.92	(2)	0.82	(1)	0.92	(3)
3		1.22	(1)	1.42	(1)	1.09	(4)	1.42	(4)
4		0.92	(3)	0.87	(3)	1.02	(2)	0.87	(2)
1	INDONESIA	0.86	(4)	1.15	(1)	1.24	(1)	0.83	(4)
2		1.16	(1)	1.10	(2)	0.88	(4)	0.93	(3)
3		1.05	(2)	0.95	(3)	0.90	(3)	1.03	(2)
4		0.93	(3)	0.80	(4)	0.98	(2)	1.20	(1)
1	MALAYSIA	0.86	(4)	1.04	(2)	1.11	(4)	0.86	(2)
2		1.17	(1)	1.22	(1)	0.93	(2)	0.85	(1)
3		1.01	(2)	1.22	(1)	0.93	(2)	0.85	(1)
4		0.96	(3)	0.88	(3)	1.03	(3)	1.16	(4)
1	PHILIPPINES	0.81	(4)	1.02	(2)	1.18	(4)	0.85	(1)
2		1.20	(1)	1.21	(1)	0.91	(1)	0.87	(2)
3		1.03	(2)	0.94	(3)	0.92	(2)	1.04	(3)
4		0.96	(3)	0.92	(4)	0.98	(3)	1.23	(4)
1	SINGAPORE	0.74	(4)	0.93	(2)	1.24	(4)	0.89	(2)
2		1.08	(2)	1.38	(1)	1.04	(3)	0.72	(1)
3		1.55	(1)	0.82	(4)	0.76	(2)	1.192	(4)
4		1.03	(3)	0.87	(3)	0.96	(2)	1.191	(3)
1	THAILAND	0.85	(4)	1.03	(2)	1.14	(4)	0.86	(2)
2		1.20	(1)	1.27	(1)	0.94	(1)	0.83	(1)
3		1.03	(2)	0.95	(3)	0.95	(2)	1.03	(3)
4		0.93	(3)	0.75	(4)	0.96	(3)	1.28	(4)

(continued)

Appendix B:

Multiplier Analysis

Sector/Country	Multiplier	(Rank)	Type IA	(Rank)	Type IB	(Rank)	Type IIA	(Rank)	Type IIB	(Rank)
1 AUSTRALIA	2.50	(4)	1.69	(4)	2.16	(2)	3.99	(2)	2.99	(2)
2	1.64	(3)	1.64	(3)	2.21	(1)	4.09	(1)	3.09	(1)
3	3.19	(1)	1.34	(1)	1.55	(3)	2.86	(3)	1.96	(3)
4	3.17	(2)	1.23	(2)	1.35	(4)	2.49	(4)	1.49	(4)
1 FIJI	2.05	(4)	1.16	(3)	1.21	(3)	1.97	(3)	1.97	(3)
2	2.06	(3)	2.31	(1)	2.66	(1)	4.33	(1)	3.33	(1)
3	2.36	(1)	1.23	(2)	1.32	(2)	2.16	(2)	1.16	(2)
4	2.25	(2)	1.12	(4)	1.13	(4)	1.85	(4)	0.85	(4)
1 NEW ZEALAND	2.35	(4)	1.77	(1)	2.36	(1)	4.01	(1)	3.01	(1)
2	2.84	(2)	1.52	(2)	1.96	(2)	3.33	(2)	2.33	(2)
3	2.83	(3)	1.36	(3)	1.55	(3)	2.64	(3)	1.64	(3)
4	2.91	(1)	1.22	(4)	1.33	(4)	2.26	(4)	1.26	(4)
1 PAPUA NEW GUINEA	1.41	(4)	1.40	(2)	1.62	(2)	2.11	(2)	1.11	(2)
2	1.98	(3)	1.79	(1)	2.20	(1)	2.86	(1)	1.86	(1)
3	2.30	(1)	1.36	(3)	1.54	(3)	2.00	(3)	1.00	(3)
4	2.12	(2)	1.13	(4)	1.19	(4)	1.55	(4)	0.55	(4)
1 INDONESIA	1.51	(4)	1.23	(2)	1.32	(2)	1.65	(2)	1.65	(2)
2	1.99	(2)	1.80	(1)	2.18	(1)	2.73	(1)	1.73	(1)
3	2.13	(1)	1.20	(3)	1.30	(3)	1.62	(3)	0.62	(3)
4	1.85	(3)	1.19	(4)	1.28	(4)	1.59	(4)	0.59	(4)

Appendix B: Multiplier Analysis (Continued)

Sector/Country	Multiplier	(Rank)	Type IA	(Rank)	Type IB	(Rank)	Type IIA	(Rank)	Type IIB	(Rank)
1 MALAYSIA	1.43	(4)	1.23	(2)	1.36	(2)	1.76	(2)	0.76	(2)
2	1.94	(3)	1.84	(1)	2.22	(1)	2.89	(1)	1.89	(1)
3	2.15	(1)	1.15	(3)	1.21	(4)	1.58	(4)	0.58	(4)
4	1.99	(2)	1.17	(4)	1.24	(3)	1.61	(3)	0.61	(3)
1 PHILIPPINES	1.86	(4)	1.10	(4)	1.18	(4)	1.58	(4)	0.58	(4)
2	2.30	(2)	2.93	(1)	3.91	(1)	5.26	(1)	4.26	(1)
3	2.41	(1)	1.19	(3)	1.35	(3)	1.82	(3)	4.26	(1)
4	2.11	(3)	1.28	(2)	1.45	(2)	1.95	(2)	0.95	(2)
1 SINGAPORE	1.45	(4)	1.38	(2)	1.61	(2)	2.84	(2)	1.89	(2)
2	2.58	(3)	1.48	(1)	1.76	(1)	3.09	(1)	2.09	(1)
3	2.41	(1)	1.19	(3)	1.35	(3)	1.82	(3)	0.82	(3)
4	2.11	(3)	1.28	(2)	1.45	(2)	1.95	(2)	0.95	(3)
1 THAILAND	1.51	(4)	1.52	(4)	1.46	(2)	1.86	(2)	0.86	(2)
2	2.16	(2)	2.16	(2)	2.22	(1)	2.84	(1)	1.84	(1)
3	2.20	(1)	2.20	(1)	1.32	(3)	1.69	(3)	0.69	(3)
4	2.14	(3)	2.14	(3)	1.22	(4)	1.56	(4)	0.56	(4)

Appendix C: Methodology of Linkages and Multipliers

Linkages and Spreads:

:	Backward linkages:	Normalized column means of Leontief inverse.
:	Forward linkages:	Normalized row means of Leontief inverse.
:	Backward spreads:	Normalized row coefficient of variation.
:	Forward spreads:	Normalized column coefficient of variation.

Normalization refers to division by grand mean or average of the means.

———————

Multipliers:

$$\text{Type IA Income} = \frac{\text{Initial} + \text{First Round effects}}{\text{Initial effects}}$$

$$\text{Type IB Income} = \frac{\text{Initial} + \text{Production Induced effects}}{\text{Initial effects}}$$

$$\text{Type IIA Income} = \frac{\text{Initial} + \text{Production induced} + \text{Consumption induced}}{\text{Initial effects}}$$

$$\text{Type IIB Income} = \frac{\text{Flow on effects}}{\text{Initial effects}}$$

Source: West and Jensen (1980).

CHAPTER 11

Towards an Information Economy—The Case of Singapore

Meheroo Jussawalla
Chee-Wah Cheah

Introduction

Advances in communications technology are transforming societies and rapidly generating an "information revolution" that equals the Industrial Revolution in its impact on the dynamics of socioeconomic evolution. The radically changing environment of communications, as dramatized by modern applications of satellites, computers, and other electronic systems, is expected to have widespread influences on the use of information in the ordinary affairs of life. With society's increasing dependence on information, significant changes in the structure and product-mix of a country's economy are bound to follow, because the unrealized potential of new technology promises a more powerful and complex communication environment.

The information component of advanced economic systems is seen to have more than just a cursory role in economic growth and development. Whether or not these experiences are shared by developing countries remains largely an empirical question. If information activities are an integral part of a nation's economy, we must begin to account for the product originating from such activities. This is the primary purpose of the present paper. In particular, we focus our attention on Singapore, in the hope that such a study will lead to an appreciation of the size and composition of an "information sector" in the context of a developing country.

Some Measures of the "Information Economy"

Structural changes associated with the advent of modern information technologies have resulted in the formation of both information-intensive and information-sensitive economies. Perhaps of greater importance are the noticeable and profound socioeconomic changes accompanying the transformation of economic organizations based on the mass production of wage-goods to those based on the mass production of symbols and patterns. In particular, the pioneering work of Machlup (1962) indicated the U.S. "knowledge industry" accounted for 29 percent of GNP and employed 31 percent of the total workforce in 1958. By Machlup's estimates, this "knowledge industry," which encompasses education, research, publishing, and broadcasting, grew at a rate of 10.6 percent per annum between 1947 and 1958. This growth rate is twice that of the GNP and is indicative of the magnitude of national resources being consumed by information activities.

These estimates are largely dependent upon the manner in which occupations are classified as information related or otherwise. Despite differences in the definition of an information workforce, each of the countries studied has experienced a marked and sustained increase in its share of human resources devoted to information activities. The general conclusion is that, at least in the cases of the advanced economies, there appears to be a common pattern of structural transformation as the economic production system responds to changes in information technologies. It is of some interest to see whether the same pattern occurs in less developed and newly industrializing countries. With the availability of comparative studies in both mature and developing economies, economists can begin to unravel the impact of information technologies and of their implications for the pricing and investment of goods and services. Similarly, with better understanding of the array of processes by which new technologies are introduced and diffused, their opportunity costs become clearer, so that decision makers can exercise a choice between alternative investment options.

An Information Sector Approach: Concept and Methodology

Empirical estimates of the size of an information economy are based on what has come to be called the "information sector" approach. At a fundamental level, information activities encompass certain features which are common to other economic activities, viz., (a) the absorption of resources, (b) claims on current production, (c) imposition of transactions costs, and (d) the function of being intermediaries to further production.

For our purposes, we conceptualize information as a bundle of symbols, words, messages, or patterns. As such, the operational notion of information employed here differs markedly from that used in information-theoretic models of decision analysis (e.g., signaling-screening, job search, or problems of constrained maximization under uncertainty). While a piece of information may be subjected to varying degrees of abstraction, we recognize that the symbols or patterns which represent information are outcomes of activities which consume scarce resources. We can, therefore, delineate an information sector as one which encompasses those activities associated with the production and distribution of information goods and services. We define information goods as those which are used primarily in the processing or transformation of information from one pattern or set of symbols to another. Information services will be defined as that bundle of activities associated with the production, processing, storage, and dissemination of symbols and patterns. Given these definitions, the information sector can be measured in terms of the value-added originating with the production and distribution of information goods and services.

This suggests the use of a "factor incomes" approach.[1] It is widely accepted that these income components are obtainable from a social accounting matrix. By using an input–output (IO) framework, we can begin to estimate the size of the information sector while still preserving those details of interindustry relationships. Aside from some restrictive assumptions, IO techniques can then be applied to study structural relationships within an information economy. This mode of analysis has been amply demonstrated in Porat's (1977) work. However, it should be clear that a direct replication of Porat's analyses is neither possible nor appropriate. Economic structures vary across countries according to their rates of growth and states of development. By implication, the information economy of a given country will be unique in its composition and intersectoral linkages. To facilitate intercountry comparisons, the derivation of an information sector must therefore proceed on the basis of a common theoretical principle, rather than on similarities in data bases.

The primary data base for our empirical exercise is Singapore's IO table for 1973 (Singapore, 1978). This table consists of 74 so-called "industry groups," each of which is defined by an activity or an aggregation of two or more activities described at the 4-digit level of Singapore's Standard Industrial Classification (SSIC) scheme (see Appendix 1). Prior to statistical estimation, we made use of the SSIC to guide us in identifying information

[1] Incomes accruing to factors of production are salaries and wages, operating surpluses (or profit-type income earned by corporations or proprietors), and indirect business taxes. These value-added components are considered more accurate measures of national wealth, since they are insensitive to production costs.

activities according to our definitions of information goods and information services given above. The resulting inventory of activities, described at the SSIC 5-digit level, were then classified into five categories, covering:[2]

1. the production of information goods, like paper, stationery, inks and print;
2. the production of "hardware" (i.e., information machines) used in processing and distributing information, such as office machinery, data processing, and telecommunication equipment;
3. the production, processing, and distribution of information services stemming from service activities like travel, finance, insurance, and private education, where information is organized, packaged, and sold as a commodity;
4. wholesale and retail trade in consumer-oriented information goods, such as books, magazines, calculators, radios, and television sets;
5. information infrastructure provided by the public sector, which includes postal, telephone, and telecommunication (PTT) services, public administration, and education.

Categories 1 to 4 make up the primary information sector; category 5 constitutes part of the secondary information sector.[3]

Using the inventory of information activities, we then designated an entire or a portion of an industry group as belonging to the information sector or otherwise (see Table 1).[4] In cases where only a portion of an industry group is information related, the relevant portion is extracted by the use of scalars. These scalars are imputed from output data obtained from various censuses published by Singapore's Department of Statistics.[5] Unfortunately, scalars for certain activities cannot be derived because of the unavailability of data. To the extent that these activities are information related, we will be overestimating the size of some noninformation sectors by default. Consequently, our estimate of the information sector will be on the conservative side.

---

[2] It is instructive to note that the 5-digit classification scheme is the highest level of disaggregation available for Singapore's published statistics.

[3] The unavailability of data prevents estimating the size of private bureaucracies which form the other part of the secondary information sector.

[4] For example, the manufacturing and repair of nonelectronic computing and data-processing equipment and accessories is classified as activity 38211 according to SSIC. This activity is aggregated within industry group 45 of the IO table. Consequently, only a portion of industry group 45 can be designated as belonging to the information sector. On the other hand, the entire industry group 64 defined by postal and telecommunications services is included in the information sector.

[5] They include the Census of Industrial Production, 1973; Census of Services, 1974; and Census of Wholesale and Retail Trades, Restaurants, and Hotels, 1973.

Table 1. Singapore's GDP by Sector of Origin, 1973 (S$ million)

	Sector	(1) Total V.A.[a]	(2) Information V.A.	(2)/(1) × 100% % of total
(1)	Agriculture, fishing, and quarrying	235.4	n.a.[b]	n.a.
(2)	Manufacturing	2249.2	573.9	26
(3)	Utilities	210.0	n.a.	n.a.
(4)	Construction	647.0	n.a.	n.a.
(5)	Wholesale and retail trades	2627.7	243.8	9
(6)	Transport and storage	969.8	317.1	33
(7)	PTT	163.4	163.4	100
(8)	Finance, insurance, and real estate	1593.8	586.5	37
(9)	Recreational, cultural, and other services	320.1	n.a.	n.a.
(10)	Government services	764.1	498.3	65
	Total	9780.5	2383.0	24

[a]Value-added. [b]Not available.

The use of scalars is admittedly a crude method for apportioning an industry group into information and noninformation activities. It is, however, compatible with the assumptions underlying the construction of an IO table. Given that each industry group employs a linear production function characterized by constant returns to scale, we may express the IO relationship for a typical industry group as follows:

$$y_i = f_i(x_1, x_2, \ldots, x_n, v_i), \tag{1}$$

where y_i is the total output of the ith group, x_j is the jth intermediate input, for $j = 1, \ldots, n$, and v_i is value added of the ith industry group. Although y_i is usually assumed to be one homogeneous output, this assumptin can be relaxed by interpreting y_i as a composite output comprising two or more items produced in fixed proportions (Baumol, 1977). Together with the additive property of a linear homogeneous production function, we may restate the activity vector in (1) as follows:

$$y_i = g_i,(I,N), \tag{2a}$$

$$= g_i(I) + g_i(N), \tag{2b}$$

$$= \lambda y_i + (1 - \lambda_i)y_i, \tag{2c}$$

where $g_i(I)$ is information-related output and $g_i(N)$ is noninformation output in industry group i, $0 \leq \lambda_i \leq 1$. Under the "industry technology" assumption, the outputs produced by an industry group have the same input structure, regardless of its product mix. This implies

$$\lambda_i y_i = f_i(\lambda_i x_1, \lambda_i x_2, \ldots, \lambda_i x_n, \lambda_i v_i), \text{ or} \tag{3a}$$

$$\lambda_i y_i = \lambda_i f_i(x_1, X_2, \ldots, x_n, v_i). \tag{3b}$$

γ_i, is therefore, the scalar that apportions the total output of an activity i into two separate outputs with the same input structure. For statistical purposes, the number of inputs is prorated according to the volume share of the outputs, respectively. Using census data on output, scalars are computed as

$$\lambda_i = g_i(I)/y_i. \tag{4}$$

In other words, the scalar λ_i is the ratio of information-related output of industry group i to total output of industry group i.

The final step in our empirical exercise deals with the reclassification of the original 74-order IO table (see Figure 1 and Appendix 2). This involves "collapsing" the original 74-order table into a 25-order IO table, with activities described at the SSIC 2-digit level. The information sector is identified as the collection of activities under the five categories described earlier. The rest of the economy consists of eight activities covering the production of noninformation goods and services, wholesale and retail trade in noninformation goods, primary production, utilities, and construction.

The Information Economy of Singapore

Singapore is a compact city-state which has mainly relied upon international trade. Singapore's economy is increasingly being redirected from an export-oriented manufacturing base to one based on the export of services. By 1979, two out of three persons employed in Singapore were working in service occupations, while more than two-thirds of the country's total output was generated through services (Singapore, 1980). In addition, her manufacturing sector is now geared to skill-intensive, technologically sophisticated output of typewriters, semi-conductors, computers, television receivers, and other information goods. Singapore is also strategically located as an important center for financial and communication flows. The operation of such an economy would require increasing specialization in information-related activites. These casual observations suggest that Singapore is proceeding towards an information economy. The results of our empirical study of Singapore's information sector are consistent with this proposition.

The gross domestic product (GDP) of Singapore in 1973 is presented in Table 1, using a conventional sectoral breakdown. Table 1 also shows the value-added originating from information activities residing in each of the conventionally defined sectors. The information component of the primary, utilities, construction and recreational, cultural, and household services sectors (i.e., sectors, 1, 3, 4, and 9 in Table 1) are not available, as the relevant output scalars were not estimable from the data on hand. We can, however, make the following observations about those sectors, for which the size of information components are estimated.

In 1973, the largest sector in terms of total value-added was the wholesale and retail sector. Nine percent of this value added originated from wholesale and retail trade in information goods like calculators, office machinery, books, magazines, etc. By contrast, more than one fourth of the total value-added in the manufacturing sector was attributable to the production of information goods. These goods included nondurables like paper and stationery products (0.4%) and newspapers and other publications (4%), as well as durables ("hardware") like nonelectronic computing and data processing equipment (3%) and electronic and telecommunication equipment (17%). The entire communication sector made up by PTT services was allocated to the information sector. In 1973 this sector's share of GDP was about 2 percent.

The conventional services sector, defined by activities in transport, storage, finance, investment, and real estate (sectors 6 and 8 in Table 1) made up 18 percent of Singapore's GDP. Over 35 percent of these services were devoted to the production and distribution of information. On its own, information value-added in transport and storage accounted for 33 percent of total value-added in that sector. In the finance, insurance, and real estate sectors, 37 percent of total value-added originated with the provision of informational services. The bulk of these services stemmed from advertising, market research, employment agencies, and consultancies, including secretarial, accounting, auditing, and data-processing services (21%). Informational services performed by stock and foreign exchange brokers accounted for another 10 percent of total value added. The rest of the information value-added in the services sector originated with services performed by agents and appraisers in real estate and insurance activities. Finally, the public sector appeared to be the most information intensive, with approximately ⅔ of all government services being information based. Public bureaucracies in administration, planning, and development agencies accounted for 49 percent of total value-added. The value-added of social services, primarily education, made up another 16 percent of the entire public sector.

As a whole the information sector comprised 24 percent of Singapore's GDP in 1973. This implies that, for every S$1 income received, more than 24 cents were paid for the production and/or dissemination of information. We consider this to be a conservative estimate, since we have not been able to extract information value-added originating from private bureaucracies as well as from the four sectors mentioned earlier. It is most likely that a sizable portion of activities in the primary and recreational and cultural services sectors are indeed informational in nature. With regard to the primary sector, such activities will include research and extension services in agriculture and fisheries. We have also excluded, by default, activities such as broadcasting, production, and distribution of motion pictures and repairs of audio and video consumer electronic equipment. All of these activities are aggregated in the sector for recreational, cultural, and other services.

Although our primary purpose has been to estimate the size of the information sector, we have also constructed an IO matrix in the process. This IO matrix offers a comprehensive description of structural relationships between the identified information activities and the rest of the economy. Suffice it to say that such a matrix will be valuable in examining a variety of policy issues involving the information sector. Research along these lines should yield additional insights to the structural composition of Singapore's information economy. In view of the apparent penetration of information activities in Singapore, we feel that such studies are sufficiently important to be researched and reported separately. As such, we have not included any detailed IO analyses in our present discussions. A follow-up study of the secondary sector, with particular attention to the size of private bureaucracies, is bound to strengthen the results obtained from our present assessment of Singapore's information sector.

The Role of Communication Economics in Assessing the Information Sector

Communication itself is a relatively new area of study that has traditionally drawn upon disciplines like psychology and sociology for its research. With the explosion in communication technology, and concomitant improvements in information handling and dissemination, an economics of communication becomes necessary for an understanding of the impact that such technology has on economic life, through its effects on production, storage, and distribution costs. According to Arrow (1980), "the amount of information that can be handled for a given cost has increased enormously and has contributed to the unprecedented growth in productivity of the last twenty-five years." Thus, with increasing cost-effectiveness, leverage of specialization, and economies of scale, communication technology is becoming an important choice variable in economic planning.

So far, communication studies mostly have been related to measuring attitude changes resulting from mass media or communication campaigns at an interpersonal level. Dordick (1982) suggests that, with the use of newer communication technology like computer networks and organized information systems, economics and communication science will have common ground in their pursuit of efficiency and equity. The allocation of nonmarketed information goods and services, like the magnetic frequency spectrum and the geostationary orbit, along with R & D that is specific to a given corporation, posts problems for resource allocation. As Arrow (1980) rightly maintains, allocation of resources that would be optimal cannot be achieved in the absence of information costs. This is the principal role of economics in assessing decisions that affect the behavior of those who participate in communication activities.

Singapore's economy is no longer based primarily on entrepot trade. It has phased out its economic policies of the colonial era and ushered in labor-saving, high value-added, and skill-intensive activities. The increasing interdependence between economic growth and telecommunications development in Singapore can be best seen from the fact that, while its growth rate has averaged 9.4 percent per annum over the last 10 years, the growth of telephones and utilization of telex services has averaged 15.8 and 52.3 percent, respectively. As such, Singapore generates more international telecommunications traffic than New Zealand or the Indian subcontinent.

Our empirical results indicated that 17 percent of Singapore's GDP originated with the production of electronic and telecommunication equipment. Such activities are deemed to be susceptible to the introduction of new technology, e.g., microprocessor-based technology. Under these circumstances, it is crucial for decision makers to be aware of the implications that new technology poses for factor incomes, production structure, and patterns of employment. These possibilities of structural changes comprise policy issues of major concern. Since the manufacture of electronic and telecommunication equipment accounts for a rather sizable share of total value-added, the lower labor requirements of a microprocessor-based technology may result in the displacement of labor and reduction in value-added in the information sector. On the other hand, the same technology may lead to process innovations and thereby lower production costs. Whether or not such innovations will raise employment and, hence, value-added, will depend on the market demand for electronic and telecommunication equipment.[6] Process innovations may also generate "new" products and services thereby contributing to the "chain" of value added in the overall economy. From a policy standpoint, this raises the issue of technical obsolescence in existing investment and consumption goods, and in the means by which replacement demands can be accelerated.

Conclusion and Suggestions for Future Research

With the type of analysis conducted in this paper, it becomes possible to identify the stages of development of the information sector. Once the sec-

[6] In particular, it depends on a positive income elasticity of demand as well as a price elasticity greater than one. In a service-oriented economy like Singapore, such elasticities may be present.

tor is identified and data analysis confirms the existence and growth of an information sector *per se,* it is possible to delineate the stages of information sector development and thus identify their implications for overall policies of economic development. As more and more developing countries become conscious of their states of communication development as distinct from their states of economic growth, there is a greater likelihood that both these considerations will be linked in the development planning process. However, less developed countries (LDC) often find their plans beset with problems of measurement of growth sectors and the determination of key indicators and investment criteria. By identifying the stage of development of the information sector, policymakers can become more aware of the penetration of information activities and the consequences these have for the economy's product mix.

As the information sector becomes more predominant, policies focusing on more traditional sectors will be inappropriate for stimulating economic growth and development. It has long been postulated that economic growth proceeds with the provision and availability of social overhead capital. In an information-intensive economy, an analogous proposition may be stated in terms of the production and provision of information infrastructure. This leads to an area of conceptualization that deserves further inquiry. If the hypothesis that information can replace capital and labor is tenable, then neoclassical economics should abandon the two-factor approach embodied in traditional Cobb-Douglas type production functions. Alternatively, the analytical problem may be one of disaggregating information from capital and labor, thereby enabling output to be treated as a function of all three factors and their marginal productivities.

Neoclassical economics concerns itself with who owns the resources for production. If information forms part of the production function, then the question arises of whether the market system underallocates resources to the production of information. If information is to be equitably distributed, then economic theory should be concerned with the ownership of communication channels. The rationale for an interventionist approach in the pricing of information goods and services will depend on how information sensitive an economy is. Moreover, the type of information produced is dependent upon the use to which available information is put. For example, a commercial firm's need for a market survey will not be particularly useful for policy prescriptions applied to public users.

The critical issue remains whether the information sector is an admissable concept in economics analysis. If it is, we must then begin to contend with questions of measurability of nonmarketed information goods and services, such as the orbital spectrum for satellites, the magnetic frequency spectrum for radio, and proprietory R & D which is corporation specific and private. Apart from these problems, we also lack a standard statistical framework for information sector accounting purposes. Existing national accounting systems, based on Keynesian economics and developed for measurement by Kuznets, need to be reexamined to accommodate data on the information value-added. It is perhaps possible or advisable to revise such accounting systems in view of empirical evidence and theoretical revisions that focus on the imminence of information economies. In addition, the need for data banks reflecting the emerging trend of information societies is crucial. As social systems move from agrarian to industrial and to information-based service economies, there is a concomitant change in the focus of policymakers and researchers. Without proper data and indicators for measurement, the impact of technological changes cannot be anticipated or planned for. It becomes imperative to replicate this type of study in other newly industrializing as well as less developed countries.

References

Arrow, K.J. (1980). The economics of information. *In* M.L. Destouzos and J. Moses (Eds.), *The computer age: A twenty-year view.* Cambridge, MA: MIT Press.

Baumol, W.J. (1977). *Economic theory and operations analysis.* (4th ed.). Englewood Cliffs, NJ: Prentice-Hall.

Dordick, H.S. (1982). On the economics of communicating behavior. *In* M. Jussawalla and D.M. Lamberton (Eds.), *Communication economics and development.* New York: Pergamon.

Machlup, F. (1962). *The production and distribution of knowledge in the United States.* Princeton, NJ: Princeton University Press.

Porat, M.U. (1977). *The information economy.* Washington, DC: Department of Commerce, Office of Telecommunications.

Singapore, (1978). *Singapore input-output tables, 1973.* Singapore: Singapore National Printers.

Singapore, (1980). *Singapore yearbook of labour statistics.* Singapore: Singapore Research and Statistics Division, Ministry of Labour.

Appendix 1
Singapore IO Table: Classification of Industry

	Industry	Description
(1)	Livestock	
(2)	Other agriculture:	Rubber, coconuts, vegetables, fruits, orchids, mixed farming, agricultural services (e.g., pest control), hunting, forestry, logging, and collection of agricultural by-products.
(3)	Fishing	
(4)	Quarrying	
(5)	Rubber processing	
(6)	Meat and meat preparations	Canning and preserving of meats.
(7)	Dairy products	
(8)	Milled cereal and cereal preparations	
(9)	Sugar and sugar confectionery	
(10)	Oils and fats	
(11)	Other food	Canning and preserving of fruits and vegetables, soybean products.
(12)	Animal feed	
(13)	Beverages	Liquor, wine, malt, carbonated and soft drinks
(14)	Tobacco products	
(15)	Textile yarn and thread	
(16)	Textile fabrics	Spinning, weaving, knitted fabrics
(17)	Textile articles	Manufacture of textile goods, carpets, rugs, cordage, rope, and twine.
(18)	Manufacture of knitted fabrics and wearing apparel.	
(19)	Footwear	
(20)	Leather and leather products	Tanneries, leather finishing, fur products, apparel.
(21)	Sawmilling	
(22)	Wood products except furniture	Wood preserving and wooden materials.
(23)	Rattan processing	
(24)	Furniture and fixtures	Both wood and metal.
(25)	Paper and paperboards	Pulp, paper, paperboard.
(26)	Producs of paper and paperboards	Containers, boxes, and paper articles.
(27)	Printing and publishing	
(28)	Paints and dyeing materials	
(29)	Medicinal and pharmaceutical products	
(30)	Toilet preparations	
(31)	Plastic and plastic products	
(32)	Other chemicals	Basic industrial chemicals, fertilizers, and waxes.
(33)	Petroleum and petroleum products	Refineries and products of coal and petroleum.
(34)	Rubber products except footwear	Tires and tubes and other rubbery products.
(35)	Pottery, china, and earthenware	
(36)	Glass and glassware	

Appendix 1 (Continued

(37)	Bricks, tiles, and other structural clay products	
(38)	Cement	
(39)	Structural cement and concrete products	
(40)	Nonmetallic minerals	Asbestos products, graphite products.
(41)	Metal ores and scraps	
(42)	Basic iron and scraps	
(43)	Nonferrous basic metals	
(44)	Fabricated metal products	Housewares, doors, grills, wire and cable products, cans, sanitaryware.
(45)	Nonelectrical machinery	Manufacture and repair of computing and data processing equipment, office machinery, household appliances, industrial machinery.
(46)	Electrical goods and machinery	Electrical motors and generators, electrical household appliances.
(47)	Insulated wires and cables	
(48)	Electronics and telecommunication	
(49)	Musical instruments	
(50)	Vehicles	
(51)	Ships and aircraft	
(52)	Watches and clocks	
(53)	Scientific and precision equipment	Engineering and scientific instruments, photographic equipment, and supplies.
(54)	Jewelery	
(55)	Other manufactures	
(56)	Gas	
(57)	Electricity	
(58)	Water	
(59)	Construction	Public works, excavating, site preparation, and piling.
(60)	Wholesale and retail trade	
(61)	Restaurants and other eating places	
(62)	Hotels and lodging houses	
(63)	Transport and storage	
(64)	Communication	Postal and telecommunications.
(65)	Financial services	Banking, investment, and other financial institutions.
(66)	Insurance	
(67)	Real estate	
(68)	Other business services:	Legal, accounting, data processing, consulting.
(69)	Owner occupied dwellings	
(70)	Social and community services:	Private educational and research, vocational training, medical and health services.
(71)	Recreational and cultural services	
(72)	Personal and household services	
(73)	Producers of government services	
(74)	Domestic services and private nonprofit organizations	

Appendix 2
Reclassification of Singapore's IO Table.[a]

		74-order IO Group no.	Scalar
(A)	The production of information goods		
	(1) Manufacture of pulp and paper	25	1.000
	(2) Manufacture of stationery, paper, and	26	0.335
	nonpaper related products	55	0.014
	(3) Printing and publishing	27	1.000
	(4) Manufacture of inks and carbon black	32	0.095
(B)	The processing and distribution of information—"hardware"		
	(5) Manufacture and repair of nonelectronic computing, data-processing, and office machinery	45	0.861
	(6) Manufacture of cables and wires	46,47	0.161
	(7) Electronic and telecommunication equipment	48	1.000
	(8) Precision instruments and devices	53	1.000
(C)	The Processing and distribution of information—"software"		
	(9) Tourist and travel agencies in air transport and shipping	63	0.327
	(10) Risk management services in finance	65	0.676
	(11) Insurance agents, appraisers, and consultants	66	0.070
	(12) Real estate agents and appraisers	67	0.135
	(13) Professional services	68	1.000
	(14) Education	70,73	0.158
(D)	Commerce		
	(15) Commerce; wholesale and retail trades in information goods	60	0.108
(E)	Information infrastructure		
	(16) Postal, telephone, and telecommunications (PTT)	64	1.000
	(17) Public administration and development services	70,73	0.494
(F)	The production of noninformation goods		
	(18) Manufacture of noninformation goods	5-24,26,28-47 49-52,54-55	
(G)	The production of noninformation services		
	(19) Services in transport storage, finance, insurance, real estate, recreation, and culture, welfare	63-69,69 70-74	

Appendix 2 (Continued)

		74-order IO Group no.	Scalar
(H)	Commerce—net of trade in information goods		
	(20) Commerce in noninformation goods, including hotels and restaurants	60,61,62	
(I)	Primary sectors		
	(21) Livestock	1	
	(22) Fishing and other agriculture	2-3	
	(23) Quarrying	4	
(J)	Utilities		
	(24) Gas, water, and electricity	56-58	
(K)	Construction		
	(25) Construction, viz., civil works and building	59	

[a] The first 17 activites are obtained by applying the relevant scalar to the corresponding IO group in the original 74-order table. For example, activity number 5 is 86.1 percent of the total output of IO group number 45. The residual or noninformation component of IO group 45 is then aggregated into activity number 18. The last eight activities portray "the rest of the economy" in six major sectors which are defined by collapsing the original 74-order table. These sectors also include residual values of noninformation components derived from the computation of the first 17 activities (see example above).

CHAPTER 12

The Primary Information Sector of the Philippines

Meheroo Jussawalla
Stephen Dworak

Introduction

Admitting an information sector concept into economic analysis is no different in practice than admitting an agricultural, manufacturing, or services sector. Indeed, one can subdivide an economy along an infinite number of lines, but what is relevant for the economist is the size of, and rate of change in, a particular subgrouping. The delineation of an information sector and its use in this study stem from the belief that this sector is large, and getting larger at an increasing rate, in all but the most severely underdeveloped nations. The consequences of this occurence hold implications for the employment patterns, factor productivities, balance of payments, and government policy variables of, not only the country focused upon in a given study, but also its trading partners and competitors. In order to fully appreciate the nature and importance of the changes in economic structure that the growth of information sectors portends for the countries of the Asia/Pacific region, a full analysis of any particular country should be set within the context of all the countries of the region. That is the purpose of the larger research program of which this study is part, with the final results encompassing a region-wide cross sectional and intertemporal view of the changing nature of the area's economies. This paper is a step in that analysis process.

The purpose of this chapter is to derive the first phase of measurements of the information sector for the Philippines, for the year 1974, by utilizing the Leontief input–output techniques to calculate the size and structure of as much of that sector as the available data permit. As such, the major focus is upon what is generally referred to as the "primary information sector." The rationale for focusing on the primary information sector is twofold: first, data on the primary information sector is discernable from a country's IO tables, given the necessary statistics for deriving the information coefficients for each industry group, while data on the secondary sector is much more difficult to obtain without in-depth micro-level statistics on industry group activity expenditures; and second, it is the development of the primary sector that most affects economic growth rates, trade patterns, and the division of labor both within the country and internationally. Secondary information sector growth tends to represent the growth of bureaucratization of the economy, which, while important for the productivity of certain industries, is of somewhat lesser consequence for overall economic growth than is the growth of the primary information sector.

Following this introduction, the second section presents the definitional basis and conceptual framework for this study, and lays out the methodology followed and mathematical derivations used. In this section, the information sector approach is depicted, and the distinction between primary and secondary information sectors made. The third section presents the results of the analysis, and gives an over-all view of the primary information sector in the context of the entire Philippine economy. The final section contains the conclusions arrived at from this study and a description of how it fits in with the larger, region-wide research program.

Concepts, Definitions, and Methodology

The concept of an information sector becomes more tractable once a distinction between quantitative and qualitative aspects is made. The information sector, as referred to in this study, deals with the quantitative aspect. It regards information as a bundle of messages, symbols, and patterns, the production, processing, and distribution of which consumes scarce resources, imposes transactions costs, and functions as an intermediary to further production, processing, and distribution. Measuring the information sector in such quantitative terms, then, involves the calculation of what percentage of a country's economic activities, or Gross Domestic Product (GDP), result from information activities, and how the various sectors and industries are related to each other in the larger framework of the entire economy. What is relevant in terms of this study is the common theoretical approach to the analysis of the primary information sector, that of using an input–output (IO) framework. This preserves the intersectoral linkages and structural relationships unique to a given country, while allowing for inter-country comparisons along the common analytical line.

Thus, an information sector has been delineated, composed of information goods and services in the same way that the agricultural and manufacturing sectors encompass their respective goods and services. And this information sector can be further divided into primary and secondary components. The primary information sector is defined to include the information hardware and software industries, the information services industries, the information goods industries, trade in information goods and services, and the information infrastructure industries. The components of these various industry groupings are more fully detailed later in this paper and in the appendix. The secondary information sector is defined to include all the information activities that are part of the internal operations of all the other industries in the economy. It thus includes firms' internal accountants, lawyers, clerks, telephone operators, etc. As stated in the introduction, the lack of available data on the internal activity expenditures of the many different businesses that comprise the Philippine economy precludes the inclusion of the secondary sector in this study. While this may appear to be a shortcoming, as it relates to a complete view of the information sector of the Philippines, it does not hamper the stated goal of the larger research program, which aims at developing a region-wide, cross-sectional intertemporal view of economic structure, composition, and change.

The "size" of the primary information sector can be measured in terms of the value of the goods and services produced and the value-added in the sector, or in terms of the size of the workforce employed in that sector and the value-added per worker. This study includes both approaches, in the hope that what emerges is a somewhat clearer representation of the true structure of the Philippine economy at the time in question, the year 1974.

The primary source of data for this particular study was the 1974 Inter-Industry (Input–Output) Accounts for the Philippines (Philippines, 1979). The table consisted of 120 industry groups, each of which was defined by an activity or aggregation of two or more activities described at the four-digit level of the Philippine Standard Industrial Classification (SIC) scheme. The SIC was used to identify those activities in each industry group deemed to be part of the primary information sector, according to the above given definitions. These results were then classified into categories, following the method of Jussawalla and Cheah (1982), giving five subsectors within the primary information sector. This classification scheme is listed in the appendix.

In those original IO industry groups where only a portion of the group was found to be attributable to the primary information sector, scalars, hereafter referred to as information coefficients, were used to extract the portions to be allocated to the information and noninformation sectors, respectively, as warranted by the definitional basis of the study. These information coefficients were derived from data in the 1975 Philippine Census of Establishments (Philippines, 1981), and, although their use is not an ideal method for apportioning an industry group into information and noninformation activities, it is consistent with the underlying assumptions of an input–output table. That is, assuming that each industry group employs a production function which can be described in a linear form at some point in time, the relevant information coefficient can be described as:

$$a_i = f_i(I)/Y_i$$

where f_i = the information output of group i,

Y_i = the total output of group i,

and $0 \leq a_i \leq 1$

The coefficient a_i, then, is the ratio of primary information sector related output of industry group i to the total output of group i. However, owing to the fact that information coefficients for certain activities could not be derived due to a lack of data, the information portions of these groups will, by default, be allocated to some noninformation group. This will result in estimates of the primary information sector size that are on the conservative side. The discrepancy between actual and estimated sector size resulting from this conservative approach is for the most part negligible.

In addition to the measurement of value-added per industry group, the same information coefficient technique was also utilized to apportion the number of workers employed in an industry group. The data base for this procedure was the 1975 Integrated Census of the Population and its Economic Activities (Philippines, 1978). This yielded the number of primary information sector and noninformation sector workers, and allowed the computation of total value-added per worker and total compensation per worker for use in comparisons between the primary information and noninformation sectors.

Finally, the now reclassified 120-order IO table, and worker per industry data, were collapsed into a 26-order table. While some potentially useful information about specific industry linkages is lost in the aggregation process that the collapsed table represents, it should be recalled that the desired goal of the research is to examine broad sectoral linkages within various economies over a region-wide intertemporal scope. Thus, while the software design used in this research allows for a finer level of disaggregation and a more industry-specific analysis (which may be carried out at some future date), for the purposes of this study the 26-order table is appropriate.

The primary information sector is identified as those activities comprising the first 17 groups of the 26-order table, with the other nine groups constituting the rest of the economy. (See appendix for a complete description of the 26 groups.)

The Primary Information Sector of the Philippines (1974)

The Philippines is a diverse group of islands and peoples which has mainly relied upon agriculture and light manufacturing for its economic base. In

1974, two out or three persons employed in the Philippines were working in occupations in agriculture, manufacturing, construction, and utilities, while a little more than 60 percent of GDP was generated in these areas. So the Philippines cannot yet be classified as an information economy, but, as this study shows, the size of the primary information sector is significant, accounting for nearly 12 percent of value-added in 1974.

The GDP of the Philippines in 1974 is shown in Table 1, using a conventional sectoral breakdown. This table also shows the portion of value-added in each traditional sector arising from information activities. However, the information components of the agriculture, mining, utilities, construction, and government services sectors are not listed, as the relevant information coefficients were not estimable from the available data sources. While this is not too problematic for most of these sectors, as their information activities are probably not a very large share of total production, this is not true for the government services sector. Many efforts were made to overcome this shortcoming, but, owing to the nature of the Philippine government's reporting techniques on government expenditures and output, no useful method of determining the information sector share of the

Table 1. Philippine GDP by Sector of Origin 1974

Sector	(1) Total Value-Added (P000's)	(2) Info Value-Added (P000's)	(2) (1) % of Total
1. Agriculture & Fishing	28,088,088	n.a.*	n.a.
2. Mining and Quarrying	3,280,453	n.a.	n.a.
3. Manufacturing	24,705,882	1,128,141	4.57
4. Utilities	1,053,964	n.a.	n.a.
5. Construction	4,259,564	n.a.	n.a.
6. Commerce	16,011,611	920,878	5.75
7. Transportation and Storage	3,173,245	491,469	15.49
8. P.T.T.	667,828	667,828	100.00
9. Finance, Insurance, and Real Estate	8,315,862	5,322,702	64.01
10. Recreation, Business, Cultural, and other Services	6,638,069	2,895,324	43.62
11. Government	4,703,000	n.a.	n.a.
12. Notional Industry	(3,032,019)	n/a**	n/a
97,865,547	11,426,342	11.68	

*) Note: n.a. = not available; that is, not available from data sources utilized in this study.

**) Note: n/a = not applicable; this sector is a dummy sector designed to account for the imputed output of financial institutions. The figure in paranthesis is negative in sign.

total government budget could be developed during the initial round of analysis. Fortunately, the larger research program of which this study is a part includes researchers in the Philippines who may be able to secure the necessary data for this sector as the project progresses into the second phase of research. With this in mind, the following observations can be made.

As Table 1 indicates, approximately 12 percent of the Philippine GDP can be attributed to the primary information sector. The majority of this information production arose in the traditional services sectors of finance, insurance, and other business services. Only 4.57 percent of manufacturing can be classified as belonging to the primary information sector. These results point to the fact that the Philippines cannot be realistically termed as anything but a noninformation, developing economy. While this result is not surprising, it should be noted that 12 percent of GDP is not an insignificant proportion of total output for a country of this type.

Table 2 presents another form of breakdown between the primary information and noninformation sectors. It shows that, while the bulk of Philippine production is of the noninformation type, there are some noticeable differences between the two sectors, primarily in the area of productivity. Workers in the information sector appear to be more productive in terms of value-added or their contribution to GDP, and they are, appropriately, better compensated than their noninformation sector counterparts. Table 3 highlights the individual sectoral value-added and compensation relations that are presented in aggregate form in Table 2. It appears that, in the Phil-

Table 2. Information and Noninformation Sectors: Analysis of Overall Relationships

	Information Sector	Noninformation Sector	Over-all Totals
1) Total Value Added	11,426,342	86,439,205	97,865,547
2) Total Number Workers	707,752	11,534,301	12,242,053
3) Total Compensation	3,320,922	31,363,014	34,683,936
4) Value-Added per Worker	16.14	7.49	7.99
5) Compensation per Worker	4.69	2.72	2.83
6) Sector Value-Added, as % of total	11.68	88.32	100.00
7) Sector Compensation, as % of total	9.57	90.43	100.00
8) Sector Workers, as % of total	5.78	94.22	100.00

Note: Numbers 1 thru 5 values are in P000's

Table 3. Value-Added and Compensation Per Worker, by Activity

Activity	Value-Added/Worker (P000's)	Compensation/Worker (P000's)
12	267.54	36.19
2	61.14	20.50
1	58.01	16.78
23	56.03	14.02
10	55.39	14.44
24	41.66	9.24
11	38.69	12.97
16	27.63	7.69
17	22.04	8.89
7	21.62	5.78
15	19.96	6.68
18	18.67	4.48
3	17.61	6.45
6	13.42	3.92
20	10.95	3.09
13	10.28	3.66
25	10.23	4.05
26	10.09	10.09
22	9.04	3.32
5	8.35	1.97
9	8.01	1.16
19	7.61	2.25
4	5.39	1.55
21	3.70	1.51
8	3.52	.97
14	2.97	1.12

Note: Estimates of the number of workers were taken from the *Integrated Census of the Population and its Economic Activities* (Philippines, 1978), by applying the same scalar method of interpretation utilized in restructuring the IO table.

ippines, workers in the education sector are not very highly compensated, ranking last in this category, a fact that seems to be prevalent in developed countries as well.

Another way of viewing the information sector's contribution to the over-all productive efforts of the economy is through the share of inputs to production that arise from the primary information sector. Table 4 presents a breakdown of these percentages. The table shows that the primary information sector seems to be more dependent on its own output than is the noninformation sector, with all of the noninformation sectors deriving less than 6 percent of their total inputs from the primary informatin sector.

The characteristics of an industry are in part described by the proportion of its output sold to other industries for intermediate uses and the proportion going to final demand, and also by the proportion of inputs bought from other industries as intermediate inputs and used directly by itself.

Table 4. **Information Sector Inputs as a Percentage of Total Activity Inputs**

Activity	Information Input (P000's)	Total Input (P000's)	Information Input/ Total Inputs (%)
2	70,152	273,644	25.64
15	162,197	756,887	21.43
1	83,631	439,759	19.02
7	73,266	416,657	17.58
3	113,866	678,128	16.79
5	7,981	67,312	11.86
9	75,534	642,437	11.76
14	87,574	908,632	9.64
17	68,257	815,530	8.37
13	174,756	2,155,459	8.11
10	274,084	3,548,232	7.72
11	93,266	1,375,531	6.78
4	7,487	113,234	6.61
6	2,550	41,451	6.15
16	63,692	1,096,440	5.81
20	1,167,206	20,752,022	5.62
19	593,748	11,273,527	5.27
8	2,210	43,034	5.14
24	96,092	1,965,770	4.89
12	57,033	1,361,423	4.19
25	324,317	8,032,412	4.04
18	2,061,671	65,676,222	3.14
23	79,891	4,235,008	1.89
21	180,182	27,633,644	.65
22	29,860	5,860,803	.51
26[a]	0	4,703,000	.00

[a] Sector 26 (government services) was not included in the IO table except for the value-added by labor component, the rest of the sector was included as a final demand vector.

Table 5 shows these ratios for the collapsed 26-order table, with the ratios defined as:

$$b_j = B_j/X_j$$
$$c_j = C_j/Z_j$$

where B_j = total purchased inputs
X_j = total domestic production
C_j = total intermediate demand
Z_j = total demand

The ratio b_j indicates the extent to which the given sector or industry group draws on the whole system of industries for its intermediate inputs. On the other hand, the ratio c_j gives the proportion of total available supply of a sector that is used by the system in production.

Table 5. Interindustry Sales and Purchases

Sector	Total Int. Pur.	Total Output	bj = Bj/Xj	Total Int. Dem.	Total Demand	CJ = CJ/Zj
1	219269	439759	.4986	560114	790286	.7087
2	182990	273644	.4714	189555	313712	.6042
3	287914	678128	.4246	372110	761150	.4888
4	65414	113234	.5777	44240	164102	.2696
5	18548	67312	.2756	26173	251215	.1042
6	24573	41451	.5928	60317	119126	.5063
7	176702	416657	.4241	56753	701649	.0809
8	23668	43034	.5500	16029	66017	.2428
9	150968	642437	.2350	145527	644692	.2257
10	579867	3548232	.1634	3345427	3548232	.9428
11	174834	1375531	.1271	820553	1479363	.5547
12	207783	1361423	.1526	350030	1375364	.2545
13	440873	2155459	.2045	1723673	2617192	.6586
14	186164	908632	.2049	62367	1015432	.0614
15	298617	756887	.3945	290934	788468	.3690
16	175562	1096440	.1601	503302	1096439	.4590
17	147702	825530	.1811	415418	840441	.4943
18	42051726	65676222	.6402	23425838	87607488	.2674
19	3139717	11273527	.2785	2669533	11639688	.2293
20	4424172	20752022	.2132	7007012	21028812	.3332
21	4796584	27633644	.1738	17816859	28926799	.6159
22	609775	5860803	.1040	704397	5861117	.1202
23	954555	4235008	.2253	4648212	8602098	.5404
24	911806	1965770	.4638	1309093	1965770	.6659
25	3772848	8032412	.4697	437185	8061142	.0542
26	0	4703000	.0000	0	4703000	.0000
Average			.3156			.3789

Note: Amounts are in P000's

Tables 6, 7, 8, and 9 present the multiplier analysis that can be derived from the Leontief inverse matrix. Table 6 presents the traditional sectoral aggregate multipliers and linkages, while Tables 7, 8, and 9 disaggregate these multiplier effects into their sectoral components according to the techniques developed by Cheah (1984). Basically, what is involved is a partitioning of the Leontief inverse into subaggregate shares of the total inverse, in this case into information and noninformation sectors, and then calculating the appropriate submultiplier. These submultipliers indicate secondary repercussions of productive activities within the other sector. The pattern of and received effects is found again in Table 9, indicating a consistency in the results as to the interrelationship between investment in the information sector vis-a-vis the noninformation sector. The information sector is more self-propagating, while the noninformation sector is more interreliant in its expansion.

Table 6. Sectoral Multipliers and Linkages in Ascending Order

Sector	Mb	Lb	Sector	Mf	Lf
26	1.0000	.6234	26	1.0000	.6234
11	1.1863	.7395	8	1.0072	.6279
22	1.1871	.7401	4	1.0175	.6343
10	1.2471	.7775	6	1.0348	.6451
12	1.2529	.7810	9	1.0591	.6602
16	1.2550	.7823	14	1.0618	.6619
21	1.2803	.7981	5	1.0753	.6703
17	1.2957	.8077	22	1.0809	.6738
13	1.3176	.8214	2	1.0825	.6748
14	1.3329	.8309	10	1.0977	.6843
20	1.3445	.8382	16	1.1021	.6870
9	1.3561	.8454	12	1.1032	.6878
23	1.4063	.8767	25	1.1243	.7009
5	1.4391	.8971	7	1.1324	.7059
19	1.4810	.9234	3	1.1692	.7289
15	1.6369	1.0204	17	1.1800	.7356
7	1.7133	1.0681	15	1.1810	.7363
3	1.7640	1.0997	11	1.2730	.7936
24	1.8415	1.1480	24	1.4550	.9070
25	1.8481	1.1521	23	1.5003	.9353
2	1.8725	1.1673	13	1.6459	1.0261
1	1.9090	1.1900	1	1.6965	1.0576
18	1.9865	1.2384	19	1.8127	1.1300
8	2.0105	1.2534	20	2.5248	1.5739
4	2.0569	1.2823	21	2.8897	1.5739
6	2.0816	1.2976	18	6.7957	4.2364

Table 7. Intrasectoral Analysis of Multipliers

	Backwards		Forwards	
Sector	Internal	External	Internal	External
1	1.231	1.019	1.640	1.025
2	1.313	1.014	1.063	1.008
3	1.202	1.017	1.127	1.014
4	1.074	1.032	1.012	1.002
5	1.133	1.011	1.073	1.001
6	1.067	1.034	1.023	1.002
7	1.204	1.016	1.057	1.031
8	1.057	1.031	1.006	1.001
9	1.131	1.008	1.040	1.006
10	1.087	1.006	1.062	1.013
11	1.075	1.004	1.165	1.036
12	1.045	1.007	1.064	1.014
13	1.090	1.009	1.434	1.069
14	1.108	1.007	1.060	1.001
15	1.255	1.013	1.157	1.010
16	1.064	1.007	1.041	1.024
17	1.095	1.007	1.133	1.015
Average	1.129	1.014	1.127	1.012

Table 8. Intersectoral Analysis of Multipliers: Inducement to Production per unit of Cross-Sectoral Input

Sector	Industry Inducing (Column Sum QCo)	Industry Receiving (Row Sum PBo)
1	.538	.015
2	.377	.006
3	.451	.019
4	.922	.002
5	.258	.001
6	.951	.008
7	.413	.001
8	.900	.000
9	.186	.009
10	.129	.014
11	.088	.049
12	.190	.016
13	.196	.096
14	.190	.001
15	.289	.008
16	.168	.020
17	.163	.002
Average	.377	.012
	(Column Sum PBo)	(Row Sum QCo)
18	.035	3.416
19	.059	.535
20	.062	.925
21	.007	.902
22	.006	.034
23	.021	.243
24	.054	.281
25	.044	.075
Average	.036	.768

Note: The first 17 sectors refer to the information sector's inducive and receptive effects due to internal effects; the last 8 refer to the noninformation sectors.

Table 9. Intersectoral Analysis of Multipliers: Inducement to Cross-Sectoral Input Activity Due to Internal Multiplier Effect

Sector	Industry Inducing (Column Sum CoP)	Industry Receiving (Row Sum BoQ)
1	.373	.019
2	.306	.009
3	.307	.023
4	.523	.003
5	.177	.001
6	.543	.009
7	.291	.001

(continued)

Table 9. (Continued)

Sector	Industry Inducing (Column Sum CoP)	Industry Receiving (Row Sum BoQ)
8	.507	.001
9	.134	.011
10	.099	.020
11	.070	.063
12	.116	.020
13	.136	.122
14	.123	.001
15	.224	.011
16	.110	.033
17	.114	.026
Average	.247	.022
	(Column Sum BoQ)	(Row Sum CoP)
18	.054	2.631
19	.065	.495
20	.065	.678
21	.013	.024
22	.010	.000
23	.030	.009
24	.073	.246
25	.064	.069
Average	.047	.519

Note: The first 17 sectors refer to the information sector's inducive and receptive effects due to cross sectoral impact; the last 8 refer to the noninformation sector.

Conclusion

The Philippine economy in 1974 was largely based on agriculture and light manufacturing; that is clear from the data presented. However, there is also a significantly large primary information sector, a sector which accounted for nearly 12 percent of GDP. Inclusion of the omitted government services sector would probably increase this conservative estimate. What is also clear from the analysis of multipliers and submultipliers is that the information sector tends to be more internalized in its growth, relying on itself in terms of input usage and of induced multiplier effects. The noninformation sector, on the other hand, tends to be more interdependent, receiving a larger multiplier effect from increases in the noninformation sector output.

As the larger research program progresses and a second set of data for the Philippines is examined, a fuller understanding of the structural relationships in the Philippine economy should be possible, and a set of growth rates for the various sectors, in the context of the entire economy, can be developed. This will also make possible some comparisons between the expected impacts of the multipliers derived in this study and the actual changes that took place over the posted 5-year period of the research program. This is not to dampen the usefulness of this preliminary "snapshot" of the economy, but to suggest that these results are but a first step in the overall process of analyzing the changes in economic structure that arise with the growth and development of the primary information sector.

References

Cheah, C.W. (1984). *Sectoral interdependencies within an information economy.* Working Paper, East-West Center, Honolulu, Hawaii.

Jussawalla, M., & Cheah, C.W. (1982). Towards an information economy: The case of Singapore. *Information Economics and Policy, 1,* (2).

Philippines, National Census and Statistics Office. (1978). *Integrated Census of the Population and its Economic Activities—1975.* Manila, Philippines: National Census and Statistics Office.

Philippines, National Census and Statistics Office. (1979). *Inter-Industry (Input-Output) Accounts of the Philippines—1974.* Manila, Philippines: National Census and Statistics Office.

Philippines, National Census and Statistics Office. (1981).*Census of establishments —1975.* Manila, Philippines: National Census and Statistics Office.

Appendix
Reclassification of Philippines IO Table A

	120-order IO Group No.	Scalar
A. *Production of Information Goods*		
1. Manufacture of pulp and paper	49	.7758
2. Manufacture of stationary, paper, and nonpaper related products	50	.2101
3. Printing and publishing	51,52	1.0000
4. Manufacture of inks, ad signs, pens,	65	.0350
and pencils, etc.	92	.0959
B. *Processing and Distribution of Information—"Hardware"*		
5. Manufacture and repair of nonelectronic computing, data-processing, and office	80	1.0000
machinery, etc.	119	.0048
6. Manufacture of cables and wires	84	.3147
7. Electronic and telecommunications equipment,	82	1.0000
radios, and televisions, etc.	85	1.0000
	119	.0390
8. Precision instruments and devices, etc.	92	.0612

(continued)

Table A Continued

C.	*Processing and Distribution of Information—"Software"*		
	9. Tourist and travel agencies in air transport and shipping, and brokerage services in same	108	.9936
	10. Risk management services in finance	100,101	1.0000
	11. Insurance agents, appraisers, and consultants	102	1.0000
	12. Real estate agents and appraisers	103	.2782
	13. Professional services (includes lawyers,	113,114	1.0000
	accountants, advertisers, etc.)	115	.4193
	14. Education	111	1.0000
	15. Production of movies, TV, radio, etc.	116	.6733
D.	*Commerce*		
	16. Commerce; wholesale and retail trade in	98	.0724
	information goods and hardware	99	.0306
E.	*Information Infrastructure*		
	17. Postal, telephone, and telecommunications (PTT)	110	1.0000
F.	*Production of Noninformation Goods*		
	18. Manufacture of noninformation goods	26-50, 53-79,81 83, 84, 86-93	
G.	*Production of Noninformation Services*		
	19. Services in transport, storage, real estate, recreation, community service	102-109, 112 116, 119	
H.	*Commerce—Net of Trade in Information Goods*		
	20. Commerce in noninformation goods, including restaurants and hotels	98, 99, 117 118	
I.	*Primary Sectors*		
	21. Agriculture and forestry	1-18, 21	
	22. Fishing	19, 20	
	23. Mining and Quarrying	22-25	
J.	*Utilities*		
	24. Electricity, gas, water	94-96	
K.	*Construction*		
	25. Construction, viz., civil works and building	97	
L.	*Government*		
	26. Government Services	120	

Note: The first 17 activities are obtained by applying the relevant scalar (information coefficient) to the corresponding IO group in the original 120-order table. For example, activity number 12 is 27.82% of the total output of IO group 103. The residual or noninformation component of IO group 103 is then aggregated into activity number 19. The last nine activities portray the rest of the economy in seven major sectors, which are defined by collapsing the original IO table. These sectors also include residual values of noninformation components derived from the computation of the first 17 activities.

CHAPTER 13

Information Economies of Indonesia, Malaysia, and Thailand

Neil D. Karunaratne
Meheroo Jussawalla

Introduction

The Association of South East Asian (ASEAN) countries have a record of economic stability and growth that distinguishes them from other crisis-ridden, stagnant developing economies. ASEAN, however, comprises a divergent panoply of six nations which include the tiny sultanate of Brunei and the massive Indonesian archipelago. Brunei, with its rich oil and gas, enjoys a per capital income that is more than five times that of Indonesia. But neither Brunei nor the much panegyrized city state of Singapore are truly representative of ASEAN. On the other hand, the larger economies of Indonesia, Malaysia, and Thailand are more typical of the ASEAN scenario, as this trio of countries accounts for nearly 90 percent of the land, 80 percent of the population, and 75% of the GOP of ASEAN (see Table 1). These economies have dualistic structures, with a predominantly rural agricultural economy coexisting with a modern urban industrial or plantation economy. They are highly specialized in the production and processing of a narrow range of primary products for export. The exigencies of primary product specialization for export led to the pursuit of import substituting industrialization (ISI) programs in the 1960s (Tan, 1984). The diminishing dynamics of ISI led ASEAN economies to embark in a decisive manner on export-led growth strategies in the 1970s. The development plans of larger ASEAN economies bear testimony to the emphasis on export-oriented industrializa-

Table 1. Profiles of ASEAN Economies

Country	Area .000^{2}km	%	Population Mid-1981 millions	%	GDP per capita $US 1981	(Rank)	AAGR (%) of per input income (1960-1981)	GDP 1981 $US billion	%	Exports as percentage of GDP 1981
Indonesia	1919	(62.6)	149.5	(56.7)	535	(5)	4.1	84.96	(42.8)	26.2
Malaysia	330	(10.8)	14.2	(54.)	1840	(2)	4.3	24.77	(12.5)	52.0
Philippines	300	(9.8)	49.6	(18.8)	790	(3)	2.8	38.90	(19.6)	14.7
Singapore	1	(0.03)	2.4	(0.9)	5240	(1)	7.4	12.91	(6.5)	162.4
Thailand	514	(16.8)	48.0	(18.2)	770	(4)	4.0	36.81	(18.6)	18.8
Total	3064	(100.0)	263.7	(100.0)	—		—	198.35	(100.0)	

Source: World Bank, (1983).

tion. The current Indonesian Five Year Plan—Repelita III (1979–84), the Fourth Malaysian Plan (1981–1985), and Thailand's Fifth National Development Plan (1981–1986) emphasize industrilization exploiting revealed comparative advantage. The ASEAN economies have maintained an impeccable growth record, cruising at a rate of over 4 percent growth per annum during the past decade, despite the excruciating effects of a world-wide recession. The adjustment of ASEAN economies to the global recession has been commendable (Naya, Kim, & James, 1984). However, despite the accolades bestowed on the high economic performance of ASEAN by neoclassical analysts, the euphoria about ASEAN success is superficial. Wide rural–urban economic disparities exist in the larger ASEAN economies, vitiating the affluence reported by broad macro-economic aggregates (Karunaratne, 1982). ASEAN economies will have to continue to grapple with the redistribution problems by planned action, as the neoclassical trickle-down process fails to deliver the basic needs to the vast majority of the people living in the rural hinterland. The deprivation of the rural people and their rising expectations, often fanned by an international demonstration effect, can be a fertile breeding ground for Communist subversion and insurrection. The threat of Communist expansion has been the major source for the reinforcement of ASEAN solidarity, which has failed to make much progress in industrial package and complementation schemes and intra-ASEAN trade liberalization. The festering internal problems of relative poverty and the inadequacy of basic needs can undermine the ASEAN facade of growth and stability, if these problems are not tackled head on as early as possible.

The fast spreading new techno-centric order, or the diffusion of the information technologies in ASEAN economies, can aggravate the internal tensions and dualism that are simmering in ASEAN. The ASEAN economies, with multinational collaboration, have embarked on information goods manufacture and electronics components assembly for export. The proliferation of computers, the electronic office, and banking transactions have caught on rapidly in ASEAN urban centers of business and commerce. The dialectics of this spreading information revolution have to be sized up to guide the ASEAN economies along the stable trajectory of redistribution with growth. The problems confronting planners are, not only lack of a wide perception of the importance of the information revolution in ASEAN, but also a dearth of basic benchmark planning data on the interdependencies, magnitude, and structure of the information economy and its constituent sectors. The filling of this data gap is an imperative first step for the formulation of national plans and policies to usher the information era in the ASEAN economies in a humanistic, developmental fashion, minimizing the traumas and tensions caused by the rapid economic and societal change which the information revolution forbodes.

The Information Revolution and Big ASEAN Countries

Megatrends clearly indicate that the developing ASEAN economies are rapidly transforming from basic agrarian structures to post-industrial or information economies. This information revolution will bring about dramatic changes, not only in the lives of citizens in the rich countries, but also in the economic status of the low income ones. *Time* magazine awarded "Man of the Year" (retitled "Machine of the Year") to the computer in 1983, stating "that the computer is so cheap and so powerful that it would enable underdeveloped nations to bypass the whole Industrial Revolution" (*Time*, 1983). The computer and telecommunications convergence, or telematics, has been growing at a phenomenal rate in the ASEAN economies. In (1981–1982), the number of computers increased by nearly 32 percent, to 1,857 in 1982, and the total investment in computer installations and related services topped the billion-dollar mark (Rahim, 1984). However, like telecommunications, the computer installations were concentrated predominantly in the metropolitan commercial hubs, providing jobs only for the urbanites, thus further widening the urban rich and rural poor income gap (see Table 2). The skewed distribution of telematics infrastructures in ASEAN economies, and the rapid diffusion of information technologies, pose severe challenges to the monopolistic public utility models of telecommunications operating in most of the ASEAN economies, except in Philippines, where private companies control the business. The Perumtel in Indonesia, the Directorate in Malaysia, and the Communications Authority (CAT) in Thailand will have to face up to the challenge of a rapid pluralization of user services, as in advanced economies. However, some observers believe that ASEAN economies are still too far from the stage of interactive telecommunications to change substantially the government-controlled monopolistic structures of telecommunications (Gregory, 1980). The thin-route rural telecommunication services, which are cross-subsidized from revenues from the other routes, could also crumble if competitive cream-skimming organizations are introduced prematurely in ASEAN.

The reluctance of domestic and international agencies to fund information infrastructures for development has been due partly to the lack of empirical evidence on the nexus between development and investment in telematics. The Agency for International Development (AID) has launched a number of experimental projects in developing economies to demonstrate the developmental benefits of rural telecommunications based on satellite technology. The Palapa system, in place in Indonesia since 1979, has served mostly the military, strategic, and commercial needs of the massive Indonesia archipelago. The AID strategy has been to give the vast Palapa network a rural development orientation. There are over 125 earth stations, two-thirds of them with less than 5-meter diameters, providing audio and video services to

Table 2. Telematic Socio-Economic Perspectives

Country	Telephones per 100 inhabitants 1980-1981	AARG 1965-1979	Urban Concentration of Telephones % of Total (1978)	Population in Main Cities	Information Workers as % of Total Workforce	(Year)	Urban Concentration of Computers	TVs per 1000 inhabitants
Indonesia	0.3	188	70.4	11.0	19.0	(1977)	69	9
Malaysia	4.4	271	58.6	10.2	24.4	(1979)	47	64
Philippines	1.3	344	93.8	19.2	20.4	(1978)	—	21
Singapore	24.0	517	100.0	100.0	41.5	(1980)	—	166
Thailand	1.1	392	82.8	14.8	13.7	(1980)	96	17

Sources: AT&T, The World Telephones; MacDonald and Mondeville (1984); Rahim (1984).

remote areas. However, much of the telecommunication of government departments has so far been geared mainly to provide telephone services. The distance education project covering ten new universitites (the Badan Kerja Sama (BKS) project) is a breakthrough in bureaucratic inertia and constraints that hamstrung the use of modern technology for development purposes. The project is expected, not only to provide cost-effective educational instructions, but also to facilitate faculty training, library development, and efficient administration (Block, Goldschmidt, Hafid, Lalor, & Velasquez, 1984).

The big ASEAN economies may be the beneficiaries of the rapidly diffusing information technologies. Only if the development orientation of the new technology to remove the blight of poverty and underdevelopment in the rural hinterlands of ASEAN is effectively programmed can the information revolution be a boon to the ASEAN economies. If not, there is the danger that the problems of income inequality and the vicious dualism in health, education, communications, and media services that plague the ASEAN economies will be exacerbated, leading to internal tensions, instability, and external interference. The information revolutions and the information infrastructures are a crucial plank in the development planning of ASEAN. Its recognition and implementation will be imperative to ensure the continuation of the spectacular growth performance of ASEAN in the decade ahead.

A Comparative Analysis of Macro-economic Indicators of ASEAN Economies

Although proxy indicators from telematics clearly suggest that the larger ASEAN economies are tagging behind the rapidly informatizing small economies such as Singapore, no data has been available heretofore to make a comparative analysis of the structures of the larger ASEAN economies. The reworking of national income and input–output statistics to generate the information economy of advanced countries such as U.S. and Europe (Porat, 1977; Organization for Economic Cooperation and Development, 1978) had to be replicated for the developing ASEAN economies. The methodology for the consistent generation of data of the primary information sector or the sector producing commodities for established markets has been detailed elsewhere (Karunaratne, 1984a). It uses the industry technology assumption, rather than market shares hypothesis of input–output economies, to estimate national income (value-added) and national expenditure (final demand) from output data. The intermediate demands have been partitioned to information and noninformation components, keeping intact the sectoral interdependencies underpinning the Leontief technology coefficients matrix.

An examination of the sectoral composition of national income (value-added) and expenditure (final demand) clearly demonstrates the dominance of the service sector in the larger ASEAN economies. Indonesia's, however, continues to be predominantly agricultural and mining, with nearly 48 percent of its value-added coming from the primary sector. One of salient characteristics of the post-industrial society is the dominance of the service economy and the emergence of the information workers as the new technocarcy (Bell, 1973). The data for ASEAN economies clearly indicate that they are on the threshold of entering the information era. In the mid-1970s, the information sectors of the larger ASEAN economies contributed about 9 to 16 percent of the total value-added and 8 to 15 percent of total final demand. Singapore's information sector outclassed the larger ASEAN economies manifold, as revealed by the performance indicators (see Table 3). Singapore also had the largest service sector among the ASEAN countries, indicating its high progression towards informatization.

The five top-ranking sectors accounted for over 80 percent of the value-added generated in the three economies. Agriculture (Sector 17), noninformation goods (Sector 13), and commerce (Sector 15) were the most prominent contributors to national income or value-added in the economies under scrutiny. The five top-ranking sectors also accounted for almost 80 percent or more final demand in the three economies. The noninformation service (Sector 14), goods (Sector 13), and construction (Sector 20) sectors were the major contributors to final demand or national expenditure. The output indicator also revealed that above 85 percent of the output in the three economies emanated from the five top-ranking sectors. Noninformation goods (Sector 13), services (Sector 14), and agriculture (Sector 17) were the largest contributors to the output performance of the economies under study. The electronics equipment sector (Sector 10) figured among the five top-most sectors in Malaysia. This is the only ASEAN economy, among the three studied, that had a high performance information sector, namely electronics. This is also the country for which the information economy contributed most to national income, expenditure, and output among the three large ASEAN economies (see Table 3). The sector classification used in the Input–Output Tables of ASEAN economies is detailed in Table 4.

Trading activities were also concentrated in the noninformation economy. For example, in Indonesia, 68 percent of the total exports emanated from mining and quarrying (i.e., petroleum) (Sector 18). Agriculture (Sector 17) was next in order of importance with respect to exports. Noninformation goods dominated the exports of both Malaysia and Thailand, registering 80 and 60 percent of the total exports, respectively. The five top-ranking sectors in all the three ASEAN economies accounted for over 95 percent of the total exports, showing the high concentration of export activity in a few noninformation sectors. The same story is repeated with respect to imports, where 85 percent of the total imports was accounted for by the

Table 3. Structure of ASEAN Economies (1975)

Percentage of Total	Value-Added					Final Demand					Output				
Sector / Country	Primary	Secondary	Tertiary	Quarternary	(Rank)	Primary	Secondary	Tertiary	Quarternary	(Rank)	Primary	Secondary	Tertiary	Quarternary	(Rank)
Indonesia	47.8	10.6	32.7	8.9	(5)	37.3	15.5	39.6	7.6	(5)	7.7	32.3	40.8	19.2	(1)
Malaysia	23.2	25.1	35.7	16.0	(2)	0.5	43.0	41.8	14.7	(2)	15.9	44.9	24.9	14.3	(3)
Philippines	29.8	18.6	38.8	12.8	(3)	9.8	35.2	44.1	10.9	(3)	20.7	41.6	28.3	9.4	(4)
Singapore	2.6	32.3	41.5	23.6	(1)	−33.4	46.5	62.3	24.6	(1)	11.8	50.9	21.4	15.9	(2)
Thailand	25.7	22.0	42.4	9.9	(4)	8.9	32.7	49.3	9.1	(4)	18.3	41.6	7.3	7.3	(5)

Source: Karunaratne (1984b).

Table 4. Sector Classification in the 20×20 Input-Output Table

Sector Code	Information Sector Name	Sector Code	Noninformation Sector Name
1	Printing and Paper	13	Goods
2	Advertising	14	Services
3	Office Machinery	15	Commerce
4	Electronics Equipment	16	Livestock
5	Infrastructure	17	Agriculture and Fishing
6	Banking and Finance	18	Mining and Quarrying
7	Insurance and Risk Management	19	Utilities
		20	Construction
8	Miscellaneous Services		
9	Business Services		
10	Education		
11	Wholesale and Retail Distribution		

five top-ranking sectors in each of the economies analysed. Noninformation goods (Sector 13) accounted for over 57 percent of the total imports. Noninformation services (Sector 14) emerged as the next highest import-dependent sector in the three ASEAN economies examined. The macro-economic indicators clearly reveal the dominance of the noninformation sectors in both the closed and open economic structures of the larger ASEAN countries.

Multipliers and Linkages in the ASEAN Economies

The responsiveness of the different sectors of the ASEAN economies to exogenous stimuli are useful to provide guidelines to planners. Consistent output and income multipliers, detailing initial, first round effects, industrial support, and consumption induced effects have been computed using the methods in Appendix C, Chapter 10. The Type I and Type II income multipliers express the income effects per unit of output change, excluding and including consumption-induced effects, respectively (Jensen & West, 1980).

The top-ranking total output multipliers for the larger economies do not show a wide variation; they range from 2.22 to 2.67. Education (Sector 10) emerges as the most attractive sector, followed by the noninformation sector construction (Sector 20), from the perspective of output multipliers. Other information sectors that get a high billing are informaiton infrastructures (Sector 5), both in Indonesia and Malaysia, and communications (Sector 12), an important information activity in both Malaysia and Thailand.

In Indonesia and Thailand, according to the various Type I and Type II income multipliers, noninformation goods (Sector 13) is the most attractive. For Malaysia, construction activity (Sector 20) is the top income-generating sector. In Thailand, the electronics industry (Sector 4) appears to offer much potential according to various income multiplier effects. Also in Indonesia and Thailand, several information sectors figure prominently in terms of various types of income multipliers. They are: information goods (Sector 1), business services (Sector 9), infrastructures (Sector 5).

The structural interdependencies in the larger ASEAN economies are found to be weak because of the narrow specialization and underdeveloped nature of the economies. The demand-stimulated intermediate input, using responses or backward linkages, and the supply-stimulated increases in domestic production inducing output use or forward linkages, have been computed according to well-known procedures (Rasmussen, 1958). The key sector that seems to demonstrate dominant backward and forward linkages is noninformation goods production (Sector 13); services (Sector 15) also emerges as a key sector (see Table 5).

Despite the predominant noninformation economic structure of the ASEAN economies, it is clear from the multiplier analyses that the information sectors are relatively important for output and income expansion and development. As far as key sectors, or sectors with strong backward and forward linkages, nurturing the noninformation sectors appears to be the best way to develop, if preserving the predominantly pre-information economic structures is a desideratum. However, the rapid technological and institutional changes that come with the adoption and diffusion of information activities portend dramatic changes. New economic activities based on information technologies will emerge, changing conventional modes of production and creating new comparative advantages for trade. ASEAN economies will have to reorient their planning strategies to harness the benefits of the information era in a more decisive manner. For effective planning, the input–output data bases and structural analyses provide vital support.

Table 5. Key Sectors in the Larger ASEAN Economies

Country	Sector	Backward Linkage	(Rank)	Forward Linkage	(Rank)	Backward Spread	(Rank)	Forward Spread	(Rank)
Indonesia	13	1.21	(7)	4.88	(2)	0.94	(7)	0.72	(6)
	14	1.41	(6)	1.76	(4)	1.19	(8)	0.64	(4)
Malaysia	13	1.10	(10)	7.23	(1)	0.77	(4)	0.57	(3)
	14	1.12	(7)	1.18	(4)	1.44	(20)	0.79	(10)
	15	1.11	(8)	1.30	(3)	0.88	(5)	0.66	(6)
Thailand	13	1.21	(8)	6.96	(1)	0.79	(2)	0.56	(3)
	14	1.19	(9)	2.35	(3)	0.99	(8)	0.68	(9)

Conclusion

The static input–output analyses, or the snapshot indicators of the larger ASEAN economies, reveal that these economies are still languishing in a pre-information age. The proxy telematic indicators, multipliers, and linkages nevertheless demonstrate that the ASEAN economies are fast acquiring the trappings of the information economy. Already the large ASEAN economies have collaborated with Western and Newly Industrialized Countries' (NICs) multinational corporations to establish electronics-based industries for export. Technology parks in the image of Silicon Valley or Route 128 Massachusetts are pursued to gate-crash or leapfrog into the hedonistic information age. The export-processing zones and technology parks operating in the ASEAN economies are by and large chip assembly rather than chip manufacturing factories. With the increasing automation of chip assembly, the advanced countries are not only recapturing the market, but are also again wresting the comparative advantage in some of the other labor intensive manufactures such as textiles and leather industries (Dordick, 1982). The information revolutin can, therefore, increase the economic dependency of developing economies on metropolitan countries by eroding the existing comparative advantages of developing economies. National economic policies that see the writing on the wall have yet to be evolved in ASEAN countries. Appropriate transfers and absorption of new information technologies will enable these countries to keep abreast of their prospective competitors. But, with inadequate information infrastructures, ASEAN economies will have a real battle on their hands in the near future. If the growth and development record of ASEAN is to be sustained, ASEAN economies will have to respond decisively to the international challenges posed by the information revolution without delay. They would have to selectively adopt the new technologies that provide an edge in a menu of tradeable commodities in the world market. Simultaneously, ASEAN planning will have to address the important tasks of growing vicious domestic dualism. The information technologies are facilitative technologies that need not necessarily widen the cleavage between the information haves and have-nots. By tackling the requirements of health, education, and communication head on, using the information technologies, basic needs delivery to the impoverished rural hinterlands of ASEAN can be vastly improved. This, in turn, will turn the heat off the need for wasteful defense build-ups. A stable domestic political and economic order will reduce the threat of external aggression to the sovereignty and territorial integrity of ASEAN. The information infrastructures, such as telecommunications, promote efficient resource mobilization through an improved division of labor (Jussawalla, 1983). Gains in allocative efficiency that information technologies bestow will strengthen the international competitiveness of ASEAN. In addition, it will promote domestic development in ASEAN economies, if these technologies are adopted in a manner appropriate to the economic and political aspirations of the vast majority of the people who dwell in the rural hinterlands of ASEAN.

References

Bell, D. (1973). *The coming of post-industrial society*. New York: Basic Books.

Block, C., Goldschmidt, D., Hafid, A., Lalor, G., & Velasquez, A. (1984). Satellite telecommunications for development: The A.I.D. Rural Satellite Program and its pilot projects in Indonesia, Peru, and the Carribean. *In* D. Wedemeyer and L.S. Harms (Eds.), *Proceedings of PTC '84*. Honolulu, Pacific Telecommunication Council.

Dordick, H.S. (1982). *Critical issues for national computerization policy*. Working Paper. Annenberg School of Communications and East-West Center.

Gregory, G. (1980). The Asian communication explosion. *Communication International,* February.

Jensen, R.C., & West, G.R. (1980). Some reflections on input-output multipliers. *Annals of Regional Science, 14*(2).

Jussawalla, M. (1983). *The future of the information economy*. (Occasional Paper 16). Asian Mass Communication Research and Information Centre.

Karunaratne, N.D. (1982). Growth euphoria, academia and the development paradigm. *Third World Quarterly, 4,* (2).

Karunaratne, N.D. (1984a). *The methodology of information economy analysis*. University of Queensland and East-West Center Collaboration Project Paper.

Karunaratne, N.D. (1984b). *Insights on the information economies of Australia and her developing neighbours*. Paper presented at the 13th Conference of Economists, W.A.I.T., Perth.

Macdonald, S., & Mandeville T. (1984). *Telecommunications in ASEAN and Australia* (ASEAN-Australia Economic Papers No. 5), ASEAN-Australia Joint Research Project, Kuala Lumpur and Canberra.

Naya, S., Kim, D.H., & James W. (1984). External shocks and policy responses: The Asian experience. *Asian Development Review, 2,* (1), 1.

Organization for Economic Cooperation and Development. (1981). *Information computer communication policy. 6 Information activities, electronics, and telecommunications technologies*. Paris: Organization for Economic Cooperation and Development.

Porat, M.U. (1977). *The information economy*. Washington, DC: Department of Commerce, Office of Telecommunications.

Rahim, S.A. (1984). *The computer and knowledge information development in ASEAN countries,* A research working paper. Honolulu: Institute of Culture and Communication, East-West Center.

Rasmussen, P.N. (1958). *Studies in intersectoral relations*. Amsterdam: North Holland.

Tan, C.H. (1984). Trade and comparative economic development in ASEAN countries. *Journal of Asian-Pacific and World Perspectives, 7,* (1), 2.

World Bank, (1983). *World development report 1983*. New York: Oxford University Press.

CHAPTER 14

The Size and Structure of Singapore's Primary Information Sector

Chee-Wah Cheah

Introduction

Empirical studies focusing on industrialized countries have vindicated the existence of information sectors in the economies of the U.S., Australia, and Japan. This raises the interesting question of whether similar economies can be found among the newly industrializing and less developed countries in the Asia/Pacific region. Among the few empirical studies made in this regard, Jussawalla and Cheah (1983) estimated that the primary information sector contributed 24 percent to Singapore's gross domestic product (GDP) in 1973.[1] Since Singapore is regarded as a strategic regional center for both financial and communication flows, it is anticipated that the operation of its economy will require further specialization in information-support activities. Whether or not this is substantiated by recent experience remains to be seen.

At present, there are indications that Singapore's economy is already shifting away from the export-oriented manufacturing of wage goods. This is reflected in the burgeoning Singaporean services sector, which accounted for 44 percent of Singapore's total output in 1978. In terms of value-added, the services sector contributed 66 percent to GDP. The change in Singapore's industrial production structure is further apparent in the increasing proportion of its workforce engaged in service occupations. By mid-1979, it was estimated that more than 60 percent of total employed persons were to be found in the commerce and services sectors. In view of the

[1] The other studies include those of Karunaratne and Cameron (1980), for the case of Papua New Guinea, and Jussawalla and Dworak (1983), for the case of the Philippines.

wide range of market- and information-support facilities in Singapore, there is reasonable expectation that its future economic growth and social stratification will be arranged in terms of productive activities centering on information and communication technologies.

The primary purpose of this chapter is to document the structural arrangements, output composition, and employment patterns associated with information-related activities in Singapore through the use of familiar input–output (IO) analytical techniques. First, an attempt is made to clarify and build upon the conceptual underpinnings and methodology that have been developed for the empirical assessment of primary information sectors. Second, the analysis of more recent data provides additional evidence on the size and composition of Singapore's primary information sector, supplementing the empirical findings of an earlier study (see Jussawalla & Cheah, 1983).

In the following section, the definitional basis and conceptual premise for the study of an information sector is delineated. Next, the theory and methodology underlying the derivation of the primary information matrix (PRINMA) is described. The data sources and initial results of the PRINMA analysis are presented in the fourth section. In particular, the primary information sector input, value added, and employment are examined and compared for their relative economic significance within the context of the conventionally defined macro-economy. A structural analysis of Singapore's macro-economy, with particular attention to the role of its primary information sector, is conducted in the fifth section. The sixth section contains brief remarks regarding the research and policy implications of the PRINMA analysis suggested by this chapter.

The Information Sector: Definitions and Concepts

The quantification of information remains problematic and imprecise, insofar as a piece of information can be subjected to varying degrees of abstraction. The measurement problem can be made more tractable by referring to the economic goods and services that are functionally associated with the production, manipulation, or dissemination of symbols and patterns. In this regard, an information good is defined as one which provides a medium whereby information can be manipulated or transformed from one pattern or set of symbols to another (e.g., writing equipment and paper). Similarly, information services are defined by activities which relate to the production, processing, storage, and dissemination of symbols and patterns (e.g., advertising). On the basis of these definitions, it is possible to delineate an information sector which encompasses all information goods and services produced within an economy.

An information sector can be divided into two subsectors, referred to as the "primary" and "secondary" information sector. This terminology is due to the work of Porat (1977). The primary information sector is made up of goods and services which are exchanged in explicit markets. These goods and services are unique in the sense that they are intrinsically used, either directly or indirectly, in the production, processing, and dissemination of both technological and market information. The secondary information sector refers to informational processes that are inherent in the conduct of all aspects of socioeconomic organization in private as well as public sectors. In particular, these processes are associated with the internal functions performed by production units in controlling, monitoring, coordinating, or, more generally, organizing productive activities.

The PRINMA Analysis: Methodology and Theoretical Support

The size of a primary information sector can be measured either in terms of the value-added originating from the production of information goods and services, or via the size of the workforce employed by the sector.[2] The former approach is facilitated by the availability of factor income components. These components can be conveniently derived from an IO accounting scheme. Aside from certain restrictive assumptions, it is felt that there are advantages to be gained from using an IO framework. In the first instance, it is recognized that an IO table is essentially the empirical counterpart of the theoretical Walrasian general equilibrium model. As such, the relevant details of interindustry relationships are maintained and reported in an economically consistent manner. Second, the analytical tools of IO techniques can be fruitfully utilized in studying the structural dependencies between the primary-information and other sectors which are unique to a given economy.

The main task of the proposed methodology is to extract the primary information sector from a given IO transactions matrix, while preserving the intricacies of interindustry dependencies. A requisite step is the generation of an inventory of information-related industrial activities through the use of a country-specific Standard Industrial Classification (SIC) scheme at the 4-digit level. The resulting inventory of activities are then categorized into five functional groups which constitute the primary information sector.

[2] On the other hand, measurements of the secondary information sector are much more difficult to obtain. This is because there are as yet no social accounting schemes which generate data on the informational activities conducted and consumed internally by the bureaucracies of both private and public firms. As such, the size of the secondary information sector cannot be possibly imputed unless a field survey of firms at the micro level is undertaken.

These functional groups are designated by the following generic labels: (1) production of information goods; (2) risk management; (3) search and coordination; (4) information and knowledge distribution; and (5) distribution of information goods.

Next, the inventory obtained from the procedure described above is used to identify and locate information-related industries within the transactions matrix, X. In practice, there are instances where only a portion of an industry defined in X (say, i) is information related. The relevant information-related component of i's output, value-added, and employment can be extracted from their respective aggregates by applying an industry-specific "information intensity ratio," P_i.[3] This admittedly crude method of proration is entirely consistent with the production technology assumed in the construction of X. More specifically, the technology of each industry i in X is described by a linearly homogenous Marx-Leontief production function characterized by fixed factor proportions such that

$$X_i = [A\ B] \begin{bmatrix} U \\ V \end{bmatrix} \tag{1}$$

where X_i is the ith industry output, A is the $(1 \times j)$ vector of intermediate input coefficients, B is the $(1 \times k)$ vector of primary input coefficients, U is the $(j \times 1)$ vector of intermediate inputs, and V is the $(k \times 1)$ vector of primary inputs.

Although X_i is usually regarded as a homogenous bundle of output, it can be reinterpreted as a composite output comprising of two or more items produced in fixed proportions (see Baumol, 1977). As such, it is possible to restate (1) as

$$X_i = P_i X_i + (1 - P_i) X_i \tag{2}$$

for the special case where X_i is a composite of information and noninformation outputs. By virtue of the "industry technology" assumption, each of the separate component in (2) can be treated as a separate industry with the same input structure as that of X_i. Thus,

$$P_i X_i = P_i K F' \tag{3a}$$

$$\text{and } (1 - P_i) X_i = (1 - P_i) K F' \tag{3b}$$

where $K = [A\ B]$ and $F = [U\ V]$. For empirical purposes, P_i is defined as the ratio of information-related output of industry i to total output of industry

[3] It is instructive to note that the ratio P_i is defined in the same manner as the scalar λ_i employed by Jussawalla and Cheah (1983). The term "scalar" is dropped in favor of "ratio" to avoid confusion in the mathematical presentation in matrix notation below.

i. This ratio can be constructed from census data on industrial production or, in its unavailability, from other disaggregated data which proxy the size of the information component within an industry.

It is clear that, in extracting the information component from each industry's aggregate value added and output, each individual cell in the transactions matrix X will have to be separated into four sub-cells to maintain the internal consistency of the IO relationships (see Karunaratne & Cameron, 1980). Thus, for each transaction x_{ij} (i.e., input from industry i used by industry j), the following interdependencies are maintained: (a) input from an information-related industry to another $\{P_iP_jx_{ij}\}$; (b) input from an information-related industry to a noninformation industry $\{P_i(1-P_j)x_{ij}\}$; (c) input from a noninformation industry to an information-related industry $\{(1-P_i)P_jx_{ij}\}$; and (d) input from a noninformation industry to another $\{(1-P_i)(1-P_j)x_{ij}\}$.[4] The four-way separation of the entire transactions table can be described compactly in matrix notation.

Suppose that the transactions matrix X is of order n. Define a n-order diagonal matrix P such that its ith diagonal element is equal to $[P_i]$. From P, the matrix (I – P) can be obtained using an identity matrix I of order n. The ith diagonal element of this matrix is equal to $[1-P_i]$. The matrices P and (I – P) are then collected into a partitioned matrix of order (2n × 2n) defined by

$$\Sigma = \left[\begin{array}{c|c} P & O \\ \hline (I-P) & O \end{array}\right] \tag{4}$$

where O is the null matrix of order n. The matrix which preserves the four-way interdependencies described above is then calculated by performing the matrix multiplication

$$\Sigma(I^* \otimes X)\Sigma' \tag{5}$$

where I* is a (2 × 2) identity matrix and $\otimes$ is the Kronecker product operator. The result of (5) is a partitioned matrix described by

$$\left[\begin{array}{c|c} PXP' & PX(I-P)' \\ \hline (I-P)XP' & (I-P)X(I-P)' \end{array}\right] \tag{6}$$

The elements of the sub-matrix PXP′ refer to transactions between information-related industries, while those in (I – P)X(I – P)′ refer to transactions between noninformation industries. Transactions between industries in the information sector and those in the noninformation sector are captured by the off-diagonal matrices.

[4] For the special case of the diagonal elements in X where i = j, the corresponding sub-cells are computed as $\{P_i^2x_{ii}\}$, $\{P_i(1-P_i)x_{ii}\}$, $\{(1-P_i)P_ix_{ii}\}$, *and* $\{(1-P_i)^2x_{ii}\}$ respectively.

The derivation of the so-called primary information matrix (PRINMA) makes up the final step in the methodology. In particular, the matrix in (6) is "collapsed" in a manner that preserves the IO structure of the primary information and noninformation sectors. This step is defensible in terms of the additive property of Marx-Leontief production functions. The primary information sector subsumed under the PRINMA is identified by a collection of industrial activities falling under the five functional categories described earlier. The rest of the economy consists of conventional industrial activities covering the production of noninformation goods and services, wholesale and retail trade in noninformation goods, primary production, utilities, and construction.

Empirical Application and Results

The methodology set out above is applied to the Singaporean 150-order IO table for 1978 (Singapore, 1983). An inventory of information-related industries is obtained from Singapore's SIC (Singapore, 1980a). The corresponding industrial activities defined in the IO transactions matrix are presented in Appendix 1 under five functional categories. The vector of information intensity ratios is constructed from published data generated by various censuses and surveys (Singapore, 1978, 1979, 1981). Ratios for primary activities in agriculture and fisheries were set to zero by default because of the lack of disaggregated data which proxy the value of research and extension services in these activities. However, this omission does not seriously affect the estimate of the primary information sector, in view of the relative unimportance of the primary sector in Singapore's economy.[5]

The extraction of the information sector is based on the computation expressed in (5). In particular, the partitioned matrix represented in (6) is reduced to a 25-order matrix to yield the PRINMA. This involves a summing up of the rows and corresponding columns of the matrix in (6). The first 17 rows (and columns) of the PRINMA correspond to the activities described in Appendix 1. The noninformation sector is portrayed by eight aggregate activities which constitute the rest of Singapore's macro-economy (see Appendix 2).

Singapore's GDP in 1978 is presented in Table 1, using a conventional sectoral format. The value-added originating from information-related activities residing in each of the conventional sector is also shown. On the whole, the primary information sector generated more than one-quarter of Singapore's GDP in 1978. This implies that, for every S$1 received, about

[5] The agricultural sector contributed only 1.2% and 1.5% of total output and value-added, respectively, in 1978.

Table 1. GDP by Sector of Origin, 1978 (S$Million)

Sector	Total Value-Added (TVA)	Information Sector Value-Added (IVA)	TVA/IVA (%)
1. Agriculture	269.2	n.a.*	n.a.*
2. Mining	21.6	—	—
3. Manufacturing	4750.9	965.0	20.3
4. Utilities	363.5	—	—
5. Construction	1093.5	—	—
6. Commerce, restaurants & hotels	4275.3	278.3	6.5
7. Transport, storage & communication	2575.8	468.0	18.2
8. Finance, insurance & real estate	1929.6	1178.0	61.1
9. Government & services	2710.2	1592.9	58.8
10. Imputed bank charges	(−737.5)	—	—
GRAND TOTAL	17252.1	4482.2	26.0

* not available

25 cents were paid for the production of information goods and services. The largerst contributing sector was government and services, where 58.8 percent of total value-added originated from the provision of informational services. The bulk of these services stemmed from public administration and education (37%). Informational services provided by professional and business agencies, such as those in advertising, market research, consultancies, and data-processing, accounted for about 6% of total value added in the sector.

The conventional finance, insurance, and real-estate sector made up 11.1 percent of GDP. Of this, almost two-thirds (61%) of total value added was derived from the informational services of financial institutions, stock brokers, insurance agents, and real-estate appraisers. The manufacturing of information goods contributed 20 percent to total value-added in the aggregate manufacturing sector. These included items such as office and computing machines, electronic consumer products, and telecommunication equipment and components. The rest of the primary information sector can be found in the conventinally defined sectors of commerce and transport, storage, and communication.

In terms of employment, more than 26 percent of Singapore's total workforce was engaged by the primary information sector. The majority of this "information workforce" can be found in public administration and education, manufacturing of electronic and telecommunication equipment, and banking and finance (Sectors 13, 4, and 7, respectively, in Table 2). Of the top five activities ranked according to compensation per worker, four

Table 2. PRINMA Sectoral Employment and Output

PRINMA Sector	Workers ('000)*	Compensation Per Worker (S$ '000)	TVA Per Worker (S$ '000)	Output (S$Million)
1. Pulp & paper	.648	4.2	10.2	20.1
2. Inks & carbon black	.434	10.6	15.2	23.6
3. Office equipment	4.737	7.1	16.4	209.4
4. Electronic components	58.328	4.4	11.7	2581.6
5. Precision instruments	.806	5.8	16.5	35.2
6. Signs & advertising displays	.119	0.8	1.7	0.4
7. Banking & finance	22.878	13.5	41.3	1310.2
8. Insurance	5.844	6.7	19.9	182.7
9. Tourist & travel agencies	4.164	9.6	20.4	234.2
10. Real estate agents	3.702	2.8	31.7	155.9
11. Professional services	14.075	19.9	31.7	854.9
12. Printing & publishing	13.150	7.0	13.4	414.2
13. Public administration & education	98.473	10.1	10.2	1818.4
14. Education	4.121	5.5	10.2	60.4
15. Culture & mass-media communication	9.692	4.9	10.2	165.0
16. Postal, telephone & telegraph services	11.418	8.8	23.5	460.5
17. Commerce allied to information goods	13.498	6.2	20.6	397.8
18. Noninformation goods	215.091	6.7	17.6	19492.5
19. Noninformation services	232.669	5.7	13.9	7627.6
20. Commerce	222.954	5.6	17.9	6256.4
21. Livestock	12.957	1.5	13.5	401.5
22. Other agriculture	2.163	5.7	43.6	156.6
23. Mining	1.518	4.6	14.2	51.4
24. Utilities	9.817	7.5	37.0	670.4
25. Construction	58.324	11.1	20.1	2574.2
GRAND TOTAL	1017.580	6.9**	16.9**	46155.2

* Derived from data published in Singapore (1980b).
** Refers to average figure.

are found in the information sector. These activities are, in descending order of magnitude, professional services (S$19.9), banking and finance (S$13.5), manufacturing of inks and carbon black (S$10.6), and public administration and education (S$10.1). Table 3 summarizes the relative importance of economic variables associated with the information sector. It can be seen that the average worker in the information sector generated as much value added as his or her counterpart in the noninformation sector. In addition, the average information sector worker tends to receive a higher compensation.

Table 3. Sectoral Comparison of Total Output, Value Added, Compensation, and Employment

Sector / Component	Information	Noninformation	Grand Total
Total Value Added (S$Million)	4482.2	12769.0	17252.1
Total Output (S$Million)	8924.5	37230.7	46155.2
Total Compensation (S$Million)	2328.8	4732.2	7061.0
Total Workers (number)	266,087	751,493	1,017,580
Sector Output (%)	19.3	80.7	100.0
Sector Value Added (%)	26.0	74.0	100.0
Sector Compensation (%)	32.9	67.1	100.0
Sector Employment (%)	26.2	73.8	100.0
Value Added per Worker (S$ '000)	16.8	16.9	16.9
Compensation per Worker (S$ '000)	8.8	6.3	6.9

While these results are indicative of the size and contribution of Singapore's information sectoral activities, it is of some interest to compare the Singaporean experience with those of other economies in the Asia/Pacific region. The relevant data drawn from Jussawalla and Cheah (1983), Jussawalla and Dworak (1983), and Karunaratne and Cameron (1981) are presented in Table 4. With the exception of the Philippines and Papua New Guinea, the base years of the other countries are sufficiently close to enable meaningful comparisons. It is observed that the Singaporean experience is remarkably similar to that of Australia. The higher proportion of information workforce in Singapore is perhaps reflective of its larger services-sector base, compared to that of Australia.

Although the size of Singapore's information sector has grown in terms of value added, the proportion of information-sector output has declined from 20.1 percent in 1973 to 19.3 percent in 1978. This is due to the higher growth rate of total output relative to that of the information sector per se (see Table 5). In terms of value added, it is interesting to note that the growth of the information sector surpassed that of the overall economy.

Table 4. Cross-Country Comparison of Primary Information Sector

Country (Year)	% Total Output	% Total Value Added	% Total Employment
Australia (1977/78)	18.9	25.5	21.1
Fiji (1977)	13.0	16.7	17.0
Philippines (1974)	10.7	11.7	5.8
Singapore (1973)	20.1	24.4	n.e.*
Singapore (1978)	19.3	26.0	26.2
Papua New Guinea (1972)	12.9	12.8	13.0

* not estimated.

Table 5. **Information Sector and Macro-Economy Growth Rates**

Year	1973	1978	Annual Growth Rate
Information Sector Value Added	2383.0	4482.2	13.5
Total Value Added	9780.5	17252.1	12.0
Information Sector Output	8200.9	8924.5	1.7
Total Output	40820.9	46155.1	2.5

This statistic testifies to the dynamic impact of economic activities relating to the production of information goods and services.

The PRINMA Structural Analysis

A structural analysis of the PRINMA is useful in revealing the demand and supply relationships of individual industries, as well as those between the aggregate information and noninformation sectors. In particular, interesting characteristics of economic structure can be discerned in the pattern of sectoral input requirements from intermediate and final sources, as well as in output distribution between intermediate and final uses. Since the PRINMA has been derived in such a manner that the first 17 activities are information related, it is possible to obtain indications about the volume of goods or services from the information sector which enters into the production structure of each activity. Table 6 presents the breakdown of sectoral purchases by origin, as a percentage of total supply. The data here are indicative of the extent to which a given industry draws on the domestic economy for its intermediate and primary inputs. The breakdown of sectoral sales by destination, as a percentage of total demand, is given in Table 7. These statistics show the proportion of a given industry's supply that is consumed by intermediate and final demand sectors.

With regards to sectoral purchases by origin, three information-related industries are observed to be relatively more dependent on the domestic economy than others (see Table 6). Out of the 43 percent of input requirements purchased by Sector 9 (informational services allied to transport) from domestic sources, more than 34 percent were drawn from the noninformation sector. Similarly, Sector 11 (professional and business services) relied more on the noninformation sector (18.1%) than it did on the information sector (12.7%) for its intermediate inputs. On the other hand, the intermediate purchases of Sector 8 (insurance) were quite evenly distributed between the information sector (16.5%) and the noninformation sector (15.7%). By contrast, the production structure of Sectors 3 (office machinery) and 4 (electronic components) were heavily dependent on external sources. About 50 percent of input requirements in Sector 3 came from imports, while those in Sector 4 made up 63 percent of its total purchases.

Table 6. Sectoral Purchases by Origin (%)*

Sector**	Information Sector	Noninformation Sector	Primary Inputs	Imports
1	1.3	23.1	32.8	42.8
2	7.0	19.3	28.0	45.8
3	4.3	8.7	37.0	50.0
4	3.0	7.4	26.5	63.1
5	8.4	15.5	38.1	38.1
6	4.5	15.0	50.0	25.0
7	14.6	9.1	72.1	4.2
8	16.5	15.7	63.8	4.1
9	8.6	34.2	36.3	20.9
10	3.4	18.3	75.2	3.0
11	12.7	18.1	52.2	17.1
12	14.3	8.3	42.5	34.9
13	2.4	12.2	55.3	30.1
14	10.5	14.3	69.7	5.5
15	16.2	12.7	60.0	11.1
16	5.3	7.8	83.2	3.7
17	9.7	14.6	70.0	5.8
18	1.8	13.8	19.4	65.0
19	14.6	22.1	42.5	20.8
20	8.7	18.1	63.9	9.3
21	2.1	37.0	43.6	17.3
22	3.5	13.9	60.2	22.5
23	9.1	32.4	42.0	16.5
24	1.0	24.2	54.2	21.0
25	1.0	27.1	42.5	29.4

* Row entries may not sum to 100% due to rounding errors.
**Refer to Appendices 1 and 2 for detailed description of sectors.

In terms of output utilization, a majority of the sectors are seen to have more than 50 percent of their outputs destined for final demand (see Table 7). These included Sectors 3 (office machinery), 4 (electronic components), 13 (government services), and 14 (education). Included among the information-related industries which contributed most to the domestic economy are Sectors 7 (banking and finance), 11 (professional and business services), and 16 (communication). About 70 percent of total output from Sector 7 was utilized by the noninformation sector, while 45.6 and 45.1 percent of the outputs of Sectors 11 and 16 were used in further production by noninformation industries. By contrast, 44.8 percent of the total output from Sector 6 (signs and advertising displays) was consumed within the information sector itself.

Aside from these direct observations, the structural analysis of the PRINMA can be extended by indices of demand-generating or multiplier effects. Sectoral output multipliers (M) are calculated by summing the respective columns in the Leontief inverse of the PRINMA. In addition, the

Table 7. Sectoral Sales by Destination (%)*

Sector**	Information Sector	Noninformation Sector	Final Demand
1	3.0	43.3	53.7
2	28.9	33.4	37.7
3	1.8	1.5	96.6
4	2.2	1.7	96.2
5	16.8	2.8	80.4
6	44.8	18.0	37.3
7	6.1	69.8	24.1
8	9.7	39.9	50.4
9	4.3	32.4	63.3
10	13.3	41.7	44.9
11	20.9	45.6	33.5
12	22.4	41.0	36.6
13	0.6	1.9	97.5
14	0.0	0.3	99.7
15	14.7	14.6	70.7
16	28.2	45.1	26.6
17	2.0	12.5	85.5
18	1.5	16.5	82.0
19	5.3	24.3	70.4
20	2.8	11.9	85.3
21	0.3	13.6	86.1
22	0.2	13.3	86.5
23	0.4	99.6	0.0
24	14.5	58.7	26.7
25	1.5	8.7	89.8

* Row entries may not add to 100% due to rounding errors.
** Refer to Appendices 1 and 2 for detailed description of sectors.

"roundaboutness of production," or degree of sectoral interdependence, can be gauged from backward and forward linkages which measure the direct and indirect repercussions of exogenous economic changes on all sectors within an economy. The backward linkage (L_b) is an index of dispersion which measures the extent to which the overall economy develops with a given expansion of a particular industry. Mathematically, L_b for each industry j is defined as

$$L_b(j) = \{\sum_{i=1}^{n} z_{ij}\}/\{n^{-1}.\sum_{i=1}^{n}\sum_{j=1}^{n} z_{ij}\} \qquad (7)$$

where $[z_{ij}]$ is the (i,j) element in the Leontief inverse. The forward linkage (L_f), on the other hand, is regarded as an index of sensitivity to dispersion which measures the extent to which a sector can expand for a given unit of expansion in the overall economy. L_f for each industry i can be defined as

$$L_f(i) = \{\sum_{j=1}^{n} z_{ij}\}/\{n^{-1}.\sum_{i=1}^{n}\sum_{j=1}^{n} z_{ij}\} \qquad (8)$$

The values and rank of M, L_b, L_f for each industry defined in the PRINMA are given in Table 8.

Of the top 10 sectors ranked by magnitude of M and L_b, five were information-related, viz., Sectors 9 (informational services allied to transport), 8 (insurance), 11 (professional and business services), 15 (cultural and mass-media communication), and 14 (education). Thus, aside from their significant multiplier effects, the productivity of these sectors are interwoven into the top productive capacity and economic growth of Singapore. In terms of the top 10 sectors ranked according to the size of L_f, four were information-related. These sectors, which included Sector 11 (professional and business services), Sector 7 (banking and finance), Sector 16 (communication), and Sector 12 (printing and publishing), can be considered "supporting" sectors in the sense that they are relatively responsive to the stimulus of economic growth within the overall economy. Perhaps of greater interest is the economic status of Sector 11 which, as indicated by its value of L_b and L_f, appeared prominently linked within Singapore's production structure. In considering that the professional and business services sector is most likely to be income elastic, this sector can be rightly identified as a "leading" sector in Singapore's economy.

Table 8. Sectoral Multipliers and Linkages Ranked by Size

Sector	M	L_b	Sector	L_f
9	1.6159	1.2065	18	2.2681
23	1.6117	1.2034	19	2.2297
19	1.5080	1.1260	20	1.3721
21	1.4817	1.1063	11	1.1898
8	1.4483	1.0814	24	1.1302
11	1.4238	1.0631	7	1.1285
15	1.4061	1.0499	16	1.0275
20	1.3722	1.0245	12	1.0056
14	1.3484	1.0068	23	0.9515
25	1.3473	1.0059	25	0.9290
2	1.3419	1.0019	15	0.8548
17	1.3404	1.0008	13	0.8451
7	1.3236	0.9883	8	0.8194
1	1.3229	0.9877	10	0.8044
5	1.3153	0.9821	9	0.7978
24	1.3068	0.9757	4	0.7930
12	1.3013	0.9717	5	0.7915
10	1.3003	0.9709	17	0.7845
6	1.2671	0.9461	2	0.7694
22	1.2283	0.9171	21	0.7587
18	1.1980	0.8945	3	0.7548
13	1.1867	0.8860	22	0.7506
16	1.1806	0.8815	1	0.7494
3	1.1744	0.8769	6	0.7481
4	1.1318	0.8450	14	0.7467

Conclusion

Even though there may be obvious policy implications in the results presented above, our intention is not to suggest options for economic growth and development in the face of an emergent information sector. Rather, the empirical exercise should be considered demonstrative of the capability and utility of the PRINMA analysis in generating data relevant for policy and planning purposes. Once the presence of an information sector is acknowledged, policymakers can become more aware of the consequences of a changing economic structure for future sectoral priorities and employment patterns. In particular, investment criteria for economic growth and structural development can be identified in the context of the appropriate technology and planned replacement demands for the newer product cycle fostered by an information economy.

There is no doubt that the bane of empirical research is the unavailability of refined data. In addition, the PRINMA analysis is afflicted by the same limitations which beset any standard IO analysis. Without denying the apparent need for better measurement techniques, the present approach can benefit from a statistical framework that incorporates data on information-related activities. In this regard, national income accountants must be persuaded to revise the Keynesian accounting scheme so as to alleviate problems of measurability, particularly in the context of nonmarketed information goods and services (i.e., the secondary information sector). Finally, it is evident that questions about the admissability of an information sector concept in economic research are now rendered academic, in view of the preponderance of empirical findings which confirm the existence of information sectors across national economies.

References

Baumol, W.J. (1977). *Economic theory and operations analysis* (4th ed.), Englewood Cliffs, NJ: Prentice Hall.

Jussawalla, M., & Cheah, C.-W. (1983). Towards and information economy: The case of Singapore. *Information Economics and Policy, 1*(2), pp. 161–176.

Jussawalla, M., & Dworak, S. (1983). The primary information sector of a developing country: The case of Philippines. Honolulu, HI: East-West Center Institute of Culture and Communication. (mimeographed.)

Karunaratne, N.D., & Cameron, A.D. (1980), Input output analysis and the Austrailian information economy. *Information and Management, 3*(5), 191–206.

Karunaratne, N.D. & Cameron, A.D. (1981). "A Comparative Analysis of the 'Information Economy' in developed and developing countries" *Journal of Information Sciences, 3,* 113–127.

Porat, M.U. (1977). *The information economy.* Washington, DC: Department of Commerce, Office of Telecommunications.

Singapore. Department of Statistics. (1978). *Report on the census of wholesale and retail trades, restaurants, and hotels, 1975.* Singapore: Department of Statistics.

Singapore. Department of Statistics. (1979). *Report on the survey of services, 1976.* Singapore: Department of Statistics.

Singapore. Department of Statistics. (1980a). *Singapore standard industrial classification 1978.* Singapore: Department of Statistics.

Singapore. Ministry of Labour. (1980b). *Report on the labour force survey of Singapore 1979.* Singapore: Research and Statistics Division, Ministry of Labour.

Singapore. Department of Statistics. (1981). *Report on the census of industrial production 1978.* Singapore: Department of Statistics.

Singapore. Department of Statistics. (1983). *Singapore input-output tables, 1978.* Singapore: Department of Statistics.

Appendix 1
PRINMA Sectoral Classification

Functional Category	Derived PRINMA Sector	Industrial Activity Components	Source IO Sector	Information Intensity Ratio
I: Production of Information Goods	1. Pulp & paper	a. manufacture of pulp & paper	048	1.000
	2. Inks & carbon black	a. manufacture of inks & carbon black	062	1.000
	3. Office machine & equipment	a. manufacture & repair, office & computing machines (both electronic and otherwise)	091	1.000
	4. Electronic equipment & components	a. electronic consumer products	097	1.000
		b. telecommunication equipment & components	098	1.000
	5. Precision instruments	a. engineering & scientific measuring and controlling devices	111	1.000
	6. Signs & advertising displays	a. manufacture of signs & advertising displays	117	0.044
II. Risk Management	7. Banking & finance	a. commercial & merchant banks	132	1.000
		b. other financial institutions	134	1.000
	8. Insurance	a. insurance agents, brokers, and companies	133	1.000
III: Search & Coordination	9. Informational services allied to	a. tourist & travel agencies	130	0.182
	10. Informational services allied to real estate	a. real estate agents and appraisers	135	0.135
	11. Professional & business services	a. legal services	136	1.000
		b. accounting & data-processing services	137	1.000
		c. architectural & technical services	138	1.000
		d. market research, advertising, & consultancies	139	0.747

Appendix 1 (Continued)

Functional Category	Derived PRINMA Sector	Industrial Activity Components	Source IO Sector	Information Intensity Ratio
IV: Information & Knowledge Distribution	12. Printing & publishing	a. printing of newspapers	053	1.000
		b. printing of books, periodicals & journals	054	0.943
	13. Government services	a. public administration & education	140	0.850
	14. Education	a. private educational institutions	142	1.000
	15. Cultural & mass-media communication	a. motion picture production and distribution	144	1.000
		b. radio & television broadcasting	145	1.000
	16. Communication	a. postal, telephone, & telecommunication	131	1.000
V: Distribution of Information Goods	17. Commerce allied to information goods	a. wholesale & retail trade in information goods	123	0.079

Appendix 2
Sectoral Reclassification of Singapore's Conventional Economy

Derived Sector	Industrial Activity Components	Source IO Sectors
18. Noninformation goods production	a. manufacture of conventional goods	005-047, 049-052, 054-061, 063-090, 092-096, 099-110, 112-118
19. Noninformation services	a. conventional services in transport, storage, recreation, culture, & welfare	126-130,135, 139-141, 143, 146-150
20. Commerce	a. wholesale & retail trade in conventional goods, restaurants & hotels	123, 124, 125
21. Livestock	a. livestock production	001
22. Fishing & other agriculture	a. fishing, forestry, logging & collection of agriculatural by-products	002-003
23. Quarrying & mining	a. quarrying & mining	004
24. Utilities	a. gas, water, & electricity	119-121
25. Construction	a. construction	122

CHAPTER 15

The Primary Information Sector of Taiwan

Hans-Juergen Engelbrecht

1. Introduction

Developed and developing countries alike are experiencing profound changes in their economies and societies due to dramatic advances in telecommunication systems which are at the heart of the information revolution. However, the impacts are most obvious in the developed countries, especially Japan, where important institutional changes have taken place recently which will help to unleash the full force of the new technologies. Because of these changes, 1984 has been dubbed "Year One of the Information Age." There is the likelihood that Japan will emerge as the leading information economy, thereby shifting the center of the world economy from North America to East Asia.

To some, the impending changes promise the full development of information as the basic raw material of economies, and its transformation into "great endless wealth" (*Far Eastern Economic Review,* Sept. 6, 1984). Others are more cautious, and emphasize the potential costs and benefits. Especially for developing countries, the potential effects of the information revolution range from increased dependency on the developed countries due to an ever-widening technological gap, and dire social and cultural consequences (Boon, 1982; Wad, 1982), to the promise of leap-frogging the development process and regarding information as a key to development (Davis, 1984).

This study measures the primary information sector (PRIS) of Taiwan in 1976, assesses its potential, and draws some tentative conclusions about its role in the future development of that economy. This is a prerequisite for any assessment of economic policies designed to reap the potential benefits of the ongoing information revolution.[1]

The economy of Taiwan has experienced enormous growth and structural change in the past. Real GDP grew at an average of 9.5 percent from 1960 to 1980 (Taiwan, 1983c, pp. 178–179). Between 1951 and 1981, the share of primary industry in GNP fell from 32 to 7 percent, and the share of secondary industry increased from 22 to 51 percent, earning it the accolade of "Newly Industrializing Country" (NIC). These changes were to a large extent induced and supported by an outward-oriented development strategy (Kuo, 1983, p. 1). Like other Pacific Basin countries, Taiwan has now embarked on a program to revolutionize its communication networks, committing massive resources to this aim. Over the next 5 years, the Directorate-General of Telecommunications has budgeted NT $210 billion (US $5.25 billion) for the first stage of a project which will eventually result in a fully integrated digital voice and data communication system (*Far Eastern Economic Review,* Sept. 6, 1984).

In order to assess the impending changes properly, a new statistical framework is used in which the PRIS is accorded its well-deserved place alongside traditional primary, secondary, and tertiary industries, under which it is currently subsumed in the National Accounts.

There is evidence to suggest that the development of the PRIS will not necessarily follow the pattern exhibited in developed countries. This will be briefly explored in Section 6 of this study. Section 2 discusses the identification of the information sector within an Input-Output (I-O) framework. This is followed in Sections 3 to 5 by a detailed assessment and structural analysis of the macro-economy, using linkages and multipliers. The methodology used, and a critical examination of its appropriateness as a means by which to assess the potential of the emerging information sector, is contained in Appendix 1.

2. Identification of the Primary Information Sector

The methodology explained in Chapter 3 was applied to the 1976 I-O Table of Taiwan (Taiwan, 1980a,b). The constituents of each I-O sector, as given in the "Sectoral Disaggregation and Explanation of Input-Output Tables of Taiwan Industries" (Taiwan, 1981) and the "Standard Classification of

[1] There are indications that the informatization of Taiwan has advanced rapidly since 1976. One such indication is the growth in teledensity, which has been remarkable in recent years.

Rate of Growth of Teledensity (Telephones/100 Persons)

1965	*1970*	*1976*	*1979*	*1982*
1.3	2.8	8.5	14.8	23.6

Source: Taiwan (1983b), p. 209.

Industries of ROC'' (Taiwan, 1983a), were checked with the OECD inventory. In some cases, the total output of an industry was designated informational. For many manufacturing industries, the information component of output had to be determined from the Census of Manufacturing (Taiwan, 1975). The 99-sector 1976 I-O table was used throughout (except for one industry, for which recourse was made to the 392-intermediate-sector table). For some sectors, data on information components was not available. In such cases, the information scalar was estimated from other studies. As a general rule, we assumed a conservative estimate.

Therefore, the contribution of the PRIS to value-added, final demand, and output, as presented in this study, is an underestimation of its true contribution, due to the nature of available data. In particular, due to lack of data, no attempt was made to estimate the following information items which could be argued to be part of the PRIS: information goods and services used in agriculture and mining, and travel and freight agents. It was felt that the neglect of these items would result in only a minor underestimation of the sector, and that the items could be regarded as part of the Secondary Information Sector (SIS).

The partitioned matrix was then rearranged and consolidated into the new I-O table, according to the sector classification scheme given in Table 1, Appendix 2. A feature of this study is that we investigate both the PRIS and the manufacturing sectors in detail. For a NIC like Taiwan, this was regarded as necessary, as the manufacturing sector has overwhelming importance for the economy. It should be noted that the manufacturing sectors referred to in this study are net of PRIS elements and therefore, are not the same as conventional manufacturing sectors. Information on the value and derivation of information scalars is provided in Table 2, Appendix 2. The 32 sectors have also been collapsed into a four-sector scheme, thereby facilitating a highly aggregated analysis which gives a clearer picture of the broad interrelationship of PRIS and noninformation sectors.[2]

3. Magnitude of the Primary Information Sector and Analysis of Direct Effects

The major findings regarding the rise of the PRIS are presented in Table 1.

The PRIS generated approximately 20 percent of value added, 17.5 percent of final demand, and 13.7 percent of output in 1976. It ranked third for

[2] The thirty-two sectors have been aggregated as follows:

	32 Sector Code
1. Primary or Agriculture	28,29
2. Secondary or Manufacturing	14-25,31,32
3. Tertiary or Services	26,27,30
4. Quaternary or Information	1-13

Table 1. Sectoral Value-added, Final Demand and Output (Million TW$)

Sector	Value Added	%	Rank	Final Demand	%	Rank	Output	%	Rank
1. Primary	91	12.5	(4)	56	5.3	(4)	260	12.9	(4)
2. Secondary	250	34.3	(1)	519	49.2	(1)	1078	53.5	(1)
3. Tertiary	242	33.2	(2)	295	28.0	(2)	400	19.9	(2)
4. Quaternary	146	20.0	(3)	184	17.5	(3)	276	13.7	(3)
Total	729	100.0		1054	100.0		2014	100.0	

all three macro-economic indicators, behind secondary and tertiary sectors. The economy of Taiwan was predominantly industrial in 1976. The secondary sector accounted for 34.3 percent of value-added, 49.2 percent of final demand, and 53.5 percent of output.

Comparing our results with those of others in this book, we find that the contribution of the PRIS of Taiwan to value-added is not as high as that found for Australia and Singapore. However, it is greater than that for New Zealand, Papua New Guinea, and the ASEAN countries. It also compares well with findings for advanced countries.

Tables 2 and 3 present the composition of total demand and total supply for the highly aggregated four-sector economy. Of each dollar total demand for the PRIS, one-third was contributed by intermediate demand, 21.74 cents by household demand, 22.93 cents by other final demand, and 22.1 cents by exports. The relatively high contributions of household demand and exports are noteworthy. Of each dollar total supply to the PRIS, 30.8

Table 2. Contributions to Total Demand in the Four-Sector Economy (in percent)

Sector	Intermediate Demand	Households	Other Final Demand	Exports	Total
1	78.46	12.31	4.23	5.00	100
2	51.76	16.05	9.83	22.26	100
3	26.50	31.50	34.00	8.25	100
4	33.33	21.74	22.83	22.10	100

Table 3. Contributions to Total Supply in the Four-Sector Economy (in percent)

Sector	Intermediate Sector	Households	Other Value Added	Imports	Total
1	30.38	21.15	13.85	34.23	100
2	60.11	9.65	13.54	16.70	100
3	37.00	29.50	31.00	2.50	100
4	30.80	30.80	22.10	16.30	100

cents each were spent on purchases from intermediate sectors and households, 22.1 cents on purchases from other value added inputs, and 16.3 cents on those from imports.

4. Structural Analysis of the 32-Sector Macro-Economy

An extensive structural analysis of the PRIS and the macro-economy as a whole was conducted. The linkages and multipliers used are explained in Appendix 1. The results give insights into the sectoral interdependencies in the PRIS and the macro-economy, and indicate the attractiveness of sectors from a growth perspective.

4.1 A Rasmussen Key Sector Analysis

The rankings of the top 25 percent of sectors, in terms of linkages and spread effects calculated from the open Leontief inverse, are presented in Table 4 (see output open). The sectors with strongest backward linkages are: (15) textiles and (16) clothing and footwear, followed by (32) undistribued, (18) paper, and (14) food. The only PRISs in the top 25 percent of sectors are (1) printing (Rank 6) and (6) information building (Rank 8). In regard to forward linkages, the results for PRISs are even more discouraging. The two top-ranking sectors are (19) chemicals and (21) metal products; the top PRIS ranks seventh.

There are seven sectors exhibiting dominant linkage effects, six of which are manufacturing sectors, and the seventh is utilities. Out of the top eight sectors having strong backward spread effecs, half are PRISs. However, only one PRIS shows strong forward spread effecs. Sectors with dominant spread effects are again manufacturing sectors, plus utilities and undistributed.

Rasmussen key sectors, i.e. sectors exhibiting simultaneously dominant linkage and spread effects, are (14) food, (15) textiles, (18) paper, and (30) utilities. These findings clearly confirm the importance of the manufacturing or secondary sector for the economy of Taiwan in 1976.

4.2 Analysis of the Influence of Trade

If imports are of importance, linkages and spread effects calculated from the open Leontief inverse may give a misleading picture of the potential of sectors for inducing development in the economy. Hence, for open economies, linkages and spread effects should be calculated from the Leontief inverse corrected for imports: $K_1 = [I - A + \hat{M}]^{-1}$. Acharya and Hazari (1971) have shown that this can result in substantially different sector rankings.

Table 4. Results of Structural Analysis Using Measures of Linkages and Spread Effects - Taiwan 1976

	Rank	Backward Linkage Sector ($L_j^B > 1$)	Forward Linkage Sector ($L_i^F > 1$)	Backward Spread Sector ($S_j^B < 1$)	Forward Spread Sector ($S_i^F < 1$)	Sectors with Dominant Linkages $L_j^B \cap L_i^F > 1$	Sectors with Dominant Spread Effects $S_j^B \cap S_i^F < 1$	Key Sectors
A:	1	(15) Textiles	(19) Chemicals	(32) Undistributed	(19) Chemicals			
Output-	2	(16) Clothing	(21) Metal Products	(6) Inf. Building	(29) Mining			
Open	3	(32) Undistributed	(28) Agriculture	(31) Construction	(21) Metal Products	14,15	14,15	14
	4	(18) Paper	(29) Mining	(16) Clothing	(28) Agriculture	18,19	17,18	15
	5	(14) Food	(15) Textiles	(2) Office Machinery	(27) Trade	21,30	20,23	18
	6	(1) Printing	(27) Trade	(5) Other Inf. Manuf.	(32) Undistributed		30,32	30
	7	(17) Wood Products	(18) Paper	(1) Printing	(30) Utilities			
	8	(6) Inf. Buildings	(14) Food	(25) Misc. Manuf.	(26) Services			
B:	1	(15) Textiles	(19) Chemicals	(5) Other Inf. Manuf.				
Output-	2	(16) Clothing	(21) Metal Products	(16) Clothing	sectors 21 and 29		1,11	14
Open	3	(18) Paper	(28) Agriculture	(2) Office Machinery	exchange places;	14,15	14,15	15
Corrected	4	(14) Food	(27) Trade	(6) Inf. Buildings	otherwise ranking	18,19	17,18	18
for	5	(1) Printing	(15) Textiles	(31) Construction	as for A	20,21	20,23	20
Imports	6	(17) Wood Products	(18) Paper	(25) Misc. Manuf.		30,32	30,32	30
	7	(31) Construction	(30) Utilities	(1) Printing				32
	8	(30) Utilities	(14) Food	(32) Undistributed				

(continued)

Table 4. (Continued)

	Rank	Backward Linkage Sector ($L_j^B > 1$)	Forward Linkage Sector ($L_i^F > 1$)	Backward Spread Sector ($S_j^B < 1$)	Forward Spread Sector ($S_i^F < 1$)	Sectors with Dominant Linkages $L_j^B \cap L_i^F > 1$	Sectors with Dominant Spread Effects $S_j^B \cap S_i^F < 1$	Key Sectors
C: Output-Open Corrected for Imports & Exports		Rank 1 to 6: as for B	same sector ranking as for B	same sector ranking as for B	same sector ranking as for A	same as for B	same as for B	same as for B
	7	(6) Wood Products						
	8	(31) Construction						
D: Income-Open	1	(12) Other Inf. Services	(12) Other Inf. Services	(32) Undistributed	same sector ranking as for A	7,8	11,14	
	2	(13) Education	(27) Trade	(10) Real Estate		12,13	15,17	
	3	(7) Inf. Trade	(28) Agriculture	(30) Utilities		26,27	18,19	None
	4	(27) Trade	(13) Education	(15) Textiles		28	20,21	
	5	(31) Construction	(26) Services	(2) Office Machinery			23,30	
	6	(6) Inf. Buildings	(19) Chemicals	(18) Paper			32	
	7	(16) Clothing	(7) Inf. Trade	(17) Wood Products				
	8	(26) Services	(9) Finance	(5) Other Inf. Manuf.				

However, in the case of "processing-type" economies, the Leontief inverse has to be corrected further to account for those imports which are induced by exports. We then obtain $K_2 = [I - A + \hat{M}^*]^{-1}$ (see Appendix 1).

It was felt imperative to calculate linkages and spread effects from both K_1 and K_2, in order to correct for the impact of trade on the domestic economy. Hopefully, this would provide evidence of whether the PRISs are more, or less, integrated into the domestic economy than other sectors.

The results obtained from the Leontief inverse K_1 and K_2 are shown for the top 25 percent of sectors in Table 4 (see 'output open corrected for imports' and 'output open corrected for imports and exports'). Again, the PRISs perform poorly in terms of linkages and spread effects. Only one activity, i.e., (1) printing, is included amongst the eight sectors exhibiting the strongest backward linkages, ranking fifth. However, they include five manufacturing sectors, among them the four top ranking sectors. A comparison of sector rankings obtained from K_1 and K_2 with those obtained from the open Leontief inverse uncorrected for trade reveals an almost identical ranking of sectors. This is a somewhat surprising result, which shows that, in terms of backward linkage effects, the top ranking sectors are well integrated into the domestic economy. The same applies to the results obtained for forward linkages and spread effects. The top-ranking sectors obtained from the three Leontief inverses do not include any PRIS. This not only implies that forward linkages of PRISs are relatively weak, but also that they are concentrated in only a few sectors.

The calculation of key sectors confirms the overwhelming importance of manufacturing sectors. The key sectors obtained from K_1 and K_2 are identical, and include sectors (14) food, (15) textiles, (18) paper, (20) mineral products, (30) utilities, and (32) undistributed. Except for the last two sectors, the result is identical to that obtained for the uncorrected open Leontief inverse.

4.3 Income-Weighted Linkages and Spreads

The linkages and spread effects discussed so far are measured in terms of intermediate output, and do not show the influence of sectoral output changes on policy variables like income and employment. Unfortunately, we were not able to calculate employment weighted indices, due to lack of appropriate data at the time this study was conducted. However, we calculated indices from the Leontief open inverse weighted by household coefficients, showing the effect of sectoral expansion on income. The results are again reported in Table 4 (see 'income open'). They vindicate the potential of the emerging PRIS: Four out of the top eight sectors ranked according to backward linkages are PRISs, including the three top ranking ones. The only manufacturing sector in this group ranks seventh! Similar results are obtained for forward linkages. Four PRIS (information distribution, communication, other information services, and education and research), and three noninformation sectors (services, trade, and agriculture), exhibit dominant linkages, but none of the manufacturing sectors do so.

In regard to spread effects, the results are almost reversed. Out of 11 sectors showing dominant spread effects, eight are manufacturing sectors; only one information activity (business services) is included. This indicates that income effects induced by PRIS output changes are transmitted to only a relatively small number of other sectors.

Because of the observed dichotomy between linkages and spread effects, there are no key sectors in the economy.

To sum up, according to the results obtained from the open output and income inverses, the PRIS has only a poor potential in terms of output creation, but a high potential for income creation. There is *no* sector which has dominant linkage effects in both cases. However, eight sectors maintain their dominant spread effects, six of which are manufacturing sectors.

4.4 Output and Income Multipliers

Jensen and West (Jensen & West, 1983; West, Morison & Jensen, 1982) multipliers were calculated to gain further insights into the structure of the economy of Taiwan in 1976.

The top 25 percent of sectors showing highest total output and income multipliers are given in Table 5. In regard to total output multipliers, half the sectors in Table 5 are PRISs. Three of the remaining four sectors are manufacturing sectors. The earlier observed importance of (16) clothing and (15) textiles is reaffirmed. The PRIS also provides half of the top ranking sectors which have high total income multipliers. Manufacturing, however, contributes only one sector, i.e., (16) clothing. Out of all 32 sectors, the PRISs (12) other information services, and (13) education and research, emerge as having both very high total output and income multipliers.

Table 5. Output and Income Multipliers

Rank	Sectors Exhibiting High Total Sector Output Multipliers		Sectors Exhibiting High Total Sector Income Multipliers	
1	(16)	Clothing	(12)	Other Inf. Services
2	(12)	Other Inf. Services	(13)	Education
3	(15)	Textiles	(7)	Inf. Distribution
4	(13)	Education	(27)	Trade
5	(1)	Printing	(31)	Construction
6	(31)	Construction	(6)	Inf. Building
7	(6)	Inf. Building	(16)	Clothing
8	(17)	Wood Products	(26)	Services

Another feature of the total output multipliers is that, for *all* manufacturing sectors, the production-induced output effect is greater than the consumption-induced output effect, the latter of which measures the economic effect of increased purchases by households which are facilitated by the increase in production and income. However, for six of the 13 PRISs, consumption-induced effects exceed production-induced effects. Indeed, sectors (12) other information services and (13) education and research have by far the highest consumption-induced output effects of all sectors. It seems that, when consumption-induced effects are included in the multiplier analysis, the disappointing results obtained for the PRIS in terms of output linkages and spread effects are not sustained. The PRISs and manufacturing sectors assume roughly equal importance in terms of potential impact response.

To sum up, the multiplier analysis vindicates the PRIS as having high potential for structural change in the economy of Taiwan. To a great extent, this is due to consumption-induced effects, which seem to be particularly strong. Out of the top ranking sectors shown in Table 5, only five have both high total sector output and income multipliers. They are sectors (12) other information services, (13) education and research, (6) information building, (31) construction, and (16) clothing.

5. Structural Analysis of the Aggregated (Four-Sector) Macro-Economy

To assess the influence of aggregation on our results, and to compare our findings to those of others, we aggregated the economy of Taiwan into four sectors (see footnote 2). The resulting input–output table is given in Table 3, Appendix 2. Table 6 presents a summary of the linkage and multiplier analysis.

Table 6 confirms our earlier observations: The secondary sector does best in terms of linkages and backward spreads. The PRIS ranks last according to the linkage criteria, but it does better on spreads. When consumption-induced effects are taken into account, the position of the PRIS improves. For both output and income multipliers, the PRIS shows the highest consumption induced effects of all sectors. The secondary sector has the lowest consumption-induced effects, but the highest production-induced effects. The observed differences between production- and consumption-induced effects have implications for the choice of criteria which should be used to assess the structural interdependence and potential of the PRIS. This is explored in Appendix 1. In short, output linkages calculated from the open Leontief inverse are especially ill suited for this task; they are measures of interdependence developed for a pre-information economy.

Table 6. Linkages, Spread Effects, and Multipliers*

Sector	B_j	Rank	F_i	Rank	S_j^b	Rank	S_i^f	Rank	Output Multiplier	Rank	Income Multiplier	Rank
1. Primary	.903	3	.899	2	.980	3	.936	3	2.474	4	.470	3
2. Secondary	1.232	1	1.551	1	1.101	1	.735	4	2.971	1	.426	4
3. Tertiary	.981	2	.780	3	.855	4	1.099	2	2.916	2	.634	2
4. Quaternary	.884	4	.769	4	1.064	2	1.230	1	2.762	3	.642	1

* Linkages and spread effects are calculated from the open Leontief inverse, multipliers from the closed Leontief inverses.
B_j = backward linkage, S_j^b = backward spread effect.
F_i = forward linkage, S_i^f = forward spread effect.

6. The Growth Pattern of the Information Sector

It is well recognized that NICs have to move into higher value-added, i.e., more knowledge- and technology-intensive, industries to counteract the loss of comparative advantage in the production of low value-added, labor-intensive manufactured goods (Yamazawa, Taniguchi & Hirata, 1983, p. 297; Uchida, Imaoka & Yanagihara, 1983, p. 24). Sunrise industries like electronics and telecommunications are being designated and supported as the new leading industries by NICs governments. Does this indicate that these NICs will experience absolute and relative growth of their PRISs over time, as have the United States and other advanced countries since the late 1940s?

There are indications that Taiwan might not follow this pattern. The economy's leading industries in the period 1971-1976 (textiles, transport equipment, electrical machinery) showed a significant decline in their relative growth rates during those years. At the same time, there was a significant deterioration in the speed of development of new leading industries (e.g., electronics), making the transition period difficult (Kuo, 1983, p. 316). This resulted in Taiwan's government adopting a two-pronged strategy, whereby traditional industries like textiles and clothing are being upgraded, while new ones, like computers and telecommunications, are targeted as "strategic industries" (*Far Eastern Economic Review,* March 22, 1984). The increasing informatization of the textile, clothing, and other manufacturing industries will not be accounted for in the PRIS but in the SIS. It might, perhaps, stimulate the PRIS through indirect effects, for example, increased demand for financial services. On the whole, however, the growth of the PRIS might stagnate, relative to that of the manufacturing sector, due to increased emphasis on SIS development. This indicates the urgent need for a combined study of both information sectors.

7. Concluding Remarks

Our analysis confirms the existence of a substantial primary information sector in Taiwan in 1976 which accounts for 20 percent of total value-added. It also confirms the growth potential of this sector in a predominantly industrial economy. Sectors having both high output and income impacts are other information services, education and research, construction (informational and non-informational), and clothing.

The importance of education and research must be emphasized. It is widely recognized that one of the greatest obstacles to economic development in Taiwan is the shortage of human capital, which is expressed in a lack of skilled manpower and weak management (Kuo, 1983, p. 324; *Far Eastern Economic Review,* March 22, 1984). This assigns a pivotal role to education and research in Taiwan's effort to diversify into new high-tech products, and to harness the full potential of the huge investments in telecommunication systems which are designed to provide the informational infrastructure for (and to keep up with) the ongoing office automation and proposed use of videotext.

Sector (8), communication, did not prove to have particularly high linkages and multipliers. However, there is evidence which suggests that its forward linkages, although less than unity, have increased steadily between 1966 and 1976 (Kuo, 1983, p. 270).

This points to the limitations of the static Leontief I-O model, which is a snapshot of the economy at a particular point in time. There is a need to analyze the development of the PRIS and its role for the economy over time. This can be done, either by applying the methodology used in this study to extract and analyze the PRIS to consecutive I-O Tables, or by constructing a dynamic I-O model. In either case, a methodology should be adopted which includes the assessment, not only of production-induced effects, but also of consumption-induced effects. Neglect of the latter will result in unwarranted pessimism in regard to the development potential of the information sector.

The measurement and structural analysis presented in this study should be regarded as a starting point for the investigation of the information economy of Taiwan. There is an urgent need to assess the secondary information sector, which seems to have assumed increasing importance in recent years. The important link between informatization and foreign trade has to be explored, as well as the new institutional requirements accompanying the informatization of Taiwan's economy.

References

Acharya, S. & Hazari, B. (1971). Linkages and imports: A comparative study of India and Pakistan. *Journal of Development Studies, 8,* 107–115.

Boon, G. (1982). Some thoughts on changing comparative advantage. *In* R. Kaplinsky (Ed.), *Comparative advantage in an automating world, IDS* Sussex Bulletin, Vol. 13, No. 2.

Chenery, H.B. & Watanabe, T. (1958). International comparisons of the structure of production. *Econometrica, 26,* 487–521.

Davis, W. (1984). Semiconductors: A key to development. *Economic Impact,* (46), 74–75.

Diamond, J. (1974). The analysis of structural constraints in developing economies: A case study. *Oxford Bulletin of Economics and Statistics,* 36, 95–108.

Institute of Developing Economies (IDE). (1982). *Input-output table Singapore, 1975.* (Statistical Data Series No. 38). Tokyo.

Jensen, R. & West, G. (1983). The nature of Australian regional input-output multipliers. *Prometheus, 1,* 202–221.

Kuo, S. (1983). *The Taiwan economy in transition.* Boulder, CO: Westview Press.
Leontief, W. (1982). The distribution of work and income, *Scientific American, 247,* (3), 152–164.
Rasmussen, P.N. (1956). *Studies in inter-sectoral relations.* Amsterdam: North Holland.
Taiwan. (1975). *The Report of 1976 Industrial and Commercial Censuses of Taiwan-Fukien District of the Republic of China, Vol. III, Book II.* The Committee on Industrial and Commercial Censuses of Taiwan-Fukien District of the Republic of China, Executive Yuan.
Taiwan (1980a). *Taiwan Input-Output Tables, Republic of China, 1976 (99 Sectors and 49 Sectors).* Overall Planning Department, Council for Economic Planning and Development, Executive Yuan, September.
Taiwan (1980b). *Taiwan Input-Output Tables, Republic of China, 1976 (394 Intermediate Input Subsectors).* Overall Planning Department, Council for Economic Planning and Development, Executive Yuan, September.
Taiwan (1981). *Sectoral Disaggregation and Explanation of Input-Output Tables for Taiwan Industries.*
Taiwan, (1983a). *Standard Classification of Industries of the Republic of China.*
Taiwan (1983b). Statistical Yearbook of the Republic of China 1983. Directorate General of Budget, Accounting and Statistics, Executive Yuan.
Taiwan (1983c). *National Income of the Republic of China: National Accounts in Taiwan for 1951-1982 and Preliminary Estimates of National Income in Taiwan for 1983.* Directorate General of Budget, Accounting and Statistics, Executive Yuan, December.
Uchida, T., Imaoka, H. & Yanagihara, T. (1983). Forecast of growth potential and factors influencing Asian development (Leading Paper). *In* T. Haseyama, Hirata, A., Yanagihara, T. (Eds.), Two decades of Asian development and outlook for the 1980s. (Institute of Developing Economies Symposium Proceedings No. 8), Tokyo, (pp. 1–30).
Wad, A. (1982). Microelectronics: Implications and strategies for the Third World. *Third World Quarterly, 4,* 677–697.
West, G., Morison, J. & Jensen, R. (1982). *An interregional input-output table for Queensland, 1978/79, GRIT III.* Report to the Department of Commercial and Industrial Development, Department of Economics, University of Queensland.
Yamazawa, I., Taniguchi, K., Hirata, A. (1983). Trade and industrial adjustment in Pacific Asian countries. *The Developing Economies, 21,* 281–312.

Appendix 1
Methodology of Linkages and Multipliers

1. Rasmussen Linkages and Spreads

Rasmussen (1956) used the Leontief inverse K to measure backward and forward linkages:

Index of backward linkage: B_j = (j-th column mean of K/m)
Index of forward linkage: F_i = (i-th row mean of K/m)
$K = [I - A]^{-1}$; m = grand mean of all elements of K.

If $B_j > 1$, sector j demands from other sectors more than an average level of intermediate inputs to sustain an expansion of its final demand. Put differently, sector j will call forth a more than average increase in output of other sectors when its final demand is increased, i.e., it exhibits a strong backward linkage. $F_i > 1$ implies that the output of sector i must expand more than average to meet increases in final demand of other sectors, i.e., it denotes a strong forward linkage.

Different weighting schemes can be applied to the linkages. Rasmussen argued that linkages should be assessed taking into account their spread effects. The latter are based on the coefficient of variation (v) to account for the degree of dispersion of sectoral technical coefficients.

Index of backward spread effect: $$S_j^b = \frac{v_j}{\frac{1}{m}\sum_{j=1}^{m} v_j}$$

Index of forward spread effect: $$S_i^f = \frac{v_i}{\frac{1}{m}\sum_{i=1}^{m} v_i}$$

S_j^b, $S_i^f < 1$ signify a more than average spread or development impact on other sectors in case of sector j's or i's expansion. Sectors for which both linkages are greater than one, or both spreads smaller than one, are said to have dominant linkage or spread effects. Rasmussen key sectors are sectors exhibiting simultaneously dominant linkages and spreads.

2. Leontief Inverses Corrected for Trade

In open economies, a substantial leakage of investment effect on development occurs through imports. Hence, the Leontief inverse has to be corrected by netting out these import leakages before calculating linkages and spreads to determine the growth potential of sectors. We therefore obtain a new matrix K_1 : $K_1 = [I - A + \hat{M}]^{-1}$, $\hat{M}$ = diagonal matrix of import coefficients. K_1 allows us to net out part of the leakage or spread which measures the economic expansion in the exporting country. However, K_1 is not appropriate in the case of "processing economies," i.e., economies which exhibit both high imports and exports at the sectoral level. In such cases, we also have to net out that part of import demand which is due to exports in order to obtain a more accurate measure of the sectoral interrelationships in the domestic economy. To correct for this, we redefine the import coefficients $m = M/X$ (M = imports; X = output) as: $m^* = M/X - E$ (E = exports) and obtain another Leontief inverse K_2 : $K_2 = [I - A + \hat{M}^*]^{-1}$ (Institute of Developing Economies, 1982, pp. xvii–xix).

3. Output and Income Multipliers

The multipliers used in this study have been developed by West, Morison, Jensen (1982). They have affinity with conventional type II multipliers in that they include consumption induced effects. Their advantage lies in the decomposition of the multiplier effect into its different impacts:

1. The *Initial Impact,* or Stimulus: this normally relates to a $1 change in sales (final demand).
2. *First Round Effects:* direct purchases by the sector experiencing the change in final demand.
3. *Industrial Support Effects:* denotes second and subsequent round effects, successive waves of output increases due to (1) and following (2); they exclude the initial impact and any increase caused by household consumption.
4. *Consumption Induced Effects:* stems from the spending of household income received directly and indirectly as renumeration for producing the increase in output.
   Production Induced Effects: first round *plus* industrial support effects.
   Flow-on Effects: production induced effects *plus* consumption induced effects. (West, Morison and Jensen, 1982, pp. 14–15).

Output multipliers show the impacts in response to a unit change in output. Income multipliers, however, show the change in income per unit of initial output change. Income effects can, however, also be expressed on a "per unit of initial income effect" basis to obtain:

$$\text{Type IA Income Ratio} = \frac{\text{Initial} + \text{First Round Effects}}{\text{Initial Income Effects}}$$

$$\text{Type IB Income Ratio} = \frac{\text{Initial} + \text{Production Induced Effects}}{\text{Initial Income Effects}}$$

$$\text{Type IIA Income Ratio} = \frac{\text{Initial} + \text{Production Induced} + \text{Consumption Induced Effects}}{\text{Initial Income Effects}}$$

$$\text{Type IIB Income Ratio} = \frac{\text{Flow-on Effects}}{\text{Initial Income Effects}}$$

The conventional Type I and Type II multipliers correspond to ratio IB and IIB, respectively.

4. A Note on the Use of Linkages and Multipliers

The use of linkage criteria to gauge the interdependence of sectors, and their attractiveness in terms of growth potential, is a well-established method in economic analysis. Criteria derived from transactions and direct coefficient matrices (Chenery & Watanabe, 1958) soon proved inadequate as they ignore indirect effects. Rasmussen (1956) used the Leontief inverse to derive linkages which remedy this shortcoming. However, as noted by Diamond (1974), Rasmussen type linkages and spreads also have serious shortcomings: (a) They neglect intersectoral linkages in demand, and (b) they are purely estimated in terms of intermediate output. To correct for (a), linkages have been calculated from closed (in terms of household) inverses. To take into account the effect on important policy variables like income and employment (instead of just output), various weighting schemes have been applied.

Multipliers are conventionally defined as either the sum of column or row elements (backward or forward multipliers). There is a straightforward relationship between these so-called Type I multipliers and linkages:

$$L_b = \frac{M_b}{\frac{1}{n}\sum_i \sum_j r_{ij}}$$

; where L_b = backward linkage, M_b = backward multiplier, n = total number of sectors, r_{ij} = elements of the open Leontief inverse.

These multipliers and linkages account only for production induced effects. Conventional Type II multipliers are equivalent to Jensen and West Type IIA Income Ratios. They do include consumption induced effects.

There are two important points to note about the adequacy of these indices to assess the attractiveness and degree of interdependence of PRISs which, if ignored, will result in an unduly pessimistic assessment:

1. If we assume that it is a general feature of PRISs to have high consumption induced effects (and of manufacturing sectors to have high production induced effects), then the calculation of output linkages and multipliers from the open Leontief Inverse $[I - A]^{-1}$ must result in a gross underestimation of the importance of PRISs.
2. Conventional Type I and Type II income multipliers are expressed on a "unit of initial effect" basis, i.e., they do *not* measure the change in income per unit of initial *output* change (as do the Jensen and West income multipliers used in our study) but the change in income per unit of initial *income* change. Therefore, if we want to measure the impact of final demand changes on PRISs we should *not* use these indices but the total Jensen and West income multipliers.

(1) explains the poor results obtained for the PRIS from our Rasmussen key sector analysis. It also explains the simultaneous occurrence of high (Jensen

and West) output multipliers and low backward linkages. The grave distortions in sector ranking due to the neglect of consumption-induced effects becomes apparent when we compare rankings based on backward linkages (L_B), the production-induced components of output multipliers (M_p), and total output multipliers (M_T):

In the 32 sector economy:

Sector	L_B,M_p	M_T	Sector	L_B,M_p	M_T
1	6	5	17	7	8
2	15	13	18	4	9
3	13	16	19	16	22
4	24	30	20	18	19
5	14	14	21	10	18
6	8	7	22	22	28
7	25	21	23	19	24
8	27	27	24	17	23
9	28	29	25	12	12
10	29	32	26	26	25
11	23	26	27	21	15
12	32	2	28	20	17
13	31	4	29	30	31
14	5	11	30	11	20
15	1	3	31	9	6
16	2	1	32	3	10

In the Four-sector economy:

Sector	L_B,M_p	M_T
1	3	4
2	1	1
3	2	2
4	4	3

Appendix 2
Table 1
Sector Code of Reclassified I-O Table

	Sectors	Source ROC I/O Sectors*
	Information	
1	Printing, Publishing, and Paper	40,42
2	Office Machinery, Office Furniture, and Repairs	39,67
3	Electronics Equipment, Parts, and Repairs	70
4	Precision Instruments and Apparatus	75
5	Other Informational Manufactures (Machinery and Products)	38,50,52,60,66,71,76
6	Informational Infrastructure Building	78,80
7	Distribution (Wholesale and Retail Trade)	90
8	Communication	89
9	Finance and Insurance	91
10	Real Estate Services	92
11	Business Services	93
12	Other Information Services	94,9520**,97,98
13	Education and Research	9510**
	Noninformation	
	Manufacturing	
14	Food, Beverages, and Tobacco	16-28
15	Textiles	29-31
16	Clothing and Footwear, Leather Products	32-35
17	Wood, Wood Products, and Furniture	36-39
18	Paper, Paper Products	40,41
19	Chemical, Rubber, Petroleum, and Coal Products	43-53
20	Non-metallic mineral products	54-57
21	Basic and Fabricated Metal Products	58-64
22	Machinery and Parts	65-68
23	Electrical Machinery	69-71
24	Transport Equipment	72-74
25	Miscellaneous Manufacturing	75,76
	Others	
26	Services	10,91,92,94,9520**, 96-98
27	Trade and Transport	84-88,90
28	Agriculture, Fishery, and Forestry	1-9
29	Mining and Quarrying	11-15
30	Utilities	81-83
31	Construction	77-80
32	Undistributed	99

* refers to sector code of 99 sector I-O table of Taiwan in 1976 (Taiwan, 1980a)
** refers to sector code of 394 intermediate Input Table of Taiwan in 1976 (Taiwan, 1980b).

Appendix 2
Table 2
Components and Value of Information Scalars

Source ROC I-O Sectors*	Scalar	Information Sectors in Reclassified I-O Table	Components
38	.033	5	TV set wooden box
39	.136	2	Nonmetallic office furniture
40	.2055	1	Newsprint paper, etc.
42	1.0	1	Printing, publishing, and bookbinding
50	.0203	5	Plastic brief case
52	.0193	5	Printing ink, carbon black
60	.0159	5	Iron and steel office furniture
66	.0218	5	Printing and bookbinding machine, etc.
67	.0123	2	Office machinery, sorting machinery
70	1.0	3	Electronic products
71	.0486	5	Communication cable
75	.97	4	Precision instruments and apparatus
76	.0971	5	Stationery, photographic film, records, and tapes
78	.15	6	Office and school construction
80	.1021	6	Telecommunication lines construction
89	1.0	8	Communications
90	.0562	7	Wholesale and retail trade in information goods
91	.9174	9	Finance and insurance
92	.16	10	Real estate services
93	1.0	11	Business services
94	.6	12	Public administration services
9510**	1.0	13	Education services
9520**	.1	12	Information component of medical and sanitary service
97	.2989	12	Informational misc. household and personal services
98	.4407	12	Misc. information services (informational nonprofit services)

* 99 sector code ** 392 sector code

Appendix 2
Table 3
Four-Sector Input–Output Table of Taiwan, 1976

Sector	1	2	3	4	H-H	O.F.D.	Exports	Total
1	17	179	7	1	32	11	13	260
2	44	391	90	33	173	106	240	1078
3	16	50	30	10	126	136	33	400
4	2	28	21	41	60	63	61	276
H-H	55	104	118	85	0	0	0	362
O.V.A.	36	146	124	61	3	11	0	382
Imports	89	180	10	45	0	0	0	324
Total	260	1078	400	276	394	327	347	0

For sector code, see footnote 2.

CHAPTER 16

The New Zealand Information Economy and Regional Cooperation

Neil D. Karunaratne
Alan Cameron

Introduction

Structural changes in the New Zealand economy in the past have been caused mainly by the diversification of the pattern and direction of trade. In the future, rapid information of the world economy poses a new challenge to the growth and change in the New Zealand economy. Unless the information revolution is recognized and New Zealand planning strategies are appropriately reoriented, the macro-economic travails that New Zealand is experiencing could be exacerbated.

The size and characteristics of New Zealand's expanding information economy are examined in terms of linkages, spreads, and multipliers. The status of the New Zealand information economy in the Oceanic region is probed. A comparison is made of the information technology and other production techniques prevailing in New Zealand and Australia. The similarity of technological structures dictates that neighboring OCEANIA countries should coordinate their trade strategies much more effectively if they are to find a niche in the rapidly accelerating information-product cycle. Past and current efforts of economic cooperation have failed to recognize the importance of the information economy in planning for development. New trade theories clearly indicate that countries such as New Zealand will have to specialize by product differentiation, and produce for a large regional or world market, to reap scale economies in new technology products or information goods and services. This chapter has quantified the magnitude of the New

Zealand information economy and some of its structural characteristics, to assist in the optimal promotion of the newly growing information economy of New Zealand.

Structural Change and Planning Strategies in New Zealand

The New Zealand economy in the pre-war (World War II) period was mainly a colonial economy, exporting farm products to metropolitan United Kingdom in exchange for finished industrial products. The exigencies of the war led to the widening of the manufacturing base and the diversification of the commodity composition and the markets for New Zealand trade. Structural change in the New Zealand economy has always been spearheaded by trade —the main engine of growth. Overcoming the balance of payments constraint spawned by the deteriorating terms of trade had been a major plank of New Zealand's development strategy until the commodity boom in the early 1970s. New Zealand's planning strategy emphasizes promotion of traditional exports and diversification of its manufacturing base to overcome the macro-economic problems confronting it in the 1980s (New Zealand Planning Council, 1978). The New Zealand planning strategies have failed to appreciate that most resource based economies, such as Australia, Canada, and the U.S., have been recording a lackluster growth performance, while resource-poor economies, such as Japan, Sweden, and Netherlands, and some of the ASEAN countries, have forged ahead despite the worldwide recession. Is the New Zealand planning strategy based on export promotion and diversification of the manufacturing base going to solve its macro-economic problems of unemployment and inflation in the 1980s? There has been a paradigm shift in the world economy, and, apparently, the New Zealand planning strategies have so far failed to perceive this. The panacea of export-led growth, which brought spectacular success to some Newly Industrialized Countries (NICs), may not be appropriate in a world that is rapidly becoming informatized. The information revolution, or the post-industrial society, has arrived, and the dynamics of the industrial revolution have petered out. Unless New Zealand plugs into the world information economy by latching on to a niche in the information product cycle, New Zealand may be pursuing a path of decline and increasing macro-economic woes in the next decade.

In the subsequent sections, we identify the magnitude of the New Zealand information economy. In Section 2, a methodology that we devised to quantify the size and structure of any information economy from an inter-industry model (Karunaratne, 1983) has been applied to New Zealand. In Section 3, the structure of the New Zealand economy is compared with that of the neighboring economies, using linkages, spread effects, and various types of multipliers. Section 4 makes a comparison of the production technologies of the information economies and macro-economies of Australia and New Zealand, and notes their similarity. Section 5 concludes by commenting on the need for closer coordination of regional economic policies of OCEANIA countries, so as to plug into an appropriate niche in the information-product cycle.

Magnitude and Structure of the New Zealand Information Economy

To plan for the development of the New Zealand information economy, it is desirable to have some idea about the size of the New Zealand information economy. The data constraints permit us to quantify only the magnitude of the primary information economy or the contribution to national income, expenditure, or output by information creation, processing, and exchange in the market. Secondary information activities, or nonmarket activities, are important, albeit no attempt has been made to impute values for these nonmarket information transactions.

In order to identify the primary information economy, the 130-sector New Zealand Inter-Industry Table 1971-1972 was processed by the methodology enunciated elsewhere (Karunaratne 1983, 1984; Karunaratne & Cameron, 1980). Information activities were identified in each of the 130-sectors, and values of these activities were estimated using Census of Manufacturing and other secondary sources of data. The ratio of information to total sectoral output (R) provided a basis to derive a four-fold typology of the New Zealand economy, after rearranging and consolidation. The four-fold typology clearly demonstrates the interdependencies between the primary information (subscripted I) and noninformation (subscripted N) sector transactions (X), as clearly depicted in matrix notation below:

$$\left[\begin{array}{c|c} X_{II} \begin{array}{c}\text{(Information}\\ \text{to}\\ \text{Information)}\end{array} & X_{IN} \begin{array}{c}\text{(Information}\\ \text{to}\\ \text{Noninformation)}\end{array} \\ \hline X_{NI} \begin{array}{c}\text{(Noninformation}\\ \text{to}\\ \text{Information}\end{array} & X_{NN} \begin{array}{c}\text{(Noninformation}\\ \text{to}\\ \text{Noninformation}\end{array} \end{array}\right] = \left[\begin{array}{c|c} \hat{R}\,X\,\hat{R} & \hat{R}\,X\,(I-\hat{R}) \\ \hline (I-\hat{R})\,X\,\hat{R} & (I-\hat{R})X(I-\hat{R}) \end{array}\right]$$

The circumflex $\wedge$ denotes diagonalized matrix of the information vector (i.e., vector of ratios R in total sectoral output).

Appendix A gives a 20-sector consolidated New Zealand Economy (1970-1971), 12 information and 8 noninformation transactions. The primary information economy in New Zealand, according to the above mentioned table, accounted for 16 percent of New Zealand Income (value-added) or 15 percent of its National Expenditure (Final Demand), and about 14.5 percent of the total Gross output. In the OCEANIA regional grouping, New Zealand ranks next to Australia in importance of the size of its information economy (see Table 1).

There is unmistakable evidence that, as the country grows, the information economy expands even faster. Although New Zealand is far behind the advanced post-industrial or information economies such as U.S. and Japan, it is inexorably being drawn into the global information economy. The failure to read these signs, and continued planning on the basis of the dwindling comparative advantage according to factor endowments, may be an error. The revealed comparative advantage in the information age has to be created—it is not bestowed by the earth's bounty. It is not endowed.

The new theories of trade clearly indicate that countries that have harnessed scale economies by specializing according to product differentiation have catered for a global market and emerged as success stories (Krugman, 1983). It is not the Heckscher-Ohlin interindustry trade, but intraindustry trade, that has provided the fuel to the trade-propelled engine of growth. Available evidence indicates that intraindustry trade in manufactures between Australia and New Zealand is about 32 percent of the total trade (Lloyd, 1971) and has grown rapidly (see Table 2). We speculate that, in the

Table 1. Size of the Information Economy

Country (Year)	(Value-added by Primary Information Economy as a % of Total Value-Added)		Information Economy Output as a % of Total Output	
		(Rank)		(Rank)
New Zealand (1971)	16%	(2)	15%	(2)
Australia (1977)	26%	(1)	19%	(1)
Fiji (1977)	12%	(4)	13%	(3)
Papua New Guinea (1972)	13%	(3)	13%	(3)

Table 2. Intraindustry Trade Coefficients* Between New Zealand and Australia

SITC 2 Digit	Average 1971-1973	Average 1972-1979
Chemical	0.181	0.208
Manufactures	0.685	0.905
Mchinery	0.282	0.610
Miscellaneous	0.600	0.871

* Intraindustry Trade Coefficient = $1 - \frac{|X_i - M_i|}{(X_i + M_i)}$

Source: Simkins (1980, p. 50).

near future, much of the increase in trade between New Zealand and her neighbors will continue to be in the area of intraindustry trade. We would also conjecture that, with the increasing strength of the information economy, or the informatization process, intraindustry trade in information goods may emerge as an important ingredient in bilateral and regional trade in the area.

A Comparative Analysis of the Morphology of the New Zealand Information Economy

An analysis of the morphology of the New Zealand economy, using the popular Chenery-Watanabe coefficients (Chenery & Watanabe, 1958) u_j and w_i, or ratios of sectoral input purchases to supply and sectoral intermediate sales to total demand, respectively, is deficient, because such ratios ignore the direct cum indirect interdependencies that exist in the economy. The linkage and spread indices computed using the Leontief inverse rectify the defects of the Chenery-Watanabe coefficients. The average linkages and spread effects calculated for the information and macro-economy for several economies indicate no statistically significant differences. This confirms the hypothesis that most of economies in OCEANIA are pre-information economies, where the information sectors do not radiate strong linkages by balances in input demands (backward linkages) or supply creations (forward linkages). However, it is noteworthy that in the case of New Zealand average forward linkages in the information economy are significantly different from those of the macro-economy. This may indicate that New Zealand's economic fortunes are predominantly determined by supply conditions in the dominant noninformation sectors, rather than in the newborn information economy (see Table 3). The spread effects of the New Zealand information economy are not significantly different from those of the macro-economy. Again, this confirms the weakness of the prevalent information economy of New Zealand. A similar story is related by spread effects calculated for the neighboring economies. The backward and forward spread effects quantify the size of the dispersal of the impact of respective backward or forward linkages. They are normalized coefficients of variations associated with the

Table 3. Average Linkages Based on Leontief Open Inverse

	Linkages-Information Economy		Linkages-Macro-Economy	
	Backward (L^b_j)	Forward (L^f_i)	Backward (L^b_j)	Forward (L^f_i)
New Zealand	1.0236	*0.2112*	0.9873	*0.5621*
Australia	0.9577	0.8188	0.9881	0.9802
Fiji	0.9663	0.8550	1.0000	1.0010
Papua New Guinea	1.0111	0.8839	1.0354	1.0021

Source: Karunaratne (1983.)

average linkage measures. The spread effects of the information and macro-economy are not different in a statistically significant manner for all the economies studied (see Table 4).

Turning the spotlight soley on the New Zealand economy, the three top-ranking sectors according to the linkage and spread criteria are tabulated in Table 5. The analysis reveals that noninformation sectors are dominant in the New Zealand economy, and that the household sector is the most important in terms of the above structural criteria.

A comparison of output and income multipliers further reinforces the hypothesis that the information economies in the OCEANIA countries are still in an embryonic stage. Furthermore, ther are no noteworthy differences between either the information economy or average macro-economy multipliers for the different economies compared (see Table 6).

Table 4. Average Linkages Based on Leontief Open Inverse

	Information Economy		Macro-Economy	
	Backward Spread	Forward Spread	Backward Spread	Forward Spread
New Zealand	1.1083	*1.0232*	1.0101	*1.0359*
Australia	0.9933	1.0928	1.0004	0.9986
Fiji	0.9397	1.0892	0.9517	1.0057
Papua New Guinea	0.9869	1.1003	1.0001	1.0000

Source: Karunaratne (1983.)

Table 5. Linkages and Spreads in the New Zealand Economy

Rank	Backward Linkages	(Sector)	Forward Linkages	(Sector)	Backward Spreads	(Sector)	Forward Spreads	(Sector)
1	Education	(1)	Household	(21)	Livestock	(16)	Household	(21)
2	Infrastructure	(5)	Services	(14)	Goods	(13)	Services	(14)
3	Household	(21)	Banking	(6)	Construction	(20)	Banking	(6)

(Sectors > (12) are Noninformation Sectors.)

Table 6. Average Multipliers

Type	Information Economy			Macro-Economy		
Economy	Output	Income Type I	Income Type II	Output	Income Type I	Income Type II
New Zealand	2.7652	1.4515	2.4515	2.7143	1.6900	2.7132
Australia	1.8913	1.4516	2.6121	2.8694	1.6548	2.9770
Fiji	1.9559	1.3393	2.1441	2.0181	1.4329	2.2938
Papua New Guinea	2.0191	1.5065	1.9130	1.9397	1.5338	1.9354

Source: Karunaratne (1983).

Production Technologies of Information Economies of New Zealand and Australia

The New Zealand economy and those of her neighbors are, by all above criteria, only fledgling information economies. Decision makers and planners in these economies have not yet recognized the importance of the rapidly informatizing global economy. Much of the macro-economic planning for structural adjustment is still conceptualized in terms of an industrial world order. In this section, an attempt is made to reveal the similarity or dissimilarities of the information and macro economies of New Zealand and her neighbors. By studying the existing nature of production technologies in these economies, we can provide more insights so as to facilitate the formulation of effective domestic as well as regional planning strategies.

Production techniques prevalent in New Zealand and Australia could be compared using the index P, which is a quotient of absolute and mean values of technical coefficients of the two economies compared (Santhanam & Patil, 1972). In matrix notation:

If $P_K = B_K[C_{KK}]^{-1}$ (i.e., column vector of dimension K)

where $B_K = i_K[A^{AUS}_{KK} - A^{NZ}_{KK}]$ (i.e., sum of absolute difference of column vectors)

and $C_K = 0.5 i_K[A^{AUS}_{KK} + A^{NZ}_{KK}]$ (i.e., mean of sum of column vectors)

Matrix *Notation:*

K: dimension. i: Unit vector. A^{AUS} and A^{NZ} are direct coefficient matrices of Australia and New Zealand respectively.

In scalar notation:

$0 < p_i < 1$ for $\forall i$.

If $p_i = 0$ implies perfect similarity of techniques.

$= 1$ implies perfect dissimilarity of techniques.

The similarity of production technologies of the two countries is given by the magnitude of p_i. If p_i is close to zero, there is a likeness of technologies used, and, as p_i approaches 1, the technological divergence increases. There is a complex of factors that interact to explain technological similarity or divergences: the sophistication of the production base, size of the market, the degree of openness of the economy, pattern of final demand, and differences in conceptual and aggregation methods.

In the comparison of New Zealand and Australian economies, there emerges a striking similarity of technologies in use in both economies. The average is $p = 0.62$ for the information sectors, and it is slightly higher for the noninformation sectors. The smallest values of p are for information sectors (6), (4) and (1), and for the noninformation sector (14), while sectors (3) and (12) exhibited the greatest divergence in sectoral technology in use (see Table 7 below).

Table 7. Similarity of Production Technologies (p) of the Information and Noninformation Sectors of New Zealand and Australia

Information Sector	p_i	Noninformation Sector	p_i
1	0.4374	13	0.7480
2	—	14	0.4318
3	1.0866	15	0.5030
4	0.3480	16	0.7840
5	0.7644	17	0.5174
6	0.3372	18	0.9260
7	0.6354	19	0.7252
8	0.5392	20	0.5968
9	0.5208		
10	0.5358		
11	0.6044		
12	1.0228		

Lessons for Regional Cooperation to Nurture the Information Economy

The similarity of production technologies in the nascent information economies of Australia and New Zealand, and the structural affinity of most economies of OCEANIA, have been confirmed by the foregoing analyses. Regional economic cooperation in the past—New Zealand Australia Free Trade Agreement (NAFTA, 1966) or the recent Closer Economic Cooperation (CER, 1983)—have been conducted in terms of liberalization of tariff and nontariff barriers for a selected range of trade in primary and manufactured commodities. Dynamic Customs Union theory predicts that closer economic cooperation between similar economies will lead to more trade creation rather than diversion, by enlargement of the market and by generating scale economies. However, the realpolitik of economic cooperation between New Zealand and her trading partners, hitherto, by focussing narrowly on agricultural and manufacturing trade exclusively, has missed recognizing a catalytic factor in the international economy—the global information revolution.

Unless small OCEANIA economies such as New Zealand perceive the importance of the emergent information economy, and attempt to reap its advantages by advanced planning at a national and regional level, international competition in the world information economy may prove to be a formidable challenge. Countries such as Australia and New Zealand should, in their regional planning on the basis of "specialization and division of labor," nominate appropriate information technologies or activities for promotion on a regional basis at an early date. Only by active planning on the basis of an enlarged regional market, and eventually by producing differentiated information products for the global market, can small economies hope to wrest a competitive edge in a rapidly informatizing world economy. The pursuit of a strategy of product differentiation to cater for a global market, so as to reap economies of scale, is consistent with guidelines offered by new trade theories. Recent empirical research further confirms that science-based technology or information technology is the main determinant of contemporary comparative advantage among advanced economies. New Zealand planning strategies have so far not clearly recognized the critical importance of the information economy. Rather, the planning strategies have emphasized export-led growth in a petering-out world industrial economy. A change in direction is imperative if New Zealand is to plug into the information revolution and reverse its declining macro-economic trends in the 1980s. The identification of the New Zealand information economy, and its structural analysis, hopefully has contributed to the search for "new ideas that will widen the horizon of our understanding of the world" (Stigler, 1983, p. 543). Such new perceptions will facilitate normative decision making in New Zealand to contribute more effectively to New Zealand's economic development in the future.

However, New Zealand, along with other countries in the Pacific such as Australia, Papua New Guinea, and Fiji, is seeking a satellite solution to its telecommunications problems. At present, it relies on Intelsat IV networks, but is negotiating with Aussat to lease a 30-watt transponder on the system's third satellite, for a reported fee of A$2.56 million per annum (Pacific Islands Monthly, April 1986). This goes to show that New Zealand is planning to integrate its markets internationally by strengthening investments in the information sector.

References

Chenery, H.B. & Watanabe, T. (1958). International comparisons of the structure of production. *Econometrica, 26,* 487–521.

Karunaratne, N.D. (1983). *Cross-country comparison of information economics.* (Preliminary Report). University of Queensland and East-West Center Project.

Karunaratne, N.D. (1984). Planning for the Australian information economy. *Information Economics and Policy, 1,* 345–367.

Karunaratne, N.D. & Cameron, A.D. (1980). Input-output analysis of the Australian information economy. *Information and Management, 3,* 191–206.

Krugman, P. (1983). New theories of trade among industrial countries. *American Economic Review, 73,* 343–347.

Lloyd, P.J. (1971). New Zealand manufacturing production and trade with Australia. *NZIER Research Paper,* (17).

New Zealand Planning Council, (1978). *Planning perspectives (1978-1983),* March.

Santhanam, K.V. & Patil, R.H. (1972). A study of the production structure of the Indian economy: An international comparison. *Econometrica, 40,* 159–176.

Simkins, G.G.F. (1980). closer economic relations between Australia and New Zealand *(Working Papers in Economics,* No. 40). Department of Economics, University of Sydney.

Stigler, G.J. (1983). Nobel lecture: The process and progress of economics. *Journal of Political Economy, 91,* 529–544.

Appendix A
Sector Code of 20-Sector I-O Table

	Information Sectors	
	(1)	Printing Paper and Paper Products
*	(2)	Advertising
	(3)	Office Machinery and Repairs
	(4)	Electronics Equipment and Repairs
	(5)	Infrastructure Building
	(6)	Banking and Finance
	(7)	Insurance and Risk Management
	(8)	Miscellaneous Information Services
	(9)	Business Services
	(10)	Education
	(11)	Distribution (Wholesale and Retail)
	(12)	Communication
	Noninformation Sectors	
	(13)	Goods
	(14)	Services
	(15)	Commerce
	(16)	Livestock
	(17)	Agriculture and Fishing
	(18)	Mining and Quarrying
	(19)	Utilities
	(20)	Construction

N.B. *(2) Advertising is not identified for the New Zealand economy in this study.

CHAPTER 17

The Emergent Information Economies of the Pacific Islands: Focus on Papua New Guinea and Fiji

Neil D. Karunaratne

Constraints on Development

The Pacific Island Nations (PINs) are dispersed over the gigantic Pacific Ocean. The geographical remoteness of the PINs from metropolitan centers, and the vast inter-island distances, are further compounded by the rugged terrain found in many of the islands. Besides, the island economies are exposed to harsh climatic vagaries and frequent natural calamities. These physical constraints on development are accentuated by the linguistic, ethnic, and cultural diversity that divides the PINs. Papua New Guinea (PNG), the largest of the PINs, has over 700 distinct dialects! It has a population of over 3 million and accounts for nearly 60 percent of the population of PINs. PNG's land mass represents nearly 80 percent of the land area covered by the PINs. The insular nature of the economies imposes a narrow resource base, and the soils vary from rich volcanics on the larger islands to infertile tracts on the coral atolls. Despite its large land area, only 25 percent of PNG's land is reported suitable for agriculture, while the Fiji islands, although smaller in area and population, has 60 percent of its land suitable for agriculture (Tsusaka, 1984, p. 66). Fiji occupies the top of the per capita income league amongst the southern PINs, with a per capita income of US$1990, or nearly two and a half times the level of PNG. Fiji is relatively more densely populated compared to PNG, which has only 7 persons per square kilometer (see Table 1). Although the PINs are sparsely populated, the rapid rate of population growth in some countries, the fragile ecosys-

Table 1. Geo-Economic Indicators of a Sample of Pacific Islands

Island	Population (1983) (Thousands)	(Rank)	GNP $million	(Rank)	Per Capita Income ($)	(Rank)	Land Area (sq. km.)	(Rank)	Population Density Per Sq. Km.	(Rank)
1. Papua New Guinea	3,130	(1)	2,560	(1)	818	(3)	462,840	(1)	7	(8)
2. Fiji	658	(2)	1,310	(2)	1,990	(1)	18,274	(3)	36	(5)
3. Solomon Islands	240	(3)	160	(3)	667	(4)	27,556	(2)	9	(7)
4. W. Samoa	158	(4)	50	(5)	136	(7)	2,842	(5)	56	(4)
5. Vanuatu	126	(5)	40	(6)	317	(8)	12,189	(4)	10	(6)
6. Tonga	97	(6)	50	(4)	515	(5)	747	(6)	130	(1)
7. Kiribati	60	(7)	30	(7)	500	(6)	716	(7)	84	(2)
8. Cook Islands	17	(8)	21	(8)	1,235	(2)	236	(8)	72	(3)

Source: Asia Development Bank (1983) *Key Indicators of Developing Member Countries* Manila.
World Bank (1983) *World Development Report*. Washington, D.C.
World Bank (1983). *World Bank Atlas*. Washington, D.C.

tem, and the limited resource base pose serious problems for their long-term development.

Beneath the veneer of the relative prosperity that PINs enjoy lie acute economic dualism and a dependence on the metropolitan countries. The high per capita income of Fiji, and even of PNG, mask the fact that a small minority of expatriates, indigenous urbanites, and rural elites appropriate themselves the lion's share of the national income. The vast majority of the population ekes out a rural subsistence living away from the bright city lights and the hustle and bustle of modern plantations or mining complexes. The dualistic structure of the island economies, with a modern monetized sector generating much of the national income and employment and a backward rural hinterland supporting the bulk of the population, creates tensions and problems for the economic development of the islands.

Another adverse economic feature that is common to most of the PINs is the extremely heavy dependence on trade. PNG and Fiji's value of exports are about one-third of the value of GDP, and the value of imports is nearly half of the GDP. The trade dependence of the PINs is precarious, because it is based on the narrow specialization of a few primary exports. These exports are directed towards a select group of metropolitan markets. PNG's commodity concentration reveals that 65 percent of its export earnings emanate from three commodities, while, for Fiji, nearly half of its export earnings come from the monocrop, sugar (see Table 2). The dramatic escalation of fuel-import prices and manufactured goods prices, coupled with the slump in commodity export prices, have immiserized growth in the PINs through adverse terms of trade effects. Most of the current planning strategies of these islands have embarked on economic diversification to overcome the narrow dependence on a few primary exports and consequent vulnerability to the vagaries of international trade. These strategies, without exception, proclaim that their goal is self-reliant development and growth with equity (Karunaratne, 1982).

Prospects and Dialectics of Rapid Development

The juxtaposing of unfavorable insular resource endowments, geographical remoteness, and severe dependence on metropolitan trade and aid could seriously jeopardize the planning zeal of PINs to promote rapid, self-reliant development. However, the promise of information technology may offer the geographically disadvantaged island economies a new critical resource. Information technologies in advanced economies have emerged as the leading engine of growth, employment, and structural change. In developing economies, this neo-technology has the potential to replace capital formation as the main growth motor.

Table 2. Trade Dependence of Some Pacific Island Nations

	Exports as % of GDP (1982)	Imports as % of GDP (1982)	Commodity Concentration of Exports	% Share of Total Exports (1982)	Major Trading Partners and Aid Donors
1. Papua New Guinea	33	44	Copper, Coffee, Gold	65	
2. Fiji	27	55	Sugar	47	Australia New Zealand UK Japan W. Germany Others
3. Solomon Islands	37	37	Fish, Timber, Palm Oil, Copra	65	
4. Tonga	7	69	Coconut Products & Vanilla Beans	63	
5. Kiribati	9	70	Copra	63	

Sources: Asian Development Bank (1983) *Key Indicators of Developing Member Countires,* Manila.

The new information technology has the capacity to deliver, in a cost-effective manner, many important services such as education, health care, agricultural extension, banking facilities, entertainment, and nation building messages (Butler, 1982). Already, Intelsat technology is in place in many island economies to integrate with suitable terrestial segments and provide teleservices in the PINs (Pelton, 1982). In these island economies, with poor infrastructure and no significant skilled manpower or investible resources, the establishment of schools, hospitals, recreational facilities, and other basic needs, with associated transport and power grid investments, is a pipe dream that cannot be realized within the life time of the present generation. But the information technology, through teleservices, offers a viable and attractive alternative way to deliver some of the basic needs and services in a cost-effective manner within a short time period.

The political leaders and decision makers of the islands have perceived the potential of the new information technology to engineer catalytic changes in the stagnant rural hinterland of the PINs. The metropolitan countries that have launched satellites to further their own strategic and commercial objectives have been addressed by PINs to channel some of their new technology to tackle their development needs. At little marginal cost to the metropolitan countries, it is possible to design satellites that can footprint, or cover, the widely dispersed island economies of the Pacific (National Aeronautics and Space Administration, 1982). The advanced countries have to be persuaded that serving the PINs is in the mutual interst of the PINs and the metropolitan powers (Bortnick, 1983). It should be noted that some of the PINs, such as PNG, have highly sophisticated telecommunication systems, established initially by loans financed by the World Bank. Now the systems are expanding on the basis of self-generated resources. These systems are technically quite advanced, with solar powered repeaters and on-line and troposcatter micro-wave links (Ranck, 1984). However, the telecommunication systems in these countries are focused to serve the pecuniary objectives of narrow urban and metropolitan vested interests. More broad based, rural-oriented development, nevertheless, could be promoted by the new technology, which is spatially flexible (i.e., as the costs do not increase with distance). The new technology will not only help to remove market fragmentation and distortions that weaken the market signals, but also will promote allocative efficiency (Leff, 1984). It will also erode the inertia of the institutions that stonewall progress. Thus, rather than graduating on a linear stages of Rostow-type development, information technology offers the prospect of catapulting neolithic societies in PNG into the information era. Such leap-frogging scenarios may be overdramatizations, as the dialectics of rapid change may involve hidden costs and social traumas for the developing island nations. There are academic hardliners in the islands strongly spearheading the resistance to rapid change.

Pitted against those who support the status quo are the villagers. The mass rural exodus to urban centers indicates that the rural folk are voting with their feet for rapid modernization and change. In addition, the transnational corporations that control the new information technologies are hard selling their wares to developing economies. In a fast-diffusing technocentric order, the transnationals perceive that the appropriability of monopoly rents is quickly diminishing, and they are eager to make quick profits at the expense of developing economies by selling inappropriate technology.

A Comparison of the Economic Structure of Fiji and PNG

The economic structures of Fiji and PNG are compared in this section to show the status of the information economy in the context of the macroeconomy in these two developing countries. The comparison is static or snapshot, based on modified input–output statistics. The input–output and national accounts statistics do not identify the fast growing information sector in their current presentations. In this study, based on census and survey data and national income statistics, the information activities were first identified. The information activities, which are diffused and hidden in a welter of conventional data, were located and rearranged to provide a clear picture of the magnitude of the information sector in both economies. The aggregated 4-sector input–output tables for Fiji and PNG are shown in Appendix A.

The current status of the information economy prevailing in both Fiji and PNG could be compared roughly to the level of informatization prevailing in the United States at the beginning of the 20th century, if we interpolate backward on the basis of a recent model (Jonscher, 1983). The information sectors of both developing economies are still in an underdeveloped or rudimentary state. Fiji, in fact, is a predominantly service economy, with nearly half of its national income (value-added) and expenditure (final demand) coming from the services sector. PNG, on the other hand, because of the dominant mining activities, generates most of its income and expenditure in the primary sector (see Table 3).

In both these developing economies, the information or quarternary sector, and the manufacturing or secondary sector, are relatively weak due to the underdeveloped nature of their respective economies. Moreover, since the information sector here refers to only the primary or market-based information activity, only a part of the modern monetized sector's importance is captured. In these economies, where planning bureaucracies both in the private and public sectors are relatively strong, one could speculate that a sizeable secondary or nonmarket information sector could coexist alongside the primary information sector. These bureaucratic or secondary infor-

Table 3. Summary Macro-Economic Indicators: Fiji and Papua New Guinea (Percent Total)

Sector		Value Added		Final Demand		Output		Employment	
		Fiji	PNG	Fiji	PNG	Fiji	PNG	Fiji	PNG
Primary	1	22.7	43.9	10.5	48.0	16.9	34.1	13.2	16.3
Secondary	2	11.3	10.6	23.2	9.8	27.1	13.6	15.9	13.9
Tertiary	3	49.3	34.3	51.2	32.7	43.0	42.7	53.9	53.5
Quarternary	4	16.7	11.2	15.1	9.4	13.0	9.0	17.0	16.3
Total (%)		100.0	100.0	100.0	100.0	100.0	100.0	100.0	100.0
Total		593.52 (F$million)	1339.98 (M. Kina)	593.5 (F$million)	1369.1 (M. Kina)	1107.62 (F$million)	24128.2 (M. Kina)	64437 (Number)	205644 (Number)

Rank Correlations

$R_{VA}^{FIJI\text{-}PNG} = 0.5837$ $R_{FD}^{FIJI\text{-}PNG} = 0.0486$ $R_{OUTPUT}^{FIJI\text{-}PNG} = 0.6367$

Source: Reworked Input Output Tables of Fiji and Papua New Guinea

mation sector activities are not reported in national income or input–output statistics, and have to be quantified on the basis of shadow pricing and imputation techniques. In the context of developing economies, a more serious sort of underestimation for structural comparison and analysis arises from the prevalance of the large subsistence and nonmonetized rural sector. This subsistence sector is fairly sizeable in PNG and, although comparatively smaller, is also important in the Fijian economy. The relative importance of this subsistence-barter or nonmonetized economy is only partially captured in national income and input–output statistics.

Another serious flaw in the structural analysis presented here is its inability to reflect the enclave nature of, and metropolitan dependence of economic activity in, both these island economies. A more disaggregated analysis will help to surface some of these features of lopsided economic structures, and the excessive influence of the foreign and external factors on the national economies of Fiji and PNG.

Sectoral Macro-economic Indicators

The disaggregated analysis of the economic structures of Fiji and PNG are conducted using a 20-sector input–output table generated by the methodology outlined in previous chapters. The 20-sector classification economy, clearly describing the noninformation sectors 1 to 12, and information sectors 13 to 20, is presented in Table 4. The relationships to the original input–output sectoral classification are also indicated. Noninformation goods (Sector 13), services (Sector 14), and trades (Sector 15) demonstrate that they are the largest contributors as a percentage of the total macro-economic indicators of Fiji. The education sector (Sector 10) is the most important contributor among the information sectors, and ranks between fifth and sixth among the various macro-indicators. PNG also shows the dominance of noninformation sectors such as fishing, services, and goods production. Education appears to be the most important sector among the sectors in the information economy of PNG (see Table 5). Rank correlations calculated on the basis of the 20-sector I–O table show that all the macro-economic indicators are strongly and positively correlated, registering over 0.8 for sectors intracountry. The information-sector correlations were markedly stronger than the noninformation-sector correlations. This, perhaps, suggests that information sectors are more closely integrated than their noninformation counterparts. The intercountry sectoral rank correlations between Fiji and PNG were also positive and significant, registering over 0.7 for the most of the macro-indicators. Again, the intercountry correlations for the information sectors were higher than for noninformation sectors, suggesting that the two economies had broadly similar sectoral configurations for the information economy (see Appendex B).

Table 4. Sectoral Classification of Fiji and Papua New Guinea

Sector	Descriptor	Fiji-I-O Sectors	Fiji I-O Descriptors	PNG I-O Sectors	PNG I-O Descriptors
1	Printing, Paper and Paper Products	36	Printing and Paper Products	45,40,45	Newsprint, Paper (various types) Printing Ink, Books, Maps, Journals, Catalogues, Lithograph
2	Advertising	35	Signs	64	Advertising Services
3	Office Machinery	37,51	Office Machines and Repairs	48	Office Equipment and Repairs
4	Electronic Equipment	37,51	Switchboards, Control Apparatus Repairs	27	Telecom Cables, Equipment and Repairs
5	Information Building Infrastructure	40	Construction Activities	50,44,57	Inf. Component of Building and Repairs Furniture & Rental of Info. Buildings
6	Banking and Finance	49	Banking	56	Actual and Imputed Bank Charges
7	Insurance and Management	49,50	Insurance and Property Management	57	Property Management Services
8	Misc. Information Services	52,19	Travel Agent, Mineral Exploration etc.	64,61,62	Consultants, Tax Agents, Auditor Bookkeeping Services Government Information Medical Consultancy
9	Business Services	50	Business Services	67	Unallocated Management and Office Expenses
10	Education	54	Education	60	Primary, Secondary and Tertiary Education
11	Wholesale & Retail Info. Distribution	42	Info-Component of Wholesale and Trade	55	Wholesale and Retail Trade
12	Communications	48	Communications	54	Communications
13	Noninfo. Goods	17	Noninfo. Manufactures	23 to 48	Manufacture of Noninfo Goods
14	Noninfo. Services	21 to 37	Transport, Storage, Recreation and Finance	51 to 68	Transport Storage, Finance Business, Culture

(continued)

Table 4. Continued

Sector	Descriptor	Fiji-I-O Sectors	Fiji I-O Descriptors	PNG I-O Sectors	PNG I-O Descriptors
15	Noninfo. Wholesale and Retail Trade	43 to 56	Wholesale and Retail	55	Wholesale and Retail Trade
16	Livestock	9,10	Dairy Trade, Livestock Components	15	Livestock
17	Fishing and other Agric.	1 to 8 and 11 to 16	Fruit, Veges, Roots, Copra, Ginger, Rice, Cereals, Fishing, Forestry	1 to 14 and 16 to 20	Copra, Cocoa, Coffee, Oil Palm, Rubber, Tea, Rice, etc. Fishing and Forestry
18	Mining and Quarrying	18,20	Mining and Quarrying	21 to 22	Mining and Quarrying
19	Utilities	38,39	Electricity, Water	49	Electricity and Garbage
20	Construction	40,41	Building and Other Construction	50	Building and Construction

Sources: Fiji. Input-Output Table 1977. Economic Analysis Unit, Ministry of Finance.
PNG. Input-Output Table 1976-1977. National Planning Office, National Statistical Office (P.F. Baxter Consultant)

Table 5. Attractive Sectors from Economic Indicator Appraisal Percentage of Total (Rank out of 20 Sectors)

(Sector)	Description	Value-Added	(Rank)	Net Final Demand	(Rank)	Output	(Rank)	Employment	(Rank)
	FIJI								
(13)	Noninformation Goods	11.27	(4)	23.15	(1)	31.38	(1)	15.89	(2)
(14)	Noninformation Services	23.69	(1)	8.19	(5)	24.63	(2)	34.19	(1)
(15)	Noninformation Trade	15.76	(3)	14.56	(2)	12.91	(3)	10.33	(4)
(10)	(Information) Education	6.42	(6)	6.97	(6)	4.65	(5)	5.71	(5)
	PNG								
(17)	Fishing & Other Agriculture	33.58	(1)	39.94	(1)	23.90	(2)	21.16	(2)
(14)	Noninformation Services	19.69	(2)	22.40	(2)	24.90	(1)	34.05	(1)
(13)	Noninformation Goods	20.44	(3)	9.62	(4)	13.59	(3)	7.92	(5)
(10)	Education	4.78	(7)	5.14	(6)	3.52	(7)	10.33	(4)

Multiplier and Key-sector Analysis

A more incisive probe of the nature of the structural interdependencies of the information and noninformation economies can be executed through multiplier analyses. Output, various types of income, and employment multipliers have been compiled for the Fijian and PNG economies. The highest multipliers of both economies are shown in Table 6. Overall, the multiplier effects, or responsiveness of the macro-economic variables to exogenous demand changes, is higher in Fiji than in PNG. The output multipliers are strong for education (Sector 10), electronic equipment (Sector 4), and noninformation services (Sector 14), with multipliers exceeding 2.5. In PNG the three highest output multipliers are recorded for livestock (Sector 16), noninformation services (Sector 14), and education (Sector 10). In each of the aforementioned sectors, the output multiplier exceeds 2.3. In Fiji, the various types of economic multipliers record their highest levels for noninformation goods (Sector 13) and livestock (Sector 16). PNG reports a similar sectoral pattern as far as income multipliers are concerned, although the magnitude of the multipliers is very much lower for PNG than for Fiji. In Fiji, fishing and other agriculture (Sector 17) and advertising (Sector 2) figure prominently with respect to employment multipliers, while, in PNG, employment figures are highest for noninformation goods (Sector 13), mining and quarrying (Sector 18), and wholesale and retail trade (Sector 11) in the information economy (see Table 6). On the basis of a composite score, the rankings for both economies suggest the noninformation sectors are the most potent with regard to multiplier effects.

Conclusion

The rapid development of the information infrastructure as a consequence of the information revolution could further promote the urban–rural imbalance in information infrastructure and its associated service provisions. Besides, it could increase the dependence of the developing island economies on the transnational corporations that supply, install, and control the new information technologies. As in the area of dominant noninformation industrial and service technology, the information technology in the PINs could be controlled and manipulated to serve the pecuniary interests of domestic and foreign commercial interests at the expense of national well being.

By perceptive planning, the PIN's decision makers could harvest a cornucopia from the new information technologies and the information revolution. However, past experience shows that linear transposition of Western technologies, based on the Schramm-Lerner model (White & McDonnell, 1983), failed, without proper cultural integration and popular participation,

Table 6. Highest Multipliers for PNG and Fiji

				Income								Employment							
Country	Rank	Output	(Sector)	IA	(Sector)	IB	(Sector)	IIA	(Sector)	IIB	(Sector)	IA	(Sector)	IB	(Sector)	IIA	(Sector)	IIB	(Sector)
Fiji	1	2.70	(10)	2.26	(13)	2.58	(13)	4.12	(13)	3.12	(13)	1.47	(7)	1.61	(17)	3.86	(17)	2.86	(17)
	2	2.53	(4)	1.55	(16)	1.99	(16)	3.18	(16)	2.18	(16)	1.46	(17)	1.61	(1)	3.12	(7)	2.12	(2)
	3	2.53	(14)	1.45	(15)	1.62	(1)	2.60	(1)	1.60	(1)	1.43	(8)	1.60	(2)	2.42	(13)	1.42	(13)
PNG	1	2.33	(16)	1.60	(15)	2.01	(16)	2.54	(16)	1.54	(16)	1.59	(13)	1.92	(13)	2.74	(18)	1.74	(18)
	2	2.32	(14)	1.60	(11)	1.98	(13)	2.51	(13)	1.51	(13)	1.56	(11)	1.82	(11)	2.58	(6)	1.53	(6)
	3	2.32	(10)	1.59	(13)	1.87	(11)	2.37	(11)	1.36	(15)	1.56	(15)	1.82	(15)	2.51	(12)	1.51	(12)

to ignite the modernization-diffusion growth process. The transnationalization of information technologies proceeds on the basis of corporate profitability objectives. Such aims may conflict with the development goals of the PINs. The present information infrastructure, by and large, serves the urban elites and expatriate hegemonic and commercial interests that are entrenched in the economies of the PINs. The proliferation of the information technologies in the Pacific (satellites, computers, telecommunications) can reinforce neocolonial dependency and exacerbate urban–rural dichotomies in these islands further. Anticipatory planning is imperative to contain the escalation of both internal and external dualism in the PINs. The national planning strategies of PINs and their planning documents are oblivious to the promise of the information revolution and its dialectics. The reports of some international institutions are more perceptive. NASA (National Aeronautics and Space Administration, 1982) documents show a healthy and balanced awareness of the developmental and humanistic benefits of the information revolution to the PINs and the commercial gains to the transnational enterprises. There is an urgent need to create an awareness among the indigenous planners and decision makers to the vast benefits of the information revolution, so that they can be harnessed for the timely delivery of basic needs to the Pacific islanders.

References

Asian Development Bank (1983). *Key Indicators of Developing Member Countries.* Manila.

Baxter, P.F. (1982). *An Input-Output Matrix for Papua New Guinea.* National Planning Office, National Statistical Office. Waigani, Papua New Guinea.

Bortnick, J. (1983). Information technology and the developing world. *The Information Society, 2,* 157–169.

Butler, R.E. (1982). Telecommunication issues in a new world information and communication order. *Pacific Island Communication Journal, 11*(2), 7–11.

Jonscher, C. (1983). Information resources and economic productivity. *Information Economics and Policy,* 1, 13–35.

Karunaratne, N.D. (1982). Development in the South Pacific. *In* B. Higgins (Ed.), *Regional Development Dialogue.* (Special Issue 1982 Regional Development in Small Island Nations) (pp. 49–64). Nagoya, Japan: UN Centre for Regional Development.

Leff, N.H. (1984). Externalities, information costs, social benefit-cost analysis for economic development: An example from telecommunication. *Economic Development and Cultural Change, 32,* (2).

National Aeronautics and Space Administration, (1982). *Satellite communication for the Pacific Islands.* (Second Year Final Project Report). Prepared by the Public Service Satellite Consortium.

Pelton, J.N. (1982). The Pacific telecommunications and socio-economic development. *Pacific Islands Communications Journal, 11,* (2), 23–46.

Ranck, S. (1984). Telecommunications in Papua New Guinea. (In Transport and communications for Pacific microstates. Issues in organization and Management). *In* C.C. Kissling, (Ed.), *The Institute of Pacific Studies of the University of the South Pacific* (pp. 49–60). Institute of Pacific Studies. The University of the South Pacific. Fiji, Suva.

Tsusaka, A. (1984). South Pacific developing countries: Development issues and challenges. *Asian Development Review, 2,* 65–82.

White, R.A. & McDonnell, J.M. (1983). Priorities for national communications policy in the Third World. *The Information Society Journal, 2,* 5–33.

World Bank. (1983). *World Development Report.* Washington, DC.

World Bank (1983). *World Bank Atlas.* Washington, D.C.

Appendix A
Input-Output Table of Fiji (1977)
($F millions)

Sector	1	2	3	4	H-H	O.F.D.	Exports	Total
1	3	93	5	0	67	10	9	187
2	2	13	33	4	108	22	118	300
3	20	13	71	14	188	139	30	476
4	4	4	21	4	62	36	12	144
H-H	71	33	191	68	1	0	0	364
O.V.A.	64	33	101	31	0	0	0	230
Imports	23	110	53	21	85	53	34	380
Total	187	300	476	144	511	260	204	0

Input-Output Table of Papua New Guinea (1976/77)
(Millions of Kina)

Sector	1	2	3	4	H-H	O.F.D.	Exports	Total
1	2	24	11	0	272	20	457	785
2	28	14	77	7	150	6	31	313
3	62	70	232	27	158	397	38	984
4	9	13	56	9	18	114	4	222
H-H	73	43	329	111	0	0	0	556
O.V.A.	515	99	130	40	1	0	17	802
Imports	97	52	148	29	177	44	1	548
Total	785	313	984	222	776	581	549	0

Sources: Ministry of Finance Economic Analysis Unit (1980).
Fiji Input-Output Table 1977, Suva. An Input-Output Matrix for Papua New Guinea (Baxter, P.F. (1982)), National Planning Office, National Statistical Office, Waigani, Papua New Guinea.

Appendix B

Sectoral Macro-Indicators (Fiji and PNG) (Percentage of Total)

(1) Value-Added (VA)	Rank	(2) Net Final Demand (FD)	Rank	(3) Output	Rank	(4) Employment	Rank	Sector	(1) Value-Added (VA)	Rank	(2) Net Final Demand (FD)	Rank	(3) Output	Rank	(4) Employment	Rank
0.11	(19)	0.14	(17)	0.27	(19)	0.22	(19)	1	0.44	(19)	0.21	(13)	0.54	(14)	0.47	(15)
0.01	(20)	0.00	(20)	0.02	(20)	0.01	(20)	2	0.00	(20)	0.0	(20)	0.00	(20)	0.0	(20)
0.19	(18)	0.08	(18)	0.04	(18)	0.37	(18)	3	0.02	(19)	0.0	(19)	0.02	(19)	0.01	(19)
0.22	(17)	0.01	(19)	0.48	(17)	0.44	(17)	4	0.06	(18)	0.01	(18)	0.52	(15)	0.05	(18)
0.45	(16)	0.93	(11)	0.75	(16)	1.13	(13)	5	0.71	(12)	0.73	(10)	0.99	(10)	1.15	(9)
2.35	(7)	2.09	(7)	1.92	(7)	1.84	(11)	6	2.03	(8)	1.24	(8)	1.63	(8)	1.57	(8)
1.57	(10)	1.03	(9)	1.38	(11)	0.58	(15)	7	0.21	(16)	0.85	(9)	0.17	(18)	0.11	(17)
0.95	(13)	0.52	(12)	1.40	(10)	0.99	(14)	8	0.19	(17)	0.23	(12)	0.17	(17)	0.45	(16)
1.31	(12)	0.40	(14)	1.28	(12)	2.30	(9)	9	0.55	(13)	0.01	(17)	0.49	(16)	0.43	(14)
6.42	(6)	6.97	(6)	4.65	(5)	5.71	(5)	10	4.78	(7)	5.14	(6)	3.52	(7)	10.33	(4)
1.76	(8)	1.62	(8)	1.44	(9)	1.15	(12)	11	0.74	(11)	0.28	(11)	0.89	(12)	0.69	(13)
1.36	(11)	0.44	(13)	1.06	(13)	2.29	(10)	12	1.34	(9)	0.13	(15)	1.17	(9)	0.99	(10)
11.27	(4)	23.15	(1)	31.38	(1)	15.89	(2)	13	10.44	(3)	9.62	(4)	13.59	(3)	7.92	(5)
23.69	(1)	8.19	(5)	24.63	(2)	34.19	(1)	14	19.69	(2)	22.40	(2)	24.90	(1)	34.05	(1)
15.76	(3)	14.56	(2)	12.91	(3)	10.33	(4)	15	6.70	(5)	2.48	(7)	7.99	(6)	6.18	(6)
0.64	(15)	0.40	(14)	0.95	(15)	0.50	(16)	16	0.34	(15)	0.10	(16)	0.67	(13)	0.89	(12)
21.24	(2)	9.93	(4)	1.76	(8)	5.32	(6)	17	33.58	(1)	39.94	(1)	23.90	(2)	21.16	(2)
0.80	(14)	1.02	(10)	1.05	(14)	2.84	(7)	18	9.38	(4)	9.94	(3)	9.51	(4)	2.24	(7)
1.71	(9)	0.16	(16)	2.14	(6)	2.76	(8)	19	1.09	(10)	0.18	(14)	0.94	(11)	0.93	(11)
8.07	(5)	13.31	(3)	10.12	(4)	11.04	(3)	20	6.66	(6)	0.54	(5)	8.86	(5)	10.57	(3)
0.11		15.05														

Rank Correlations (Fiji)

$R_{(VA)(FD)} = 0.8919$

$R_{(VA)(OUTPUT)} = 0.9459$

$R_{FD.OUTPUT} = 0.9008$

$R_{VA.EMPLOYMENT} = 0.8842$

$R_{FD.EMPLOYMENT} = 0.8166$

$R_{OUTPUT.EMPLOYMENT} = 0.8554$

Rank Correlations (PNG)

$R_{VA.FD} = 0.8847$

$R_{VA.OUTPUT} = 0.9729$

$R_{FD.OUTPUT} = 0.866$

$R_{VA.EMPLOYMENT} = 0.9534$

$R_{FD.EMPLOYMENT} = 0.8677$

$R_{OUTPUT.EMPLOYMENT} = 0.9234$

Author Index

Subject Index